VOYA PRESS

Library Collections for TEENS

Manga and Graphic Novels

Kristin Fletcher-Spear and
Merideth Jenson-Benjamin

E L Kurdyla Publishing LLC
Bowie, Maryland
in association with
Neal-Schuman Publishers, Inc.
New York • London

Published by Neal-Schuman Publishers, Inc.
100 William St., Suite 2004
New York, NY 10038

In association with VOYA Press
E L Kurdyla Publishing LLC
16211 Oxford Ct.
Bowie, MD 20715

Printed and bound in the United States of America.

The paper used in this publication meets the minimum requirements of American National Standard for Information Sciences—Permanence of Paper for Printed Library Materials, ANSI Z39.48-1992.

Library of Congress Cataloging-in-Publication Data

Fletcher-Spear, Kristen.
    Library collections for teens : manga and graphic novels / Kristen Fletcher-Spear and Merideth Jenson-Benjamin.
        p. cm
    Includes bibliographical references and index.
    ISBN 978-1-55570-745-3 (alk. paper)
    1. Libraries—Special collections—Graphic novels. 2. Libraries—Special collections—Comic books, strips, etc. 3. Young adults' libraries—Collection development—United States. 4. Graphic novels—History and criticism. 5. Comic books, strips, etc.—History and criticism. 6. Teenagers—Books and reading—United States. I. Jenson-Benjamin, Merideth. II. Title.

Z692.G7F58 2011
025.2'77415—dc22
                                                                        2010040895

Acknowledgements and Thanks

First off, the authors would like to thank their husbands, Jason Spear and Andy Benjamin, for their patience and support. It's a good thing you guys like this stuff as much as we do, or our marriages would not have survived. Thank you, Jason, for introducing me to the wonderful world of anime and manga. This wouldn't have happened without you.

Next we'd like to thank Karen Reed and Pam Jenson for serving as "beta readers" and grammar cops. We have issues with commas and semi-colons. Thanks for pointing that out.

Susan Murray, Catherine Morgan, Karen Marie Allen and Kathy Pastores get a big thank you for giving us the time we needed to work on this manuscript. We'll make up those desk hours at some point, we promise.

And finally, the authors would like to dedicate this book to Mari Benjamin, who was there at the start, and Charlie Spear, who got here in time for the finish.

Contents

Acknowledgements iii

Chapter 1   How to Use this Book and What Is a Graphic Novel 1

Chapter 2   History of American Comics and Graphic Novels 5

Chapter 3   The Evolution of Manga 23

Chapter 4   Benefits of Graphic Novels 49

Chapter 5   Collection Development and Management 59

Chapter 6   Evaluating a Graphic Novel for Purchase 87

Chapter 7   Purchasing Options 101

Chapter 8   Mending 113

Chapter 9   Programming with Graphic Novels 119

Chapter 10   Recommended Graphic Novels 151

Glossary 185

Subject Index 193

Manga and Graphic Novel Title and Creator Index 195

About the Authors 200

1

How to Use this Book and What Is a Graphic Novel

How to Use this Book

Even though graphic novels have been heavily promoted in libraries these past several years, we have noticed, through speaking to people, presenting at conferences, reading e-mails, and taking phone calls, that there is still a lot of confusion about graphic novels and their place in the library. Comics, graphic novels, and manga can have an "inside baseball" feel to them—they have their own language, they have issues that are unique to the format, and they have a cliquey and insular fanbase. Navigating this without a map can be scary and frustrating. This book provides a way in. To begin we cover some very basic concepts: a quick look at the history of American comics and manga, the similarities and differences between the two, and the benefits that these materials have for readers. Next, we take on some issues that are specific to libraries— the nuts and bolts of defending, ordering, and placing graphic novels in a library. Finally, we will round out the discussion with a look at programming with graphic novels, and end with some lists of the authors' favorite books. We have designed these materials to be useful to those who jump right in and flip to the areas that interest them, or as we call them, the "Kristin-type" readers. But we have also tried to make the book flow chronologically to work for the "Merideths" of this world, those who begin at the begining and work through to the end.

What is a Graphic Novel?

What is a graphic novel? This question pops up wherever graphic novels are discussed: at conferences, at conventions, in Web forums, and on listservs. Get more than three fans of the format together and you will probably get at least three different definitions. Therefore, we will begin this book by carefully defining exactly what it is we are discussing. A common definition is that a graphic novel is a book-length comic book. Graphic novels are bound, either in a trade paperback format or in hardback, and are between sixty and two hundred pages long. This definition, while useful for beginning a discussion of the format, is also problematic.

The problem begins with the words "comic book." Comic books have negative connotations for some librarians and educators. Many closely identify comic books with superheroes, and superheroes are closely identified, fairly or not, with a lack of literary and artistic quality. Therefore, librarians may believe that graphic novels, which they perceive as long-form comic books, are not quality materials. Also contributing to some librarians' discomfort with graphic novels is their belief that comics and cartoons are intended for a juvenile audience. This mental shorthand of "comics = kids" makes adult librarians reluctant to add graphic novels to their collections, feeling that they are intended for a younger audience. Because of this perception, a more neutral and complete definition of graphic

---

Parts of a Graphic Novel

See the glossary for more terms.

Comics. Generically used to refer to any story that combines sequential art and text. Comics usually refer to staple bound monthly publications, later bound into trade paperback graphic novels

Gutter. The white space in-between the panels on a comics page or the white space in the margins of a comic.

Panel. A box that contains comics art. It is not necessarily square, and sometimes the entire page is a single panel. Panels are used sequentially to forward the story.

Sequential Art. Static images placed in a progression to impart meaning, such as the passage of time, a specific action, or an event.

novels is needed. This definition must remove the phrase "comic book" but still describe the visual element that is an essential part of all graphic novels.

The artwork found in graphic novels is unique. The images themselves are static, but are ordered to convey movement, the passage of time, or the unfolding of a series of events. Static images arranged in a progression to convey meaning is called sequential art. All graphic novels feature sequential art. The sequential art found in comics is distinctive, as it works in synergy with the textual elements of the work. This is in contrast to picture books, for example, where the artwork may convey meaning, but reiterates or contradicts the text. The term sequential art should be central to any definition of graphic novels.

The issues of quality and content in graphic novels are simple to address in a definition. While it is certain that graphic novels featuring superheroes are some of the most popular and visible comics in American culture, it is important to remember that not all comics or graphic novels are about superheroes. In order to illustrate this, let us compare graphic novels to another format frequently found in libraries: audiobooks[1]. Like graphic novels, audiobooks are a unique format. Many public libraries choose to shelve their audiobooks separately from other print materials, but the information contained within audiobooks is often nearly identical to its print counterpart. As a format, audiobooks can be of any genre, can be any length, and can be of varying quality. Graphic novels, as a format, exhibit a similar diversity. For example, National Book Award nominee *Stitches* is a harrowing tale of childhood abuse, Michael L. Printz Award winner *American Born Chinese* is a coming of age story intertwined with Chinese mythology, and teen favorite *The Umbrella Academy* is the story of a dysfunctional family that features superheroes. It is clear that any definition of a graphic novel must respect and reflect the vast diversity present in the format. A common mantra amongst the graphic novel librarian community that sums this up nicely is "Graphic novels are format, not a genre."

Much more difficult to address than the content of graphic novels is the perception that comics are for kids. This attitude, one that is very prevalent in American culture, has proven difficult to uproot, but remains patently untrue. As an illustration of this, let us look at the top selling graphic novels of 2009, as purchased from Amazon.com.[2] The top two best selling graphic novels from Amazon.com in 2009 were part of the popular *Diary of a Wimpy Kid* series by Jeff Kinney. However, since the art in these books is not sequential and functions much like the art in a picture book, reaffirming the text, these two books (*The Last Straw* and *Dog Days*) would actually not be considered graphic novels. Moving down the list, we see *The Book of Genesis* by R. Crumb. This book, which reprints the biblical text word for word and is vividly illustrated by the renowned underground artist's distinct visual style, is considered by many critics to be a masterwork. The fact that it exists on the same bestseller list as the two children's books, an epic zombie tale (*The Walking Dead*), the novelization of a cult TV show (*Buffy the Vampire Slayer, Season 8: The Time of Your Life*), and a biography of mathematician and philosopher Bertrand Russell (*Logicomix*) serves as only the barest illustration of the wide variety of materials available for adults and teens in the graphic novel format.

Considering the above facts, we can fine tune and complete the definition of a graphic novel. **A graphic novel is a book-length narrative, of any genre, for any audience, which uses sequential art, either by itself or in combination with text elements, in order to tell a story.** Using this definition, it is possible to widen the field of graphic novels to many materials that were not originally conceived of as graphic novels, such as the wordless picture book *Flotsam* by David Weisner and Audrey Niffenegger's illustrated novel *The Three Incestuous Sisters*. We are aware of the issues with this wide-ranging definition, but believe it most fully encompasses the field of graphic novels as it pertains to our discussion. For the purposes of this book, graphic novels will be further divided into two categories: American graphic novels and manga. Manga, which is the Japanese word for comics, is exactly that: English translations of Japanese graphic material. Having established our definition, we will spend the rest of the book helping you make sense of the world of graphic novels.

---

1 Fletcher-Spear, Kristin, Merideth Jenson-Benjamin, and Teresa Copeland. "The Truth about Graphic Novels: A Format, Not a Genre." ALAN Review 32.2 (2005): 37-44. Print.

2 "Best Graphic Novels of 2009 from B&N and Amazon." ICV2. GCO, LLC, 15 Dec. 2009. *http://www.icv2.com/articles/news/16491.html.* (6 March 2010)

History of American Comics and Graphic Novels

What follows is an incredibly brief summary of the history of American comic books and graphic novels. In preparing this chapter, two books proved invaluable; *Comics, Comix, & Graphic Novels: A History of Comic Art* by Roger Sabin, and *Faster than a Speeding Bullet: The Rise of the Graphic Novel* by Stephen Weiner. The authors highly recommend these two volumes for those looking for a more in-depth review of this topic.

Sequential art is almost as old as humanity itself, and indeed, you will find comics historians who argue that Egyptian hieroglyphics, Mayan murals and the Bayeux Tapestry are early examples of comics[1]. But it wasn't until the Middle Ages, and the advent of printing in Europe, that led to images produced for a mass audience. Earlier sequential art creations could not be distributed; people had to travel to see them.[2] While European comics can trace their lineage directly to broadsheets printed from woodcuts and distributed at public executions, in the United States, the history of comics is intertwined with newspapers.[3] In 1754, Benjamin Franklin created the first cartoon published in an American newspaper: a severed snake, representing the states, with the legend "JOIN, or DIE".[4]

"JOIN, or DIE," cartoon in *The Pennsylvania Gazette*, Benjamin Franklin, Library Company of Philadelphia.

Pre-1931: *The Yellow Kid* and Other Newspaper Strips

While cartoons appeared in American newspapers from the mid-eighteenth century on, it wasn't until the late 1800s that cartoons became a major element in American newspapers, with the introduction of *The Yellow Kid*. First published in 1897, *The Yellow Kid*, created by R.F. Outcault, is often considered the first comic strip.

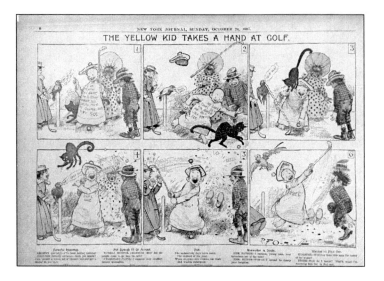

Debuting in *The New York World*, the strip proved to be wildly popular, and kicked off a "circulation war" which featured hundreds of comic strips in newspapers all over the country.[5] Comic strips were included in newspapers in large cities in order to reach immigrant populations who spoke and read little English and younger readers, often in four-to-eight page full-color supplements. Winsor McKay, creator of *Little Nemo*, Lyonel Feininger who wrote and drew *The Kin-Der-Kids*, and George Herriman, creator of the classic cartoon *Krazy Kat*, are standout comic strip originators of this period.

Given the popularity of newspaper comic strips, it is surprising that the first four-color comic publication to be sold on a newsstand didn't appear until 1929: "The Funnies" #1, a tabloid-sized collection of original strips.[6] It failed, largely because people were unwilling to pay for something that they thought should come free with their newspaper.[7] It wasn't until 1934 that publishers figured out the magic format for selling comics. *Famous Funnies,* a magazine reprinting newspaper strips, sized at a quarter of a Sunday comics page (roughly 7.5" x 10"), with a high percentage of color comics and a price of ten cents, was an unexpected success.[8] Hard on the heels of *Famous Funnies* came *New Fun Comics,* a collection of original comic strips, again mostly in color, with a trim size of 7.5" x 10", which first appeared in 1935.[9] More original humor anthologies followed and remained similar in tone and content to the popular newspaper strips.

The 1930s and 1940s: The Golden Age of Comics

The face of the comics market changed forever in 1938, when *Action Comics* featured the debut of Superman, created by Jerry Siegel and Joe Shuster. Looking to create a newspaper strip, the two created a caped hero with an 'S' on his chest, who uses his extraordinary abilities for good. After being turned down repeatedly by a number of comic syndicates, the pair took Superman to comic book publisher National Allied Publications, later known as DC Comics. Gambling on an untested idea, DC unwittingly kicked off the "Golden Age" of superhero comics.[10]

Together with Batman, who made his appearance in *Detective Comics* in 1939, Superman opened the floodgates for superhero characters. As superhero titles proliferated, comics featuring reprinted newspaper strips became a minority.[11] The popularity of the superhero comic in wartime America is not difficult to understand. The superheroes of the Golden Age were uncomplicated: Superman, Captain America, Wonder Woman, the Flash and their brethren were always on the side of right, fighting for "truth, justice, and the American way" in a time when the American way was thought to be threatened by foes from without and within. Since comics publishers had long since known that children in particular were a primary market for comics, many of the heroes were given teen sidekicks—Robin for Batman, Bucky for Captain America, Speedy for Green Arrow, etc. —in order to more fully appeal to children.[12]

The Early 1950s: Teens, *MAD* and *Seduction of the Innocent*

After World War II, the popularity of the superhero waned. The war was over, there were no more clear-cut "bad guys," and many of the costumed heroes either faded into obscurity or were stuck fighting the cold war. However, a new market was discovered for comics: teenagers. The teens of the 1950s were the first generation of kids who had grown up with comics and who continued to read them as they grew older.[13] Some comics, such as *Archie*, centered on high school life, while others featured funny animals, most notably those using Disney characters published by Dell, but the most popular comics were those in the crime and horror genres.

The horror and crime comics of the 1950s were a mixed bunch. Some, if not most, were produced for sheer shock value, with lurid drawings and sensational storylines. The notable exceptions were the horror titles published by EC comics, which distinguished themselves through creative storytelling and superior artwork. EC took storylines from the best pulp fiction of the day, and, perhaps more importantly, paid artists faster and better than their competitors.[14] William Gaines, the owner of EC Comics, had inherited the EC company from his father and moved the company away from the educational comics it had originally produced. Once known for such titles as *Picture Stories from American History,* EC soon began publishing such titles as *Tales from the Crypt* and *The Haunt of Fear.*[15]

Despite the popularity of their horror and crime comics, perhaps EC's greatest contribution to comics history is *MAD Magazine,* which revolutionized the genre of satire comics. *MAD* was notable for quality artwork and the contributions of Harvey Kurtzman. Kurtzman, a freelance artist during the early days of the comic book industry, worked as an editor on several EC titles and wanted to create an original humor comic.[16] The result was *MAD,* which began as a spoof of other comics, but soon expanded to saterize all aspects of popular culture. Kurtzman's early 1950s work, principally *MAD,* is still considered among the medium's finest.

While teenagers loved the dark and subversive stories and often lurid drawings featured in horror and crime comics, those same elements did not go unnoticed by authority figures. In 1954, psychiatrist Fredric Wertham published *Seduction of the Innocent,* which claimed that these comics were responsible for the decay of American youth. Wertham believed that they would ruin an adolescent's taste for fine literature; that comics were too violent, too sexual, and showed open disrespect for authority. This idea of "subversion" fit nicely with the anti-communist sentiment that prevailed in the United States at the time, and the U.S. Senate held hearings on comic books and youth.[17] Wertham's work ultimately lead to the adoption by the comics industry of the Comics Code: forty-one editorial guidelines for depicting—or rather, not depicting—sex, crime, horror, and violence within comics.[18]

The Late 1950s: The Silver Age of Comics

This intense scrutiny and the subsequent adoption of the Comics Code devastated the American comic industry. Horror comics virtually disappeared, but all genres of comics felt the impact. Many titles disappeared altogether, and several publishers went out of business. EC left the comics industry altogether and focused instead on *MAD*, which was being published in magazine format, and therefore not subject to the limits of the Comics Code.[19] A strangely positive side effect of the "Comics Code" was a rise in quality among comics, both in terms of art and storytelling, since many of the more sensationalistic, poorly produced comics simply disappeared.[20] Surprisingly enough, superhero comics were one of the few popular types of comics that proved able to adapt to the strict policies of the Comics Code authority.[21] The comics market came to be dominated by DC comics, publishers of Batman and Superman, and Marvel, another superhero publisher, whose comics had appeared under various corporate names.

While DC Comics went back in time, reintroducing some comic heroes and creating new characters based on the Golden Age model, Marvel comics, led by head writer and editor, Stan Lee, created a new type of superhero. Lee wanted the Marvel heroes to be as grounded in reality as much as possible, to face everyday problems as well as costumed super-villains.[22] Marvel heroes were, and still are, conflicted, angsty, and faced with the unforgiving prospect of balancing an everyday existence against the need to use their extraordinary gifts. While Lee is often credited as the driving force behind the creation of the Marvel universe, he in no way acted alone. Lee was supported by many talented artists, most notably Jack Kirby and Steve Ditko. [23] Kirby, a comic book illustrator since the 1940s, was the principal artist for the Marvel characters. During the Golden Age, Kirby's skill as an artist with innovative panel layouts energized the comics industry, imparting a new visual energy to the medium, which had been obsessed with realism.[24] His work on the Marvel characters of the 1960s showed innovation and flair. Steve Ditko's skilled figure drawings brought a distinctive look and feel to the comics that Marvel produced, particularly their most popular creation, Spider-man.[25]

The 1960s: Underground Comix and Comic Fandom

The Comics Code, with its strict guidelines and obsession with "morality," may have reinvigorated the superhero genre, but the youth of the 1960s were not looking for square jawed heroes who upheld the American way. The children of the Baby Boom were seeking to change the world, and spandex-wearing traditionalists did not speak to the radical social and demographic changes sweeping the country. In short, the ground was ripe for a new type of comic—the underground comic.

The underground comics or "comix" were humorous, hippie-inspired, and politically radical. The underground comics produced in the late 1960s, primarily by artists working in the San Francisco Bay area, defied the Comics Code, and wore their liberal ideology proudly, often addressing the social issues of the day. Haphazardly produced on irregular schedules and informally distributed on street corners and in head shops, these comics spoke to the counter-culture, and dealt with subjects such as drugs, Vietnam, rock music, and sex. Many comics historians believe underground comics reached their peak in 1968 with the appearance of R. Crumb's Zap.

With a unique artwork style and content that included lots of sex, drugs, and libertarian politics, *Zap* began its life containing content created solely by Crumb, but soon evolved into a continuing anthology, with contributions from other cartoonists.[26] R. Crumb's influence on the underground comix scene cannot be underestimated. In fact, for a time, the terms underground comics and zap comics were used interchangeably.[27]

Underground comics provided a fertile breeding ground for talented artist and writers, who produced unique, ground-breaking graphic materials. However, the comics of the underground suffered from a virulent sexism that sometimes crossed the line to outright misogyny, an aspect of the underground movement that is often overlooked by historians of the period. Some female comics creators entered the field, most notably Trina Robbins, and while the work of female underground comics creators sometimes mirrored the sexism previously found in comix, their contributions did bring some balance and new perspectives to a male dominated field.

The 1960s saw one other important development in the history of comics: the birth of comic fandom. Comics fans began to gather in hotels to discuss and buy comics, as well as meet comic creators. These fans were adults, who would organize regular comics markets or create "fanzines" or magazines about comics.[28] Comics fans owed a huge debt to the more established culture of science fiction fandom, and in fact, the two cultures often overlapped, as many comics readers were also sci-fi fans, and the two remain closely linked.[29] The publication of *The Great Comic Book Heroes,* a memoir of author Jules Feiffer's childhood love of comics that also contained reprinted stories from the DC Archives, gave comics fandom a huge boost. The book received favorable critical attention, sold well, and inched comics closer to being accepted by the mainstream.[30]

The 1970s: *A Contract with God* and Comics Specialty Stores

With the end of the Vietnam War, underground comics creators no longer had a central issue around which to converge. Contributing to the decline of the underground comics scene was the disappearance of head shops, which served as distribution points for comix, but were often driven out of business by laws outlawing drug paraphernalia. The post-1960s period is referred to by some comics historians as the "Dark Ages."[31] Very few mainstream comics of note appeared during this decade, although there were some limited successes, such as *Conan the Barbarian.* Although it may seem as though the 1970s were indeed a dark time for comics, the decade is important in the history of comics for two reasons: one is the rise of the comic book store as a distribution center for comics; the other is the publication of *A Contract with God.*

In 1978, when Will Eisner's *A Contract with God* was published, it was a watershed moment in the history of comics. Eisner is often credited with the creation of the term "graphic novel," and while that is open to debate, there is no denying that the publication of *A Contract with God* is a defining moment for comics, for a variety of reasons. First, and perhaps most important, *A Contact with God* popularized the term "graphic novel." In many ways, "graphic novel" is little more than a marketing tool, as novel length comic stories had been around since the 1940s.[32] Eisner himself used the term in an attempt to interest a book publisher, Bantam, in publishing *A Contract With God.* Bantam passed, but the term remained, and eventually came to be applied to any collection of thematically connected comics stories, published in a bound format. It is worth noting that *A Contract with God,* the (disputably) first book to carry the "Graphic Novel" term, was not a novel, in the traditional sense, but rather a set of interlinked short stories. Of course, as discussed in the previous chapter, "graphic novel" has come to mean any book length comics publication. Secondly, *A Contract with God* was the first American "comic book" to be published by a non-comics publisher. The small publishing house Baronet Publishing first published Eisner's novel in 1978.[33] Although Baronet folded, and the publication of *A Contract with God* was first taken over by independent publisher Kitchen Sink Press, and then later by DC Comics, the original publication helped lead the way to the acceptance of comics-form stories by publishers, bookstores, and librarians. Finally, *A Contract with God* is notable simply for being an outstanding book. Often, the first of a kind is celebrated simply for being the first, regardless of quality. However, Eisner's powerful tales of life in a 1930's era Jewish tenement, brought to life by expressive, clean artwork, served as an inspiration to other comics creators, and vividly illustrated the possibilities of the graphic medium.

The other notable development in American comics in the 1970s was the emergence of the comics specialty store. Comic book fans had found each other in the 1960s with the birth of the comic convention; shops catering specifically to the interests of comics readers were the next logical step. Often growing out of mail order businesses, comics specialty stores usually sold comics as well as sci-fi merchandise.[34] Since comics specialty stores grew out of the comics fan movement, which was primarily interested in superheroes, there was little room for underground comics in the racks of the local comics store, which combined with irregular publishing schedules, signaled the death knell for the comix movement.[35]

Comic specialty stores provided a locus for the new fan community, and offered unique advantages to comics publishers. By supplying the shops directly, distributors could cut costs, as there were no returns from this "direct market."[36] Armed with a newfound knowledge of who was actually reading comics, as comic print runs were determined, at least in part by the orders placed by retailers, publishers began experimenting with materials aimed at older readers.[37] With a new marketplace created by the specialty store, more publishers came about, providing more options for comics readers.

The 1980s: Small Presses and Revisions

At the beginning of the 1980s, comic book specialty stores were the main point of distribution for comics. With a clearer idea of who was actually buying and reading comics, smaller scale and non-superhero publishers flourished. Some were underground publishers, such as Kitchen Sink Press, which moved to the mainstream; the European comics scene influenced other publishers, such as NBM. A third variant of the "gremlin" publishing company was the creator-owned company, such as WARP Graphics, which published the popular *Elfquest* series, or Aardvark-Vanaheim's *Cerebrus*.[38] With smaller companies taking up more and more of the marketplace, the "Big Two"—Marvel and DC— were forced to re-evaluate the superhero comics each publisher was built on. Aimed at youth and teens, these comics were unlikely to draw in the adult audience that read the underground comix of the 1960s or the independently produced black and white comics that were now appearing at every turn.

Marvel was the first to attempt to woo back an older audience, by hiring British writer Frank Miller to re-imagine a second tier hero, Daredevil. Originally a blind but acrobatic Spider-Man clone, under Miller's guidance, Daredevil became a martial arts master, who fell in love with Elektra, a Ninja-assassin/femme fatale who worked for Daredevil's greatest enemy. Miller, acting as both writer and artist, created a more "realistic" superhero story, one that was closer in tone to crime fiction than the "derring-do" of previous superhero stories.

DC also began tinkering with its slate of characters and hired another Englishman, writer Alan Moore, to update the plant-man Swamp Thing. During Moore's tenure, Swamp Thing became a tortured and emotional hero, one concerned with hot-button issues such as feminism, drug use, gun control, and environmental protection.[39] Although a number of artists worked with Moore, most notably Steve Bissette and John Totleben, it was universally accepted that Moore was the primary creative force on the title.[40] This marked a landmark shift in the thinking of most comics fans; prior to this, the artist was considered to be the most important creator on a comic.

Swamp Thing and *Daredevil* were successes, both critically and commercially. DC and Marvel realized that comics readers had matured and wanted more realistic and complex comics. Moore and Miller (who had been lured to DC), enjoyed a great deal of freedom in their work, due to their critical acclaim and high visibility in the comics world, and both continued to experiment with traditional heroes.[41] This trend of revisionism—re-imagining canonical superheroes to better fit with the tastes and trends of the times, is one that continues today.

Perhaps the best known and most successful of the revisionist stories was penned by Frank Miller. It is a sign of the esteem comics fans held Frank Miller in that he was allowed to re-imagine one of the most popular and lucrative heroes in the DC Universe: Batman. In 1986, *The Dark Knight Returns* was published; this graphic novel is often credited with redefining the superhero.[42] In *The Dark Knight Returns*, a cynical and aged Batman comes out of retirement to once again save Gotham from the Joker. Miller introduced the concept that Batman does not have a strictly altruistic motive for wearing the cape and cowl; he is compelled to do so for deeply seated psychological reasons, and for the thrill it gives him.[43] Dark is the key word for *The Dark Knight Returns*, in terms of not only the storyline, but also the artwork. Drawing the book himself, and making full use of the talents of Klaus Janson on inks and Lynn Varley on colors, Gotham City turned into a shadowy nightmare that is disorienting, frightening, and strange.

Another germinal work in the field of "Mature Readers" comics is *Watchmen* by Alan Moore. Although technically not a revisionist story, since Moore does not use any pre-existing characters, *Watchmen* does take a more realistic look at superheroes and how they might function in the real world. Set in an alternate-history United States, where President Nixon was never impeached, a forty-something group of former heroes must cope with the disappearance of one of their own. As with his work on *Swamp Thing*, Moore gave his characters rich psychological backgrounds and added a complex story structure, with each chapter redefining the one before. Although often overlooked in critical discussions of *Watchmen*, artist Dave Gibbons used a deceptively simple style and disciplined panel layouts to further the narrative and create a sense of immediacy and urgency within the story.[44]

Aside from being fantastic works of graphic storytelling on their own, *Watchman* and *The Dark Knight Returns* brought new readers, or at least new attention, to the comics marketplace. Articles about the two titles appeared in mainstream media such as *Vanity Fair* and *Rolling Stone* magazines. In 1988, *Watchmen* won the Hugo Award for science fiction.[45] Although *Watchmen* offered a far more hopeful, less cynical outlook, *The Dark Knight Returns* received more media attention and enjoyed better sales, probably due to the high recognition factor of Batman.[46]

In addition to the revisionist successes of Marvel and DC, the late 1980s also saw the publication of what is probably the best known comic of all time, at least in literary and library circles, Art Spiegelman's *Maus*. *Maus* is an epic story, which recounts the tale of Spiegelman's father and his experience as a Jew in Nazi Poland, as told by anthropomorphized animals: Jews are mice, Nazis are cats, and Poles are pigs. While the compilation of *Maus* was the average reader's introduction to Spiegelman's work, he had been active in the comics industry since the early days of the underground movement, and *Maus* made its first appearance as a feature in *Raw*, a comics anthology published by Spiegelman and his wife, Françoise Mouly. A "graphix magazine" that highlighted the work of avant-garde comics artists and foreign material, mostly from Europe, *Raw* was not only important for publishing *Maus*, but for highlighting the work of independent creators.[47]

Maus was eventually collected into a graphic novel by Pantheon, a trade book publisher, in 1986. Pantheon expected average sales for the novel and was taken aback by the overwhelming response it received.[48] Spiegelman's story, which covers not only his father's experiences during the Holocaust, but also Spiegelman's difficult relationship with his parents and their inability to cope with the horrors of their past, is deeply affecting, and is made all the more so by the use of anthropomorphic animals. However, *Maus* confused many critics, and the critical response to the book was decidedly mixed.[49] Nonetheless, the impact *Maus* had on the way the general public thought about comics was earth shattering. Here was a comic that used "funny animals" to tell a decidedly unfunny story. It proved comics could be more than about "men in tights," and now is often required reading in college and high school courses. Until the late 1990s, *Maus* might have been the only graphic novel to be found on the shelves of the average public library.

The 1990s to the Present: Comics Diversify and Come to Libraries!

Coming into the 1990s, comics had grown up, and this fact had been trumpeted by innumerable newspaper and magazine articles, most of which focused on *The Dark Knight Returns, Watchmen,* and *Maus.* DC Comics, looking to continue its string of successes, turned to another British writer, Neil Gaiman, to invigorate a fairly obscure superhero, the Sandman. What they got, however, was not a superhero revision, but a fantasy series, one that drew on the mythic tradition of many cultures, literature, history, and Gaiman's own fertile imagination. *Sandman* was a departure from other "mature readers" comics produced by a mainstream publisher in that it was not a superhero comic.

Historically Important Graphic Novels

Thanks to reprints and archive editions, many of the comics mentioned in this chapter are available to read today.

Busiek, Kurt and Alex Ross. *Marvels*. New York: Marvel Comics, 2008.

Crumb, Robert. *The Complete Crumb Comics Vol. 1: Early Years of Bitter Struggle*. Seattle, WA: Fantagraphics Books, 2001.

Eisner, Will. *A Contract with God*. New York: W. W. Norton, 2006.

Feiffer, Jules. *The Great Comic Book Heroes*. Seattle, WA: Fantagraphics Books, 2003. (Author's Note: This reprint of the 1965 edition omits the reprints of comics from the DC archives included in the original work, but Feiffer's text remains intact.)

Feldstein, Al, Wally Wood, Johnny Craig, Graham Ingels, and Jack Kamen. *The EC Archives: Vault of Horror Volume 1*. York, PA: Gemstone Publishing, 2007.

Finger, Bill and Bob Kane. *The Batman Chronicles: Volume 1*. New York: DC Comics, 2005.

Gaiman, Neil, Sam Kieth, Mike Dringenberg, and Malcolm Jones, III. *The Sandman Volume I: Preludes and Nocturnes*. New York: DC Comics, 1993.

Herriman, George. *Krazy and Ignatz 1916-1918*. Seattle: Fantagraphics Books, 2010.

Lee, Stan, and Steve Ditko. *Marvel Masterworks: Amazing Spider-Man Vol. 1*. New York: Marvel Comics, 2009.

Los Bros. Hernandez. *Maggie the Mechanic (A Love and Rockets Book)*. Seattle, WA: Fantagraphics Books, 2007.

McCay, Windsor. *Little Nemo in Slumberland 1906-1907*. Scotts Valley: CreateSpace, 2009.

McFarlane, Todd. *Spawn Origins Volume 1*. Berkeley, CA: Image Comics, 2009.

Mad About the Fifties. New York: MAD, 2005.

Miller, Frank. *Daredevil, Vol. 1*. New York: Marvel Comics, 2008.

Miller, Frank. *The Hard Goodbye. (Sin City Book 1)*. Milwaukie, OR: Dark Horse, 2005.

Miller, Frank, Klaus Janson, and Lynn Varley. *Batman: The Dark Knight Returns*. New York: DC Comics, 1997.

Moore, Alan and Dave Gibbons. *Watchmen*. New York: DC Comics, 2008.

Moore, Alan and Eddie Campbell. *From Hell: Being a Melodrama in Sixteen Parts*. Marietta, GA: Top Shelf Productions, 2000.

Moore, Alan, Stephen Bissette and John Totleben. *Saga of the Swamp Thing, Book 1*. New York: DC Comics, 2009.

Moore, Terry. *Strangers in Paradise, Pocket Book 1*. Houston, TX: Abstract Studio, 2004.

Outcault, Richard Fenton. *R.F. Outcault's The Yellow Kid: A Centennial Celebration of the Kid Who Started the Comics*. Northampton, MA: Kitchen Sink Press, 1995. (Out of Print)

Pini, Wendy and Richard Pini. *Elfquest: The Grand Quest Volume One*. New York: DC Comics, 2004.

Sacco, Joe. *Palestine*. Seattle, WA: Fantagraphics, 2002.

Siegel, Jerry and Joe Shuster. *The Superman Chronicles: Volume 1*. New York: DC Comics, 2006.

Sim, Dave. *Cerebrus, Volume 1*. Kitchener, Ontario, Canada: Aardvark-Vanaheim, 1991.

Smith, Jeff. *Bone Volume 1: Out from Boneville*. New York: Scholastic, 2005.

Spielgeman, Art. *Maus I: A Survivor's Tale: My Father Bleeds History*. New York: Pantheon, 1986.

In his original incarnation, the Sandman was a pulp-inspired green fedora-wearing superhero of the Golden Age, who used a knockout gas to defeat villains. In Gaiman's re-imagining of the character, the Sandman was Dream, one of the Endless, a family of anthropomorphized aspects of the universe that also includes Destiny, Death, Destruction, Despair, Desire, and Delirium. *Sandman* told the story of these siblings, moving back and forth in time, interacting with characters both real and imaginary.

Sandman was a tremendous success, critically and commercially. Aside from receiving eight Eisner Awards for comics excellence, it received attention in the non-comics press, and in 1991, was the first comic ever to win a World Fantasy Award.[50] *Sandman* proved that sequential art was capable of telling rich and complex stories, in a variety of genres.

Although DC and Marvel had tremendous successes, they were by no means alone in the comics marketplace. The rise of the comics specialty store saw a rise in smaller companies, and by the 1990s, these independents were beginning to claim a larger place in the comics field. Dark Horse Comics, which had always had a reputation for quality comics, found financial success with movie-tie ins such as *Terminator* and *Aliens,* and also became well known for publishing the original work of Frank Miller, most notably, the *Sin City* series of noir-crime comics.[51] Image Comics, a publishing company founded by disgruntled former Marvel artists, including fan favorites Todd McFarlane, Jim Lee, and Rob Liefeld, also entered the marketplace in 1992. In its early days, the Image line consisted mostly of superhero teams, such as Lee's *Wild C.A.T.s,* and Liefeld's *Brigade,* or monstrous super-heroes, such as McFarlane's *Spawn.*[52] These stories, featuring unique artwork colored by computer, were popular with fans, probably because they deviated little from the established superhero formula.[53] Image is a source of controversy in the comics industry, as the creator-founders of the company were all former Marvel artists, who minimized the importance of writers in comics, a reversal of the modern trend. Also, the tremendous anticipation and speculation, both critical and financial, that surrounded Image and its titles remains a point of division among comics fans.[54]

Other publishers, offering more "alternative" (i.e. non-superhero) stories were also active. A prime example of these books is *Bone,* an epic fantasy that is most often described as "Pogo-meets-*The-Lord-of-the-Rings.*" *Bone* was created and published by Jeff Smith as an irregularly produced comic. It ran for thirteen years, was collected into ten graphic novels, and produced two spinoffs.[55] In 2005, the entire series was collected into a massive "One Volume Edition" that clocked in at an impressive thirteen hundred pages. Scholastic's Graphix publishing line re-published the series with new colorized editions beginning in 2005. *Bone* is a true all-ages title, one that appeals to both children and adults.

Other independent publishers took advantage of the burgeoning "mature readers" market and published work specifically aimed for the adult market. The series *Love and Rockets*, published by Fantagraphics, started publication in 1982, but only began receiving critical and commercial attention in the 1990s. Created by Gilbert and Jaime Hernandez, who published their work under the moniker "Los Bros. Hernandez," *Love and Rockets* took full advantage of the freedom offered by an alternative press. An adult comic in almost every sense of those words, it not only featured "adult" content such as sexuality, but also complex storylines and rich characterizations. *Love and Rockets* also featured women of color who were "tall and short, gorgeous and plain, of various and multiple sexual appetites, all instantly recognizable both visually and emotionally."[56]

Throughout the 1990s, mainstream and alternative publishers continued to bring out graphic novels of both quality and depth. In 1992, Art Spiegelman wrote the followup to *Maus*, *Maus II: And Here My Troubles Began*, and received a special Pulitzer Prize. Alan Moore and Eddie Cambpell dove into the world of Victorian England and produced *From Hell*, a sixteen- part melodrama that investigated Jack the Ripper and the Whitechappel Murders. Kurt Busiek and Alex Ross examined the origins of the Marvel heroes through the eyes of an "everyman" in *Marvels*. The two creators expanded this concept in their original series *Astro City*. Joe Sacco, a comics artist and writer, traveled to Israel and the Palestinian territories, and produced *Palestine*—a collection of long and short comics stories, some autobiographical, others dramatizations of stories he was told—which received an American Book Award in 1996. Mark Waid looked at the potential future of the DC universe in the Elseworlds story, *Kingdom Come*. Terry Moore introduced the world to the trials of lesbian best friends Katchoo and Francine in the series *Strangers in Paradise*.

These titles in no way represent the whole of comics, or graphic novel publishing during the 1990s; they simply represent some of the most innovative and recognizable work in the field. Creators such as Neil Gaiman, Frank Miller, Todd McFarlane, and Jim Lee continued to produce comics, and other creators such as Garth Ennis, Matt Wagner, Daniel Clowes, Chris Ware, and Greg Rucka began to receive wider recognition for their work. Some of this recognition even came from libraries and librarians.

Many librarians had been comic fans from the beginning. With the increased media attention on comics, and with more and more quality materials being produced, many librarians started adding graphic novels to their collections. Others were drawn to graphic novels by witnessing the popularity of the materials themselves, or by hearing testimonials from other librarians. Graphic novels in libraries were given a boost by a rising interest in the importance of teen services in libraries, since, despite the number of "mature readers" titles being produced, comics are still thought of as a juvenile medium. Another factor in adding graphic novels to library collections was the tremendous interest in manga and anime, again, particularly by teen patrons. In October 1999, GNLIB-L, the first listserv for librarians discussing graphic novels, was born. As of March 2010, the list has more than seven hundred members. Perhaps the germinal moment in graphic novels achieving acceptance among librarians was in 2002, when the American Library Association held a preconference entitled "Get Graphic @ Your Library," which featured such luminaries as Neil Gaiman and Jeff Smith. This acceptance was reaffirmed in 2007, when Gene Luen Yang won the Printz Award for Excellence in Young Adult Literature for his coming of age tale *American Born Chinese*. The creation of the YALSA Great Graphic Novels for Teens list, also in 2007, guarantees that teen librarians attention stays focused on the format.

It is worth mentioning that America does not have a monopoly on graphic materials. Europe, particularly France, also has an active graphic novel community. The excellent *Epileptic* by David B., *Persepolis* by Marjane Satrapi, and the well-beloved *Asterix: The Gaul* are translations of French materials. For the purposes of this book, European titles will be grouped in with American produced works. Unfortunately, a more compete description of these materials falls outside the range of this discussion.

---

1   Indeed, the venerable Scott McCloud is one such historian, who argues the case for all of these objects as comics in *Understanding Comics: The Invisible Art* (New York: Harper, 2004).

2   Sabin, Roger. *Comics, Comix & Graphic Novels: A History of Comic Art*. London: Phaidon Press, 1996. Print. 11.

3   Sabin, 14.

4   "Timeline." *Comic Book Legal Defense Fund*. Comic Book Legal Defense Fund, 2008. *http://www.cbldf.org/timeline/index.shtml*. (6 March 2010)

5   Sabin, 20.

6   Comic Book Legal Defense Fund.

7   Sabin, 35.

8   Sabin, 35.

9   Sabin, 35.

10   "Superman." *The Superhero Book: The Ultimate Encyclopedia of Comic-Book Icons and Hollywood Heroes.* Ed. Gina Misiroglu and David A. Roach. Detroit: Omnigraphics, 2005. 538.

11   Harvey, Robert C. *The Art of the Comic Book: An Aesthetic History.* Jackson: University Press of Mississippi, 1996. 23.

12   Weiner, Stephen. *Faster than a Speeding Bullet: The Rise of the Graphic Novel.* New York: NBM Publishing, 2003. 3.

13   Weiner, 3.

14   Harvey, 129.

15   Weiner, 6.

16   Harvey, 136.

17   Weiner, 8.

18   Misiroglu, 151.

19   Weiner, 8.

20   Weiner, 9.

21   Sabin, 69.

22   Weiner, 11.

23   Weiner, 10.

24   Harvey, 35.

25   Weiner, 11.

26   Sabin, 95.

27   Weiner, 12.

28   Weiner, 11.

29   Sabin, 157.

30   Weiner, 11.

31   Sabin, 115.

32   Sabin, 165.

33   Weiner, 20.

34   Sabin, 157.

35   Weiner, 14.

36   Sabin, 158.

37   Weiner, 16.

38   Weiner, 26.

39   Sabin, 160.

40   Weiner, 30.

41   Weiner, 32.

42   Comic Book Legal Defense Fund.

43   Weiner, 32.

44   Sabin, 165.

45   The Hugo Award (By Year)." *World Science Fiction Society/WorldCon.* World Science Fiction Society, 2005. *http://worldcon.org/hy.html#88.* (6 March 2010)

46   Weiner, 34.

47   Sabin, 188.

48   Weiner, 38.

49   Sabin, 188.

50 "1991 World Fantasy Award Winners and Nominees." *World Fantasy Convention.* Ed. Sharon Sbarsky. World Fantasy Board., n.d. *http://www.worldfantasy.org/awards/1991.html* (6 March 2010)

51 Sabin, 173.

52 Dean, Michael. "The Image Story." *The Comics Journal: Newswatch.* Fantagraphics Books, 25 October 2005. *http://archives.tcj.com/3_online/n_image1.html* (6 March 2010)

53 Sabin, 174.

54 Dean, "The Image Story."

55 Smith briefly published *Bone* through Image, but ultimately returned to self-publishing through his company, Cartoon Books.

56 Chang, Jeff. "Locas rule: Los Bros Hernandez, Love and Rockets is back, and the timing has never been better…" *Color Lines Magazine* 22 March 2002. *http://www.thefreelibrary.com/* (6 Mar. 2010)

The Evolution of Manga

This chapter is to help you gain a background in manga. We will begin with a brief history of its origins in Japan. Then we will move across the ocean to the United States and give you a look at its history here. Once the history lesson is over, we will then break down the components of manga, so that you can understand some of the conventions used in the art form. Finally, we will discuss the different sub-genres specific to manga such *shojo*, *shonen*, and *shonen-ai* or boys' love.

Japanese manga has its own unique history, similar to the history of American and European comics. Visual art that tells a story has been in the Japanese culture since as early as the 12th century. During that time, large paper scrolls (up to twenty feet long) were created by Buddhist monks depicting legends and daily events, though the activity was not limited to them[1]. The Buddhist monk, Bishop Toba, is credited

---

Manga History at a Glance

12th Century: Wall Scroll Artwork.
1814: *Ukiyo-e* artist, Hokusai Katsushika, coins the term "manga."
Late 19th century: Western influences invade Japanese comics.
1930s: Children's magazines add serial comics.
1937-1945: Japanese government control the media.
1947: First "Red Cover" manga was published in Osaka.
1959: First weekly comic magazines were published.
Late 1960s: Women artists begin creating *shojo* manga.
1978: *Barefoot Gen* is translated and brought to America.
1987: VIZ Media, LLC is created.
2002: TOKYOPOP begins their "Authentic" manga line.

with creating the most well-known of these scrolls called *Chojugiga*—"Scroll of Frolicking Animals." This collection of scrolls depicts a humorous side to the Buddhist scrolls. Some of the stories included monks as animals bathing to prepare for a ceremony, men wrestling, and a monkey thief running from frogs. The importance of this scroll collection is due to its storytelling convention. It is considered the first Japanese scroll to use sequential artwork to convey a story. Read right to left, which is still how the Japanese read their text today, the stories slowly unveil themselves.

While only monks created or even saw most of these scrolls for hundreds of years, secular audiences discovered this style through the Buddhist amulets they purchased for traveling. Eventually, these amulets expanded into other depictions in the artwork such as demons, beautiful women, and other stock figures that could be reproduced easily. [2]

Moving from scrollwork into mass produced product occured in the 17th century with woodblock printing.[3] Of these mass produced prints, the most popular were the *Ukiyo-e* prints, which depicted the pleasures and pastimes of the red light district in Edo (now Tokyo). Eventually *ukiyo-e* prints explored more themes, but were always about the popular culture of the day. They encompassed humor and satire and popular culture, including prints of sumo wrestlers, kabuki actors, and courtesans. For a large sampling of *ukiyo-e* prints, the Tokyo Metropolitan Library has an online image database, which the library has been entrusted to preserve by the Japanese government. Over ten thousand of the entrusted prints have been digitally scanned for the public to view.[4] In 1814, the famous woodblock print artist, Hokusai Katsuhika, best known for his print *The Great Wave of Kanagawa*, coined the term "manga" for the first time.[5] The Chinese characters making up the word manga, were *man*—meaning "involuntary" or "in spite of oneself"—and *ga* for "pictures." Hokusai was describing the fantastical nature of his prints, which is how manga came to represent "whimsical pictures."

Western Influences

Before the mid-19th century, Japan was an isolated country. Very few foreigners were welcome on Japanese soil, but that changed when Commodore Matthew C. Perry forcefully opened Japan to foreign Western trade. Westerners brought with them comics and political cartooning from America and Europe. These western comics had artistic techniques different from the Japanese way of art—specifically shading, anatomy, and perspectives. Over the next fifty or so years, the Japanese artists adapted these influences into their traditional art, creating something wholly unique. Without this western influence and the Japanese visual history, manga would not be what it is today.

1930s to World War II

What most people consider manga—Japanese comics—really started forming in the 1930s when children's magazines added serialized comics in their issues.[6] Like manga produced today in Japan, these comics were first serialized in magazines and then, if popularity demanded, were compiled later in book form. Unlike today's manga, these stories were mostly published in color and highlighted traditional morals in a naïve style.[7] One of the most famous comic serials of this time period was *Norakuro*, about a dog who wanted to be a world famous general. The collected adventures bound together in a book format sold more than a million copies before the start of World War II (WWII).[8] Today, Norakuro is a famous icon in Japan, even having its own museum.

The drawing style of 1930s comics was theatrical, with a viewpoint as if the reader was watching a stage of actors performing.[9] Characters were drawn from head to toe. While American newspaper comic strips were beginning to play with camera angles, realism, and dramatic themes, Japanese comics did not venture down this path until after WWII.

When WWII began, the Japanese comic industry changed drastically. The government completely controlled the media and forced conformity on the artists, who were left with a handful of choices: quit being a comic artist, create harmless family comic strips, create single panels like political cartoons that vilified the enemy, or work within the government to create propaganda.[10]

Post World War II: The Beginnings of Modern Manga

Modern manga began after WWII. The Allied Occupation allowed more freedom of speech than the wartime Japanese government had, but the country itself was very subdued. Inexpensive entertainment was a high commodity for children and young adults after the war. Serialized comics for children began publication again and comic strips portrayed people trying to pick up the pieces and recreate their lives. In Osaka, professional booklending publishers—known as the "red cover" or "red book" comics, due to their red book covers—provided affordable cheap paperback compilations of comics. [11]

"Osamu Tezuka's manga techniques, which revolutionalized the comics of Japan, are still used today." [Photo credit: Tezuka Productions Co., Ltd. / Osama Tezuka, creator of Astro Boy]

The artists working in the "red cover" industry were paid very little, but were given creative freedom. One such artist was Osamu Tezuka. The only manga artist to be called "*Manga no Kami-sama*" (The God of Manga), Tezuka was to manga what Walt Disney was to American animation. His *New Treasure Island* is considered the first "Red Cover" manga produced after WWII .[12] Tezuka created *New Treasure Island* using the techniques that would quickly become the main style of manga. *New Treasure Island,* a novel-length comic book, used stylized frames, page layouts, and sound effects to create a story that made readers feel like they were watching a film. Tezuka was greatly influenced by cinema—particularly early American animation. His manga later incorporated cinematic techniques such as close-ups, different angles, and expanding action sequences from just one art panel art to multiple panels or even pages.[13] This expansion of sequences is one of the main differences in style between American comics and manga. Tezuka created a style that allows the art to show the action and emotion, rather than relying on words in text boxes and balloons. In addition to the cinematic techniques he incorporated into his artwork, Tezuka also was influenced by the character designs in the animation, in particular the large eyes of cartoon characters. This is another example of Japanese artists merging Western influences with their traditional styles to create something new and unique. Considered the most influential manga artist of all time, Tezuka's work can be found in every genre of manga and has inspired young comic artists throughout the decades.

By the late 1950s, more and more adults were reading comics that were originally intended for children and young teenagers. Fresh comic talent in the pay library industry in Osaka, which essentially became an alternative comics movement for the young adult reader, developed and polished a darker kind of manga called *gekiga* or "dramatic pictures"[14] that contrasted with the cartoonish appearance of the early modern manga. Instead of growing up and out of comics by the teenage years, comic readers and new comic creators embraced *gekiga* and its sophisticated style. To sample *gekiga* from that period, read *Golgo 13* by Takao Saito.

"*Golgo 13* is one of the oldest types of *gekiga* still being published in Japan."

Eventually, the mainstream manga accepted the diversity of *gekiga* and has since become a term that is used minimally in Japan. The terms manga and the *komikku* (comic) are used more in Japan's publishing world.

Eventually the market of the pay libraries or booklending companies in Osaka faded and manga artists worked and lived primarily in Tokyo to work for the major book publishers of Japan that had begun creating manga anthologies. The 1960s saw the magazines go from monthly issues to weekly issues, which are still the release schedule for most manga magazines today in Japan.

Today in Japan

Today's Japanese manga publishing industry creates manga for practically every age and in every genre imaginable. It holds its own against television, film, and video games. In fact, manga's animated counterpart, anime, continues to have a hold on Japan's television and film industry. Many anime are derived from manga originally, while others are co-conceived with manga for cross-marketing strategy.

First Manga Magazines

In 1959, two major manga publishers—still major publishers today—Kodansha and Shogakukan, released the first weekly comic anthology magazines. Apparently, the rivalry to be the first was so much that both publishers released their weekly magazines, *Shonen Sunday* and *Shonen Magazine*, ahead of schedule on the same day, March 17, 1959.

For example, a year before *Sailor Moon* was created, editorial meetings were held to create the basic storyline and arranged the timing of the television show to coincide with the manga magazine release.[15] Even some video games have manga counterparts!

Similar to the American critics' criticism that more technology and action means less plot and acting in movies, some opponents feel that cross-marketing creates an emphasis on a more action-oriented field of manga rather than a plot-oriented one. This commercialization through various mediums allows high visible marketing for these particular manga titles. These titles are at the core of Japanese popular culture, but are only a few of the many types of manga available.

Today's manga is still published initially in magazines, and the black and white manga are printed on different colored newsprint paper. The "telephone book" magazines can run hundreds of pages long with "chapters" from dozens of different stories. The most popular stories will then be collected into *tankobons*, graphic novels. This serialization within magazines allows for readership growth and input into the series. The magazines hold reader polls in almost every issue. The titles that receive more fan mail and poll responses may be highlighted with full color pages or cover art. The publishers' interactivity with the readers allows for more fan ownership and the influence of making something more or less popular.

Manga books and magazines make up an astronomical 25 percent of the Japanese publishing market.[16] As such, it is not hard to imagine that one major publisher, Shogakukan, publishes eighteen different comic magazines, some weekly while others are bi-weekly or monthly.[17] Another publishing company, Shueisha, has the most popular weekly comic magazine called *Weekly Shonen Jump*. This magazine has had astonishing circulation figures over the years. It has a circulation of 2.8 million copies per week.[18] To compare this with an American popular culture magazine, *Entertainment Weekly* has a circulation of 1.8 million copies per week and *Sports Illustrated* sells 3.3 million copies per month.[19] A series originally released in *Weekly Shonen Jump* currently holds the record for the highest initial print run of a graphic novel in Japan. At a whopping 2.85 million copies, a single volume of *One Piece* by Eiichiro Oda had the highest initial print run of a graphic novel in Japan.[20] A recent survey by Nomura Research Institute claims that manga *otaku* (fanatics) will spend eighty-three billion yen (around $700 million) a year on manga.[21] In 2004, more than eleven thousand volumes of manga were produced in Japan. Some of these volumes were series titles while others were stand-alone works. In 2003, the manga industry published over 6,700 different series.[22] Series can include a short-run piece, with only a small amount of volumes, or they can be epics with more than one hundred volumes. The lengths in series vary, because the creators own the stories and characters and ultimately decide when to end them—even at the height of a series' popularity, if they so choose. This differs from mainstream American comics. For example, the character Batman is owned by DC Comics. When one artist or writer finishes with Batman, another continues it. Company ownership allows for a long continuum that can span decades. In manga, the creators can make stories last a long time, but once the artist stops creating, the story stops. There are exceptions to this, but not many.

Manga in Japanese Libraries

With such a huge popular culture medium like manga in their country, one would think that manga is in every Japanese library. In actuality, very few libraries actually stock the *tankobons*, graphic novels, of the manga series. However, the cultural mindset toward manga is slowly evolving. At first, manga was seen as a passing leisure—not something a library should collect, since—once the series are completed—no one would enjoy reading them again. Then, manga was seen as ephemeral in nature. Now, Japan sees manga (and its animation counterpart, anime) as cultural exports. Libraries are taking this factor seriously and are working to change the library field's viewpoint of manga.

In fall 2005, Kristin went to Japan to tour libraries as the eighth Horner Fellow. This fellowship partners the Arizona Library Association and the Japanese Library Association, allowing librarians to visit one another's libraries. Kristin spent a wonderful three weeks visiting libraries in Tokyo, Kyoto, Osaka, and Hiroshima. She spent time in school, public, and university libraries that had manga in their collections. The varieties of how manga is being used in the libraries are interesting to note.

Some libraries, like the National Diet Library—the Japanese equivalent of the Library of Congress—are carrying manga material for research purposes. Publishers are requested to send a copy of every title they publish to be preserved in the Diet Library. The manga collection fills their closed stacks.

The stacks are arranged in the order in which a title is received. For a patron, this would be a terrible set-up, but because of the closed stacks, it allows the staff to build up their collection without have to continually shift their collection to insert new titles.

The Kyoto Seika University Library and Information Center, home to one of the few manga artist college programs, has two browsing collections for manga readers. Their manga collection is divided into two collections: one for the male readers and one for the female. The male collection is front and center, when one first walks through the door. It is completely packed with students reading. The female collection is hidden away in the basement stacks of the library, but is also filled with readers. The collection houses thirty thousand popular manga volumes, and is organized by the magazine anthology the manga was released in, then the artist's names in alphabetical order. This is similar to how the Japanese bookstores also organize their manga.

A junior high boys' school library in the Meiji area of Tokyo has a collection of graphic novels for their students to read. The school librarian found that it brought boys into the library who would not necessarily come in otherwise. She decided to focus her collection with specific rules: 1) The series had to be completed. 2) The series had to be recommended either by professional sources or by a staff member. The collection had a special emphasis on any manga that was set in the Meiji area, as this had special appeal to the teens.

There are two Japanese public libraries that stand out for their manga collections: the Chofu City Library and the Hiroshima City Library.

Photo credit: Kristin Fletcher-Spear

"Library users can borrow a bag with multiple volumes of a completed series like *Swan* by Kyoko Ariyoshi."

The Chofu City Library System in Tokyo has a large collection of manga. Library users can check out a bag of several continuous volumes of a completed manga series. For ongoing series, the individual volumes are available for regular checkout and are held in a separate area. The librarians have a clearly defined manga collection policy and a separate healthy budget for their manga purchases. The paraphrased translation of the collection policy is found at the end of this chapter.

The Hiroshima City Library System, which has a whole library just for manga, houses over eighty-one thousand volumes of manga and manga-related items. In addition to open stacks of manga interfiled by alphabetical order, they have a browsing area, a quiet reading room, a rare book collection, a most requested collection,

"The Manga Library of the Hiroshima City Library System has over 80,000 volumes of manga and manga-related nonfiction."

and manga anthology magazines. This superb collection has a hands-on approach to collection development. Every new series is hand evaluated by staff before purchasing and for each series that is added, subsequent volumes will be purchased for the collection. Because of success stories like these, many more Japanese libraries are considering new collections of manga.

Manga in America

With all the press manga has received the past few years, one would imagine that manga had just been discovered here in America. That would be untrue. In 1978, a group of activists translated *Barefoot Gen*, the first manga for America. *Barefoot Gen*'s anti-war message motivated the activists in Japan and California to have it translated and published.[23] It quickly went out of print and only recently has been revived by the publishing company, The Last Gasp.

The late 1980s saw an influx of black and white art in the American field of comics, making manga an easy fit for the market. In May 1987, the arrival of translated manga truly began. First Comics released *Lone Wolf and Cub*. At the same time, a new translating and publishing company, VIZ, partnered with Eclipse Comics to release *Mai the Psychic Girl, Kamui,* and *Area 88.*[24] In 1988, VIZ began to publish titles solo and began with *Grey*. At this time, VIZ became the fifth largest comics publisher in the US.[25]

Slowly other manga began trickling into America's comic specialty stores. Up until the mid-1990s, manga was "flipped"—meaning the manga would read like an American book—from left to right. At first, this sounds simple to do. It is just a mirror image, right? But a mirror image of the panel work would cause everything to appear backwards; characters would be left handed instead of right. Cars would be driven on the wrong side of the road. Clothes would be tied incorrectly. Particularly humorous to those "in the know" are the kimono. Kimono are always wrapped with the left side over the right, unless the person is dead; then it is the opposite. When a manga featuring characters wearing kimono is flipped to be Americanized, it inadvertently suggests that the characters are the walking dead, or zombies. While these might be viewed as minor details to most people, hardcore fans believe that such flipping alters the artist's work and intent.

Another way to create the "flipped" manga would be to cut out each panel and re-format it on the page. This takes a lot of time and requires touch-ups to the art. Dark Horse Comics made the effort to flip the artwork in *Blade of the Immortal* by Hiroaki Samura by using this technique. Manji, the main character, wears a swastika on the back of his clothing. If Dark Horse Comics had featured a mirror image of the artwork, instead of cutting each panel apart and replacing it in its proper order from left to right, then the symbol would have been viewed as the Nazi swastika, an offensive Through the late 80s and early 90s, manga was reaching more consumers in the comic specialty market. When one found manga in a store, it looked more similar to American comics than they do now. Manga had the same oversized graphic novels as the superhero comics of DC or Marvel. Manga could also be found in single issue comic books like the American comics. Then in 1996, a big name in manga publishing, TOKYOPOP arrived on the scene. Starting out as Mixx Entertainment, the company created *Mixxzine*, a manga anthology, and soon afterwards *Smile*, a manga anthology featuring *shojo* manga. After beginning to release their manga into graphic novels, TOKYOPOP did something unexpected. They revamped their graphic novel publishing line and instituted the "authentic manga." Authentic manga is simply manga that has not been "flipped," but instead kept in the right to left Japanese format. They also formatted the books to be smaller, more like the Japanese *tankobon*, graphic novels. By doing so, TOKYOPOP led the market in a new direction.

Today's manga is much easier and less time consuming to publish in comparison to the flipped manga. Because of this, it is less expensive for the consumer, dropping in price from $16-$18 a volume down to

$8-$12. Today, few manga are published in the "flipped" format. Older editions of titles may still be in print in this format but, depending upon their contract stipulations, many publishers are re-releasing the titles in the Japanese style. This all depends on negotiations with their Japanese publisher counterpart.

TOKYOPOP also led the market in another new direction—bookstores. Comic specialty stores had been the primary place to buy comics, but chain bookstores like Barnes & Noble and Borders have begun to emphasize their graphic novels, particularly manga. When graphic novels became one of the fastest growing segments in the publishing field, major bookstores had to start taking notice. In four years, graphic novels have more than doubled their market.[26] Bookstores account for the majority of that quick growth.

For example, in 2000 a Borders store in Glendale, Arizona, had a small graphic novel collection at the end of the science fiction section. It was badly out of order and consisted mainly of media tie-in products or superhero graphic novels. Six years later, their collection was displayed in an entirely different manner: The graphic novels were housed at the beginning of the art section, with shelves upon shelves of product, and more than 75 percent of those were manga. The section also had several comfy chairs, which enticed customers to sit and examine their merchandise. Four years after that, the section's appearance changed yet again. Now the marketing emphasis is on teen patrons, so the manga section leads into the teen area connecting science fiction and fantasy with the teen literature section. This particular Borders also has multiple display spaces for manga, American graphic novels, and novelty merchandise that would appeal to the manga reader, as well as knowledgeable staff to assist customers. While this Borders is definitely the ideal for manga readers, it is not represent the norm. But it does indicate that bookstores are listening and adapting to the graphic novel shopper. Teen librarians should take note of bookstore users, because the majority of them are teens and girls.

Many publishing companies have stated that libraries in America helped lead the legitimizing of graphic novels to the public. First came the Young Adult Library Services Association's 2002 preconference program "Getting Graphic @ Your Library," which featured a daylong professional development seminar on graphic novels and artists. Then, library professional journals featured articles on graphic novels; which explained why they needed to be in libraries and offered suggested lists of titles. The library continued to legitimize graphic novels by housing them not just in the children's department, but also in the teen and adult areas of libraries.

Overview of Manga

Now that you have a grasp on the history behind manga both in the U.S. and in Japan, we will look at manga itself. First, we will cover the characteristics of manga, highlighting some of its distinctive qualities, as well as, how to read a manga. Then we will explain the different categories of manga used in Japan.

Characteristics of Manga

Manga is often the area of graphic novels in which many librarians feel the least comfortable. In every sense possible, it feels foreign to many librarians. The titles are odd, the artists' and characters' names are foreign and can be difficult to pronounce, and just holding a volume in your hands seems awkward when you're not used to it. It's understandable. It's also something a librarian can get used to as she or he becomes more accustomed to manga. Manga has three major characteristics that librarians picking it up for the first time will notice: the way it is published, its artwork, and its art style.

When facing a graphic novel section of a bookstore or library, the first detail a person will notice is that the manga have a uniform appearance on the shelves. The volumes are all the same height and have approximately the same number of pages, and the spines in a series all have the same artwork with only the volume number distinguishing one from another.

Currently, in the United States, manga is published in a Japanese style. This means that the publishers have kept the book in its original right to left format, which makes the book look "backwards" to an American audience. The back of the book, at least as far as Americans are concerned, is actually the front. This can cause confusion in not only reading the book but cataloging it as well.

Manga reads from the right page's top right panel inward and downward and then it repeats on the left page. In anticipation of new readers who might be confused by the format, publishers of manga in the U.S. typically include a warning message: "Stop! You're Reading in the Wrong Direction!" This helpful page then provides a mini-lesson on how to read the manga. Kristin still remembers getting her hands on a Japanese manga magazine years ago that had the last chapters of *Rurouni Kenshin* in it.

Even though she doesn't read Japanese she thought she could at least have a basic idea of the ending of one of her favorite series through the pictures. Unfortunately, she forgot that the books were published differently in Japan. It did not make sense whatsoever—until a kind Japanese waiter told her to start from the right side not the left. So take note, even the librarians who read manga on a regular basis stumble with this sometimes!

The next item librarians may notice about these volumes is their lack of color. Manga is usually drawn and published in black and white. In Japan, manga is published originally in newsprint magazines that use colored paper to distinguish one story from another but very rarely contains any color artwork besides the occasional poster insert and cover artwork. This is in contrast to mainstream American comics, which are almost always published in color. If your idea of comics is limited to the colorful adventures of superheroes, the stark black and white artwork of manga may come as a surprise.

Finally, the most notable characteristic of manga that librarians will observe is of the character designs: the characters usually appear more Caucasian than Japanese. A distinctive set of facial characteristics is one of the most visible elements of manga, a visual style formed after years of melding Eastern and Western conventions of beauty. While this is a generalization, manga characters have unusually large eyes and small triangular noses that are not depicted when the character is drawn face on. The "big eyes" look was adopted from the look of Disney characters and other American animation

---

Manga Conventions

Explanations to help you understand some of the manga conventions regularly used.

- Black background used in the gutter space (the space between the panels) = flashback scene.
- Super-deformed characters (also called chibi) = huge heads, short bodies, and a some-what childlike appearance; used for comedic parodies.
- When a character scratches the back of their head = the character is embarrassed.
- A character has a giant sweatdrop on their head = the character is stressed.
- Blood gushes from a character's nose = they are sexually aroused.
- Bubble coming out of a character's nose = the character is sleeping.
- A character gives someone the "finger" = the character is acting defiant, but this is not as crude or vulgar as in America.
- Like in America, flowers have symbolic meanings. Artists use flowers in the background to help convey some of the emotions of the scene.

from the 1930s and 40s. Another stylistic feature in many manga titles is lanky character designs which make the characters appear tall. When familiar with the style, one will be able to distinguish manga from other countries' comics.

Once readers delve into the world of manga, they will discover that manga are generally character-driven stories that emphasize action and emotion, depending on the genre of the material. Artists use a cinematic approach to comic storytelling, using different "camera" angles, different point of views, setting the scenery, and showing the motion of a character.

Manga Categories

With the vast amount of material produced over manga's fifty plus years of existence, it should come as no surprise that every genre of literature, including nonfiction, can be found in the manga format. What may be surprising is that manga is categorized by age and sex groupings. There is overlap among these groupings, but the five most predominant ones are *kodomo, shonen, shojo, seinen,* and *josei.* The Japanese age groupings are more of a marketing strategy than a ratings guide. In other words, the manga is given an age grouping to market to a specific audience and not because it has something "naughty" or "innocent" in it. The American publisher VIZ comes closest to using these terms in their publishing of manga, particularly with their usage of *shojo* and *shonen.* However, these age groupings are not the same as our recommended ratings for manga released in America. Also, when it comes to gender-based marketing of manga, it is important to note that there will be many titles that appeal to both male and female readers. Just as with prose novels, a good book is a good book and will appeal to many different types and ages of readers.

Kodomo

Kodomo manga are published for young children. *Kodomo* can be for beginning readers through elementary school. This age category of manga has limited appeal in the American market,, but there are several titles available. Many manga titles that were not originally published as a *kodomo* manga may have been released here in the United States as an "all ages" title. For example, *Angelic Layer* by CLAMP was not published as a *kodomo* manga in Japan, but a *shonen* title. TOKYOPOP released the American version as an all ages title. This illustrates the overlap in the groupings as well as helps emphasize the importance of placing material in different areas of the library. American publishers have started publishing lines for children's manga. Udon Kids has released titles for the elementary aged. VIZ created their VIZ Kids line to market to this audience as well. In addition to their manga titles, they also have chapter books of their most popular manga series *Naruto*. This publishing line has what is probably the most famous *kodomo* manga available in the United States, *Pokémon*. In Japan, there are a handful of manga magazines for the elementary aged. The best known is CoroCoro Comic, which publishes the famous *Doraemon* manga.

> ### *Kodomo* Manga Titles
>
> Examples of children's manga titles.
>
> *Bakegyamon* by Mitsuhisa Tamura
> *Chi's Sweet Home* by Kanata Konami
> *Cowa* by Akira Toriyama
> *Dinosaur Hour!* by Hitoshi Shioya
> *Happy Happy Clover* by Sayuri Tatsuyama
> *Kilala Princess* by Rika Tanaka and Nao Kodaka
> *Ninja Baseball Kyuma* by Shunshin Maeda
> *Pokemon Diamond and Pearl Adventures* by Shigekatsu Ihara
> *Yotsuba&!* by Kiyohiko Azuma

Shonen

Shonen manga are simply comics created for, and marketed to, boys, ages ten to twenty. Many of the most popular manga series come from *shonen* comics like *Naruto, Dragon Ball Z, Bleach, Rurouni Kenshin,* and *Yu-Gi-Oh!* The most famous manga magazine is *Shukan Shonen Jump*, or in English, *Weekly Boys' Jump*. This magazine is one of the best selling weekly magazines in the world. It has a firm editorial policy of three themes: friendship, effort, and victory.[27] Without these themes, a story will not be published in the magazine. The themes may be why the popularity of *shonen* manga ranges

> ### *Shonen* Titles that Break Gender Barriers
>
> Titles that appeal to both sexes.
>
> *Angelic Layer* by CLAMP
> *Bleach* by Tite Kubo
> *InuYasha* by Rumiko Takahashi
> *Naruto* by Masashi Kishimoto
> *Prince of Tennis* by Takeshi Konomi
> *Ranma ½* by Rumiko Takahashi
> *Rurouni Kenshin* by Nobuhiro Watsuki

"VIZ's SJ spine label can be useful for a reader's advisory."

from elementary aged students to middle aged "salarymen" (Japanese businessmen). In 1991, a *Jump* editor, Hiroki Gato stated that *shonen* manga "shows that if you work hard you can accomplish anything…And that philosophy appeals to both children and adults."[28] The American publisher, VIZ, has a partnership with the Japanese *Shonen Jump* publishing company, which allows VIZ to publish these manga titles exclusively. VIZ has kept the *Shonen Jump* name—both for a monthly manga anthology and for its publishing line SJ and SJ Advanced. If a reader likes one title from the SJ line, then he will like many others and can easily look for the spine artwork of SJ. The SJ Advanced line may also appeal to similar readers, but are geared towards a more mature teen. The artwork VIZ provides on the spines of their graphic novels is a helpful tool to advise readers.

"*Shonen* manga emphasizes action, but also shows hard work and determination like in *Flame of Recca* by Nobuyuki Anzai."

Shonen manga is available in a wide range of genres. However, one element is a constant: In this genre, the characters train hard in order to defeat the enemy. Sports manga, like the immensely famous *Slam Dunk* by Inoue Takehito and *Captain Tsubasa* series, are known for their motivation of young people to take up a sport. *Captain Tsubasa*, a soccer manga currently not available in the United States, influenced many members of the Japanese 2002 World Cup team to play soccer.[29] One particular sports manga, *Ashita no Joe* (*Tomorrow's Joe*), had a huge following. When an arch-rival of Joe's died at the end of a boxing match in the manga, more than seven hundred fans gathered to hold a "funeral" for him.[30]

Shonen manga include mysteries, comedies, historical fiction, horror, and many other sub-genres, but they all emphasize action and spend less time on the emotions of the character. *Shonen* manga is the largest type of manga available in Japan. It is also the easiest to tie-in to other merchandise and media productions.

Seinen

Seinen, or men's comics, are written for older teens and adult men. Varieties of this include crime dramas, sex comedies, historical fiction, or hardcore fantasies. *Bastard!* by Kazushi Hagiwara and the manga of Ryoichi Ikegami are examples of *seinen*. Ikegami's manga series are penned by a manga writer in order to tell his story more succinctly and focuses on crime drama with realistic artwork. VIZ has a publishing line, Signature, and a web–based magazine, *IKKI*, that are "manga for grown-ups." The stories in *seinen* tend to lean in two directions—more action-oriented like Rei Hiroe's *Black Lagoon* series or more serious in nature like Naoki Urasawa's *20ᵗʰ Century Boys*. When published in America, these titles usually receive a rating of older teen or mature.

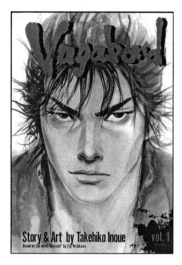

"Takehiko's Inoue's *Vagabond* is a fictional account of Miyamoto Musashi's life."

Shojo

Shojo manga are comics created for girl readers from ten to twenty years of age. Unlike *shonen* manga, *shojo* manga emphasizes the emotions and relationships of the characters. The story is typically about relationships, and whatever action that takes place during the story is a backdrop for the relationship. For example, *Fushigi Yûgi* by Yu Watase concerns the action of the main character, Miaka, who is transported into a book set in ancient China. There are many action segments in this series, but all are in relation to Miaka's feelings of love for the male lead, Tamahome, or her grief and helplessness on behalf of her best friend, Yui.

"In *shojo* manga, whatever action takes place during the story is just a backdrop for the relationships."

 Shojo manga began in 1953 when Osamu Tezuka, the most revered creator of manga, produced *Ribon no Kishi* (*Princess Knight*). This title is considered the first *shojo* narrative.[31] Until the late 1960s, *shojo* manga was created by men and contained what the creators thought girls should want to read.[32]

This usually meant the stories dealt with an idealized romance, marriage, and ultimately motherhood. The early 1970s brought a change, when women began creating *shojo* manga. Commonly called "The Magnificent 24s," a handful of women artists— Moto Hagio, Riyoko Ikeda, Yumiko Oshima, among others— completely transformed *shojo* manga. The Magnificent 24s wrote untraditional *shojo* stories that did not have specific subjects that would only be of interest to girls, and even produced work that men wanted to read.

Shojo Titles That Cross Gender Barriers

Titles that appeal to both sexes.

Banana Fish by Akimi Yoshida
Crimson Hero by Mitsuba Takanashi
D.N. Angel by Yukiru Sugisaki
Fruits Basket by Natsuki Takaya
Ouran High School Host Club by Bisco Hatori
Tsubasa RESERVoir CHRoNiCLE by CLAMP

Even the women artists who wrote traditional relationship stories for *shojo* magazines at this time were changing the way things were done. *Shojo* artists began playing with the layout of the story. Panels would be disrupted, frame sizes were manipulated, and symbolism was thrown into the artwork. This effective use of space led to dynamic changes in the way stories were read. The artists used the space manipulation to help evoke whatever emotion they wanted to convey.[33] The whole page was the story, not just frame by frame, because everything had meaning. The panel manipulation also facilitated flashbacks and dream sequences. This artistic style allows readers to respond to the emotions of the characters, just like the readers respond to the action in *shonen* titles.[34]

The typical *shojo* character look—big eyes, lanky arms and legs, petite noses, mouths, breasts, and hips—combines Japanese and European concepts of beauty.[35] The big eye look originally was a mimic of the Disney style and now is used to show the emotion of the character, literally the eyes are the windows to the soul.

While *shojo* titles deal with relationships, they still are represented by different genres. They can be historical fiction like the *shinsengumi* story *Kaze Hikaru* by Taeko Watanabe or fantasy like *Vampire Knight* by Matsuri Hino. The majority of them will be contemporary stories like *S. A* (*Special A*) by Maki Minami. These contemporary stories may throw twists into the

"*Shojo* manga gender-bend quite easily like in *W Juliet* by Emura in which a boy dresses as a girl and a girl is mistaken for a boy quite often."

plotlines, such as a subgenre of cross-dressing. *Shojo* manga can also gender-bend quite easily. Both *Hana Kimi* by Hisaya Nakajo and *W Juliet* by Emura are good examples of this subgenre. VIZ has a publishing line called *Shojo Beat* named after a defunct Japanese manga anthology. Their spine label, SB, is an easy source for a reader's advisory, as many girl readers who like one of these manga titles, will like most of the others.

"Like the SJ line, VIZ's SB spine artwork is handy for a reader's advisory."

Boys' Love *(Shonen-ai)*

A side category in *shojo* and *josei* manga that needs to be discussed separately is *shonen-ai* or "Boys' Love" (BL) manga. *Shonen-ai* literally means "boy love" but is a passé term for this category in Japan. This material is homosexual in nature, but is written for women and almost exclusively produced by women artists. Sometimes this manga is referred to as *Yaoi*, which has an American connotation indicating the material contains explicit homosexual sex. In Japan, *yaoi* actually refers to *doujinshi* (fan comics) that presents two male characters in a homosexual relationship. *Yaoi* is an acronym for *yama nashi, ochi nashi, imi nashi* ("without climax, without ending, without meaning").[36] As a librarian

---

Suggested Boys' Love Manga

Trying to figure out what this is all about? Try some of these titles to help you on your path to boys' love enlightenment. The titles run the gamut from light BL references to BL for adult readers. For other Boys' Love titles, check out Digital Manga Publishing's Doki Doki and June publishing lines. For American and other countries' boys love, check out NetComics and Drama Queen.

Boy Princess by Seyoung Kim
Cantarella by You Higuri
Dear Myself by Eiki Eiki
Earthian by Yun Kouga
Eerie Queerie by Shuri Shiozu
Fake by Sanami Matoh
Gorgeous Carat by You Higuri
Graviation by Maki Murakami
Hands Off! by Katsumoto Kasane
Il Gato Sul G by Tohko Miyagi
Invisible Boy by Hotaru Odagiri
Kimi-Shiruya: Dost Thou Know? by Satoru Ishihara
La Esperança by Chigusa Kawai
Loveless by Yun Kouga
The Moon and the Sandals by Fumi Yoshinaga
Only the Ring Finger Knows by Satoru Kannagi
Rin! by Satoru Kannagi
Same Cell Organism by Tohko Miyagi
Time Lag by Shinobu Gotoh
*Train*Train* by Eiki Eiki
Until the Full Moon by Sanami Matoh
Yellow by Makoto Tateno

you may hear all of these different terms, but the terminology Boys' Love (or BL) is the most acceptable term to use with fans.

Not all Boys' Love stories are explicit, and many teen girls and adult women flock to this genre of manga. There are many discussions about why this material is of interest to women, the most common assumption being that such manga represent female fantasies. Toshihiko Sagawa, an editor for the comic company that produces the *June* comics line, theorizes that the characters are an "ideal that combine assumed or desired attributes of both males and females.[37] What this means is that while the characters are males, they are the embodiment of female ideals. In a survey administered by Robin Brenner, she found that some readers responded more to the male characters than the stereotypical *shojo* main female character, and also that there are two pretty boys to look at rather than only one![38] The same survey revealed that 25 percent of respondents were gay males who read BL manga. So while Boy's Love titles do not necessarily provide realistic portrayals of gay relationships, their romantic fantasies are of interest toA note of caution about these BL titles: Due to the controversial nature of the books, the age ratings assigned by their publishers can be skewed. A boys' love title may receive a rating of 16+, but only contains a single kiss in the story. But if a title is rated 18+ or M for mature, then this is usually an indicator that the material contains sexually explicit content. Examples of popular Boys' Love manga are *Gravitation* by Maki Murakami and *Only the Ring Finger Knows* by Satoru Kannagi and Hotaru Odagiri.

Josei

Josei, or women's comics, are geared towards older teen and adult women. The majority of the comic artists, *manga-ka*, who create this age range of comics are women. These comics deal with realistic relationships and women's lives—particularly single women. There is a crossover of *shojo* and *josei* beyond the boys' love genre. Ai Yazawa's *Nana* is a *josei* title about two twenty-somethings who struggle to survive in Tokyo, but many consider it *shojo* because it was published under Viz's Shojo Beat line. Some other examples of *josei* include Erica Sakurazawa's *Angel* and

"*Happy Mania* by Moyoco Anno is a search for love that has been called manga's version of *Sex in the City*."

Moyoco Anno's *Happy Mania*. When published in the U.S., these graphic novels are usually marketed as older teen or mature titles.

At a Glance: Differences between Manga and American Comics	
Manga is…	**American Comics are…**
read from right to left. Some manga published in the US has been "flipped" for publication, and now reads left to right.	read from left to right like all English language materials.
most often published with a trim size of 5"x7".	often published with a typical trim size of 8"x 12", however, trim sizes can vary widely.
almost always produced in black and white.	usually published in color if they are from a mainstream press; however, many independent presses prefer to publish in black and white.
the work of one manga-ka and many uncredited assistants; in most manga, you will see only one name on the credits page.	often a collaboration between more than five creators; including a writer, a penciler, a colorist, a letterer, and original covers artist. However, many independent comics artists create their works all on their own.
known to feature a fluid panel layout.	much more likely to be a progression of squares.
more reliant on visual cues to further the story, with text acting as dialog and clarification.	wordy in comparison to most manga.
often told from a first-person perspective.	often told from a third-person perspective.
known for a distinctive style of artwork, particularly in character design. Manga characters typically have unusually large eyes and small triangular noses that sometimes disappear when the character is drawn face on.	produced in a variety of art styles, which can differ widely from artist to artist.

1   Gravett, Paul. *Manga: Sixty Years of Japanese Comics.* New York: Collins Design, 2004. Print. 18.

2   Schodt, Frederik L. *Manga! Manga! The World of Japanese Comics.* New York: Kodansha International, 1983. Print. 32.

3   Schodt, *Manga! Manga!,* 33.

4   Tokyo Metropolitan Library. *Image Database.* Tokyo Metropolitan Lib., 2004. Web. *http://metro.tokyo.opac.jp/tml/tpic/resprint_d/all/isbn001_0_100/isbn001_001_001.html.* (16 March 2010)

5   Schodt, *Manga! Manga!,* 35.

6   Schodt, *Manga! Manga!,* 51.

7   Schodt, *Manga! Manga!,* 54.

8   Gravett, *Manga,* 23.

9   Gravett, *Manga,* 23.

10   Schodt, *Manga! Manga!,* 56.

11   Schodt, *Manga! Manga!,* 66.

12   Shimizu, Isao. "Red Comic Books: The Origins of Modern Japanese Manga." *Illustrating Asia: Comics, Humor Magazines, and Picture Books.* Ed. John A. Lent. Honolulu: University of Hawai'i Press, 2001. 137-150. Print. 150.

13   Schodt, *Manga! Manga!,* 62-63.

14   Gravett, *Manga,* 38.

15   Schodt, Frederik. *Dreamland Japan: Writings on Modern Manga.* Berkeley: Stone Bridge Press, 1996. Print. 93.

16   JETRO: Japan External Trade Organization. "Manga Industry in Japan ." 2008. PDF file. *http://www.jetro.org/trends/market_info_manga.pdf* (10 March 2010)

17   Shogakukan Online. Shogakukan Inc., n.d. Web. *http://comics.shogakukan.co.jp/.* (16 Mar. 2010)

18   "Comic Magazine for Boys." *JMPA Magazine Data.* Japan Magazine Publishers Association, 2007. Web. http://www.j-magazine.or.jp/data_001/index.html. 16 Mar. 2010.

19   "Circulation Facts and Figures." *2004 Avg. Circulation for Top 100 ABC Magazines.* Magazine Publishers of America, 2004. Web. *http://www.magazine.org/consumer_marketing/circ_trends/.* (9 February 2006)

20   Williams, Joshua. "One Piece Vol. 56 to set publishing record for comic books." *Japan Headlines Examiner.* Clarity Digital Group, n.d. Web. *http://www.examiner.com/x-16352-Japan-Headlines-Examiner~y2009m11d27-One-Piece-Vol-56-to-set-publishing-record-for-comic-books.* (16 March 2010)

21   "1.72 Million Otaku in Japan." *Anime News Network.* Anime News Network, 10 Oct. 2005. Web. *http://www.animenewsnetwork.com/news/2005-10-10/1.72-million-otaku-in-japan.* (16 March 2010)

22   "The Fantastic World of Japanese Manga." *Shogakukan Online.* Shogakukan, Inc. , 20 Jan. 2003. Web. *http://www.shogakukan.co.jp/english/htm/m_manga_essei.html.* (19 Mar. 2005)

23   Gravett, *Manga,* 154

24   Gravett, *Manga,* 155.

25   *Manga/Anime 101.* San Francisco: Viz, LLC., 2004. Print. 22.

26   "Graphic Novels Grow 25% in 2004." *ICv2 Retailers Guide to Graphic Novels #4.* 2005: Print. 4.

27   Schodt, *Dreamland Japan,* 89.

28   Gravett, *Manga,* 59.

29   Gravett, *Manga,* 54.

30   Gravett, *Manga,* 52.

31   Fusami Ogi, "Gender Insubordination in Japanese Comics (Manga) for Girls," *Illustrating Asia: Comics, Humor Magazines, and Picture Books.* Ed. John A. Lent. Honolulu: University of Hawai'i Press, 2001. 171-86. Print. 184.

32   Gravett, *Manga,* 74.

33 Gravett, *Manga,* 79.

34 Gravett, *Manga,* 79.

35 Gravett, *Manga,* 76.

36 Fusami, 186.

37 Schodt, *Dreamland Japan,* 122.

38 Brenner, Robin. *Understanding Manga and Anime.* Westport: Libraries Unlimited, 2007. Print. 136-7.

Chofu City Library's Manga Collection Development Policy as of September, 2004

Translated by Daisuke Komuku

Simplified by Kristin Fletcher-Spear

What They Do Not Collect:

- Manga specifically aimed at children only, except for learning and study material in manga format. The children librarian staff order those titles specifically.

- Practical Manga that are learning and educational tools for adults

- *Dojinshi* (fan comics) that are unpublished

- Weekly and Monthly Magazines

Criteria for the Collection:

- Socially recognized manga are important, as are manga that represents each era

- A wide range of readership is required.

- Titles that have been reviewed and already published are eligible.

- For those series just being published, copyright protection must be confirmed.

- Award-winning titles

- Completed long run series are housed in sets

- Even if the work is by a well-acclaimed author or illustrator, the book is still evaluated.

- Media tie-in manga will be considered but must be evaluated first. The decision to buy is not based upon the original medium, whether movie, theater, or television.

- Vivid visuals portraying violence, sexual explicitness, anti-social and immoral topics, racism, and violation of human rights will be taken into serious consideration.

- Patron requests are not accepted for manga titles, because special effort is required to get out of print material.

Circulation Criteria:

- Manga titles are not eligible for interlibrary loan.

- Due to the printing nature of graphic novels, a title may become too difficult to buy additional copies, so the policy of purchasing extra copies for large holds is not valid for manga titles.

Benefits of Graphic Novels

Now that you have some background information on comics in general and manga in particular, we want to discuss the educational benefits of graphic novels. Many librarians have had to defend graphic novel collections to their administrations and have explained the various benefits that graphic novels can provide as a rationale for their inclusion in a public or school library collection. Note that the authors are not reading specialists, teachers, or cognitive scientists, and what follows is both a review of the literature and observations made by the authors.

Visual Literacy

Commenters often mention "visual literacy" in connection with graphic novels. Visual literacy is defined as the ability to understand, create, and use visual images.[1] As media becomes more integrated, the ability to decipher meaning from imagery becomes more important. Unfortunately, visual literacy may get ignored in schools and other settings once children begin to read on their own. Graphic novels offer a new medium for literacy, one that acknowledges the impact of visuals.[2] In any subject area, graphic novels can bring media literacy into the curriculum, as students explore the medium itself. For example, the use of color and its effect on mood and emotion would be one avenue of discussion. How realism, or the lack thereof, can affect the message of the work would be another.[3] Graphic novels also can keep students actively involved in their reading, since the students have to combine the text and their interpretations of the images to get the full story of a graphic novel. Using graphic novels to learn how to interpret meanings conveyed by visual imagery is a skill that may translate easily in today's world of visual media.

In addition to teaching visual literacy to students, graphic novels can assist students who are already adept at visual literacy with their studies. Many teenagers intuitively grasp the concept of visual literacy by playing video games, because such games successfully incorporate the combination of text, visuals, and symbolic cues which the player must decipher in order to win. Students may not, however, understand how to transfer the skills they use in gaming into school work. For teens who struggle in classes, they may benefit from graphic novels that aid in understanding information. For example, many classic novels have been adapted into graphic novels that may ease the struggling student's understanding, because such adaptations are not bogged down by heavily-worded descriptions. A math student dealing with statistics may feel more at ease with *The Manga Guide to Statistics* by Shin Takahashi rather than a standard academic textbook.

Reluctant Readers

Another benefit to graphic novels is their usefulness in reaching reluctant readers. The authors want to be very clear in this discussion of reluctant readers, that we are referring to those teens who *can* read, but choose not to—the alliterate, rather than the illiterate, teens who cannot read.

Perhaps the greatest appeal of graphic novels to reluctant readers is that they are cool. This means that many teens will read them of their own volition, with no pushing required. The myriad movie adaptations of action and superhero comics and anime television shows that are based on or tied into graphic novels and manga increase their teen appeal. Graphic materials are of high interest, and teens will work to read them.

Some teachers have discovered the power of comics as teaching tools. In the article "Comics in the Classroom," Robert A. Burns discusses using comics to teach literary terminology and figurative language. He notes that the use of comics "brings the subject down to earth" and takes advantage of a material that kids actually read.[4] Many reluctant readers have difficulty concentrating for long periods of time on a prose novel; for those readers, the graphic novel provides an opportunity to complete a book and have a successful reading experience.[5]

Many teachers and librarians are concerned that the textual element of comics may be too unsophisticated for a teen audience; in short, the words are not "at grade level." However, graphic novels, in general, have a wide variety of reading levels. Donald P. Hayes, a sociologist at Cornell University, conducted a lexicographical survey of a variety of printed media— including newspapers, novels, and comic books—and found that many comics are written at a junior high school reading level. He also found that comics contained an average of 53.5 rare words per one thousand words. This is in comparison to the 30.9 rare words found in children's books and the 52.7 in adult books[6]. Stephen Krashen, in *The Power of Reading*, found a similar reading level, particularly in the superhero genre.[7]— no doubt because scientific terminology and topics are often prevalent in such material. Although not every graphic novel is at a teen's reading level, it is worth noting that one of the most popular teen novels of all time, *Twilight,* is written at a fourth grade reading level[8]. What is important to keep in mind is the amount of reading a teen does. In 1988, researchers determined that one million words per year outside of school was the average dose of reading for a middle class child.[9] This number correlates to approximately twenty minutes of independent reading outside schoolwork each day[10]. While graphic novels contain fewer words than prose novels, there is still a significant amount of reading being done, especially taking into account the voracious nature of graphic novel readers.

Imagery, a key component of graphic novels, may assist reluctant readers in another way. Many reluctant readers, for a variety of reasons, cannot create a mental image of what they are reading. Lower ability readers do not employ mental imagery, and for students who don't see what they read, visual art may be an aid that provides a "concrete metacoginitve marking point" by which readers can see what they understand and begin to explore what they do not.[11] In other words, lacking the skill to create imagery out of words, reluctant readers may find graphic novels easier to read because the imagery is explicit—the reader does not need to create it themselves.

English Language Learners

Graphic novels are a valuable tool for English language learners. As with reluctant readers, visual cues aid the learner in comprehending the story. Unlike many novels, graphic novels more accurately portray what language sounds like in the real world by employing sound, slang, and idioms.[12] For example, many people realize that each country or language has their own sounds for commonplace noises. In Japan, the sound a chick makes is "piyo, piyo," While in America, it is "cheep, cheep." Slang and idioms are something one picks up as he or she begins using the language fluently. Graphic novels assist in this to show these examples of phrases in proper usage. Like the idiom says, "A picture paints a thousand words." Graphic novels can also teach phrases and aspects of cultural English like nonverbal language, new topic signals, ellipses, the appropriate use of language in different social contexts, and even body language.[13] English language learners are likely to benefit from graphic novels in many of the same ways as the reluctant reader. The most significant similarity is that like reluctant readers, English language learners become emotionally invested in the graphic novels because of the engaging content. In *Going Graphic*, author Stephen Cary provides frequent anecdotal evidence that English language learners see graphic novels as non-threatening reading, so the learners feel more relaxed while reading them.

Expansion Effect

A benefit of having graphic novels in your collection is one that we like to call the expansion effect. Graphic novels often serve as a gateway to more reading. Because of the collaborative nature of graphic novels, particularly American graphic novels, they lend themselves to "literary exploration"— discovering connections among books, authors, illustrators, and other creators.

The story of Bill[14], a seventeen-year-old patron at the Main Library in Glendale (AZ), serves as a good example of the expansion effect. At one of the librarian's recommendation, Bill read the first Sandman graphic novel, *Preludes and Nocturnes.* Bill is a voracious reader with a wide variety of interests. Having thoroughly enjoyed *Preludes and Nocturnes,* he proceeded to read the other nine books in the Sandman series, as well as the companion books *The Sandman: The Dream Hunters* and *The Sandman: Endless Nights.* A little catalog searching on Bill's part revealed to him that Gaiman had written two spin-off books, *Death: The Time of Your Life* and *Death: The High Cost of Living,* featuring a major character from Sandman. Bill then read those. Another catalog search turned up several more Gaiman graphic novels, all of which Bill sought out. Having exhausted Gaiman's graphic input, Bill then turned to his prose works, *Neverwhere, Stardust, American Gods, Anansi Boys* and the short story collection *Smoke and Mirrors.* Having exhausted Gaiman's output for the time being, Bill backtracked and found three more spin-off graphic novels from the *Sandman* series, none of which were written by Gaiman. Again, after reading those, he noticed one of the authors, Caitlin R. Kiernan, also wrote horror novels, and another writer, Bill Willingham, wrote a comic series called *Fables.* After seeking these out,

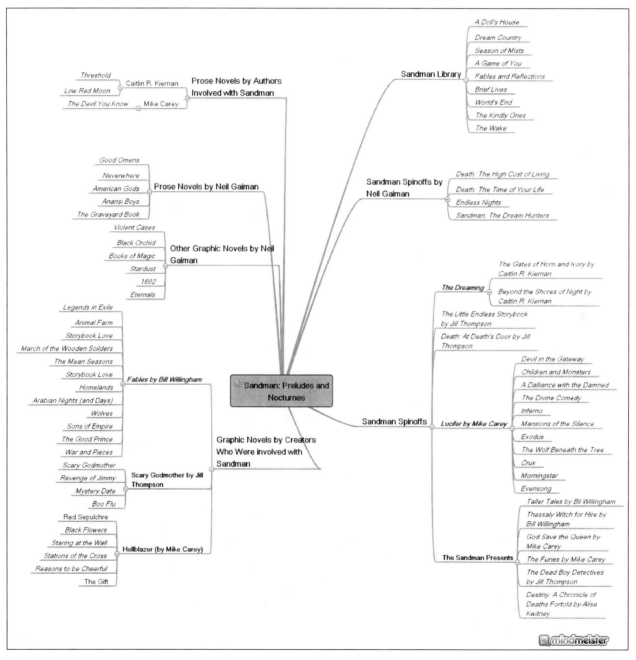

"The sum total of Bill's reading through the expansion effect can be seen in this chart."

Bill discovered that some of the artists on *Sandman,* Michael Zulli, P. Craig Russell, and Jill Thompson had created comics of their own. Again, Bill found the books and read them. Eight years later, Bill has since read more than forty graphic novels, novels, and short story collections on the strength of one recommendation several year ago.

While Gaiman and *Sandman* provide the most dramatic illustration of the expansion effect, they are by no means the only example. Teens that enjoy Brad Meltzer's work on *Justice League* seek out his mystery novels. More than one *Batman* fan has been spotted with a Greg Rucka book, both graphic and prose, stuck under his or her arm. Fans of the webcomic *Megatokyo* often find the collections of this comic in the library, and then seek out the manga titles discussed by the protagonists. Because of the collaborative nature of American graphic novel production, there are nearly limitless opportunities for teens to seek out new reading options, both graphic and not.

The expansion effect can also be illustrated with manga, but it works in a different way. As many librarians who carry manga in their collections can attest to, manga readers typically devour nearly all the manga, regardless of genre or topic. Granted, some will prefer one type of manga to another, but the majority of readers prefer manga to other types of graphic novels. That being said, manga lends itself well to the expansion effect. The first expansion effect of manga upon readers is those attracted to a specific genre. This is the manga reader who reads anything within the genre— whether it is VIZ's Shonen Jump line or samurai period pieces. This type of manga reader is most likely not going to have a favorite manga creator, but will have a favorite type of manga—shonen, shojo, fantasy, sports, et cetera. Manga readers can quickly devour a genre by working their way through one book at a time. Considering that the majority of manga being published in America are multi-volume series, it is no real surprise that the manga reader will end up reading hundreds of volumes.

The second manga expansion effect is with the library's nonfiction collection. Many times readers become interested in a cultural aspect of a manga. For example, many who have read *Rurouni Kenshin,* a Meiji Period manga series, then seek nonfiction books about that era, particularly about Commodore Perry, whom some think caused Tokugawa Shogunate to fall and the Meiji Period to begin. One particular work that appeals to such readers is *Commodore Perry in the Land of the Shogun* by Rhoda

Blumberg. Another example is the samurai period manga series. Any of these series can motivate teens into reading nonfiction about the samurai, but one series in particular, *Vagabond* by Takehiko Inoue, inspires teens into reading the prose version. *Vagabond* is the graphic novel adaptation of Eiji Yoshikawa's *Musashi*, a fictionalized biography about Miyamoto Musashi, and is one of the most well known Japanese novels. *Vagabond* also leads readers to Musashi's own work, *The Book of Five Rings*. The expansion effect from manga into nonfiction can work with most titles. *Naruto* readers learn about ninjas and martial arts, while *Fruits Basket* readers learn about the Chinese Zodiac. Manga introduces cultural references to teens that can send them to nonfiction to learn more.

Another expansion effect of manga is through the various prose novels that are either based on or are the basis for a manga or anime. *Battle Royale* was one of the first, but almost every major manga publisher has at least dabbled in translating these novels into English. These companies know that if the readers like the story in the manga format, they will either want to learn more of the story, if they can get their hands on it, or will pursue the original material the manga was based upon.

The final manga expansion effect is the incentive to read anime and comic magazines like *Newtype USA* and to inspire some readers to produce their own creations, often seeking how-to-draw books for guidance. Unlike the majority of prose readers, manga and graphic novel readers participate in an active and enthusastic fan culture. Many manga and comics fans produce "fan art" based on their favorite series or even create their own characters. Take a moment to peruse *http://www.deviantart.com* and see the many options of manga/anime style artwork—both fan art and original creations—that are available. Those who cannot draw, write fan fiction. A quick glance at *http://www.fanfiction.net* shows literally thousands of pieces of original fiction based on manga, anime, and comics.

Some fans of the format even envision themselves not just as consumers, but also as creators of manga and comics. This is one of the major differences between the readers of primarily prose novels and the readers of primarily graphic novels. A person who thoroughly enjoys historical novels is not likely to subscribe to a magazine focused solely on historical fiction, nor will the majority of readers try writing their own novel. However, because many graphic novel readers can see themselves creating a graphic novel, magazines devoted to manga and comics are some of the most requested periodicals in public libraries. What is especially encouraging is that many of these "wannabe" comics creators are girls, who, thanks to the rise of manga, have no qualms about entering the traditionally "boys only" field of comics creation.

Active vs. Passive Readers

Teens who read graphic novels are more active readers, not only in the act of reading, but also in terms of seeking out reading material. At its most basic level, reading a comic involves following a dual narrative of images and text.[15] Graphic novels rely on an interdependency of text and visuals; in order for the whole story to be told, words and imagery must be read in concert. Therefore, reading comics requires a negotiation of textual and visual forms.[16] Teens who read graphic novels must balance "graphic literacies"—expository print, dialog balloons, and purely visual elements.[17] This activity requires a demanding cognitive process. Reading comics may be quick, but it is wrong to assume that it is easy.

Reading comics is an individual experience, one that requires a great deal of imaginative input from the reader. Much of the action in comics must be imagined by the readers, as it is not explicitly depicted on the page. The reader fills in their mind the action occurring between different panels as their eyes flow over the gutter space between the panels. This is in contrast to film, where the action is shown in complete scenes to the viewer, or to reading prose novels, where the action is often described for the reader. In either case, in both books and film, the viewer/reader is taking part in an objective process, observing or reading what is being acted out or portrayed. In reading comics, the readers must extrapolate action from the surrounding art and text, and using this information create their own meaning—their own explanation of what is occurring, but not shown or described. Scott McCloud called this process "closure," while other researchers in the area of visual literacy refer to this mental leap as synecdoche—using a part to determine the whole. The comics reader must perform this act of closure automatically in order to follow the story being told. The authors think that teens, in particular, can perform these acts of cognition instinctively, as teens are the product of a culture that is increasingly "icon driven" and have a high level of visual literacy. Teens are used to providing meaning for visual imagery; they do it every time they log on to the Internet or use their cell phones. Teens gravitate to comics, because the act of closure is automatic for them—they don't have to think about it. Conversely, the reasons many librarians struggle with comics is that, being strong textual readers, they may lack the skills necessary to extrapolate meaning from the combination of art and text. Synecdoche is less intuitive for them, so they struggle to make the cognitive leap that makes reading comics possible.

---

1   Kovalik, Cindy and Peggy King. "Visual Literacy" *Visual Literacy. http://www.educ.kent.edu/community/VLO/literacy/ index.html* (7 December 2005)

2   Schwarz, Gretchen E. "Graphic Novels for Multiple Literacies." *Journal of Adolescent and Adult Literacy.* 46, no 3. 262-266.

3   Schwartz, 263

4   Burns, Robert A. "Comics in the Classroom" Exercise Exchange; a journal for Teachers of English in High Schools and Colleges. 45:1 (1999) 31-32.

5   Cary, Stephen. *Going Graphic: Comics at Work in the Multilingual Classroom.* Portsmouth: Heinemann, 2004, 146.

6   Cunningham, Anne E, and Keith E. Stanovich. "What Reading Does for the Mind." *American Educator.* 22, no.1-2, 1998. 9-10.

7   Krashen, Stephen D. *The Power of Reading: Insights from the Research.* Englewood: Libraries Unlimited, 1993, 53.

8   Popular accelerated reader company Renaissance Learning puts the ATOS Level of *Twilight* at 4.9, which means the text could likely be read independently by a student whose reading skills are at the level of a typical fourth grader during the ninth month of school. (*http://www.arbookfind.com*). The website, *http://www.lexile.com* puts the book's lexile level at 720, which is average for a 4th grade reader. (*http://www.lexile.com/about-lexile/grade-equivalent/grade-equivalent-chart/*)

9   Krashen, *The Power of Reading*, 9.

10   Cunningham, Anne E, and Keith E. Stanovich. "What Reading Does for the Mind," 11.

11   Wilhelm, Jeffrey D. "Reading is Seeing: Using a Visual Response to Improve the Literary Reading of Reluctant Readers." *Journal of Reading Behavior.* 27:4 (1995), 467-503.

12   Cary, *Going Graphic*, 156.

13   Cary, *Going Graphic*, 33.

14   All names have been changed.

15   Wilhelm, Jeffrey D. "Reading is Seeing: Using Visual Response to Improve the Literary Reading of Reluctant Readers," 467-503.

16   Murray, Chris. "Reading Comics: Narrative and Visual Discourse in Comic Art." Paper presented at 1997 SWIG Conference. *http://www2.rgu.ac.uk/criad/swig/SWIGWEBMURRAY.html.*

17   Freeman, Matt. "The Case for Comics." *Reading Today.* 15:3 (Dec 1997/Jan 1998), 3-6.

Collection Development and Management

A well-written collection development policy is an absolute necessity, particularly when dealing with graphic novels. In our experience, however, these policies seem to be the exception rather than the rule. Very few libraries mention graphic novels in their collection development policy, and fewer still have policies specifically dealing with graphic novels. In this section, we will define what should be included in a collection development policy for graphic novels.

User Group and Age

The first element of a graphic novels' collection development policy is defining your user group. Graphic novels have the ability to reach across age groups and reading levels. It is not unusual to find adults browsing in the teen collection for the latest manga and superhero comics; nor is it strange to find teens seeking out *Bone* in the youth department. By defining your user group in your policy, you can maintain a clear focus on exactly for whom you are buying. This is particularly useful when answering the questions of patrons who want to know why you are purchasing certain titles and not others. For example, when the graphic novel collection at the Main Library at the Glendale (AZ) Public Library was first begun, it was designed with older teen readers in mind. Therefore, the collection contained many titles, such as *Sandman, Hellblazer,* and *Lone Wolf and Cub* that would not be appropriate in a youth collection. By clearly defining our intended user group—older teens—before beginning to purchase, we were able to deflect any potential challenges, both by the public and the staff.

Selection Criteria

The next area that needs addressing is selection criteria or how to decide what to buy. You should consider addressing the quality of the materials you intend to buy in your policy. Do you plan to focus only on well-reviewed titles, and is a review necessary for purchase? Will your collection include award winners or the works of particularly well-respected or popular creative teams? Also, consider the issue of diversity in your collection. Will your collection focus on more independent and alternative presses, as opposed to more mainstream offerings? Will you focus on manga, American materials, or a mix of both? Consider these issues before you begin to purchase graphic novels, or reevaluate them as you craft a policy. As you consider quality, remember that graphic novels are a popular medium, both in terms of content and usage. You may have more requests for graphic novels than you will be able to fill. Therefore, in your collection development policy, you want to specifically address the issues of patron requests and local interests. Will your collection seek to fulfill patron requests, regardless of quality? As every librarian knows, popularity and quality do not always go hand in hand, and if your collection development policy states you will only purchase well-reviewed or award-winning titles, you may disappoint some patrons.

With the recent boom in films and television shows based on graphic novels, the user awareness of these materials has increased. In the summer of 2008, Glendale (AZ) Public Library had a run on *Batman* and *Iron Man*, because of the feature films based on these comics. Even less popular movies, such as *The Surrogates* and *Wanted*, caused an increase in interest for graphic novels that were their sources. Your collection development policy needs to consider graphic novels' increased profile in films, television, and other media.

As we stated in an earlier chapter, our definition of a graphic novel (a book length narrative, of any genre, for any audience that uses sequential art, either by itself or in combination with text elements in order to tell a story) leaves a lot of room for inclusion of non-comic material. Your collection development policy should address if your collection will include newspaper strips, how-to-draw books, books about graphic novel creators, books about the format, illustrated fiction, or other materials that are not traditionally thought of as graphic novels. The last several years have seen an increase in the publishing of art books, special editions, making-of books, and graphic novel criticism. It would be wise to consider these materials in your policy, lest you find yourself swimming in a seemingly endless sea of peripheral materials.

Series

Your collection development policy should state how you intend to collect series titles. Most manga are multiple volume series that are dependent upon each other, so volume three only makes sense if the reader is familiar with volumes one and two. This would necessitate purchasing multiple volumes in a series. Some libraries have chosen to purchase the first several volumes of a manga series and then leave it up to the patrons to either buy the series themselves or to interlibrary loan the material. In this case, the library sees itself as introducing the patron to the series. This may be beneficial to the budget, as the first volumes of series are typically more popular than the later volumes. When dealing with manga series, an unofficial policy might consider continuing a series if the volumes are consistently being checked out. There are some titles that become "backburners," meaning volumes will be purchased when extra funds become available, but they are not an essential graphic novel purchase—even if a patron requests it. Remember that when considering the voracious manga reader, an interlibrary loan may be your best option.

Most manga series contain multiple story arcs, so a library may choose to collect only a portion of a series. Even if you do not plan to purchase an entire series, you can still purchase enough volumes that feature an entire story arc. Purchasing manga in this way tends to placate readers more than just randomly buying a few volumes would, as the end of a story arc at least brings some closure to the story.

The concept of the story arc is also important in American graphic novels. These books are often compilations of monthly series, which go on indefinitely until low sales or creator issues cause the series to end. The result of this is dozens of graphic novels that feature the same character, some of which are interdependent and some of which are downright contradictory. It may not be possible for a library to collect all of the titles in a series. For example, the DC Comics Web site lists more than one hundred Batman graphic novels, but very few libraries have the budget or the space to purchase all of these.

However, a library could easily purchase *Batman: RIP, Batman: Heart of Hush, Whatever Happened to the Caped Crusader?*, and *Batman: Battle for the Cowl*, which together create a complete story arc.

Related to the issue of series are "event" graphic novels. Often, a publisher will have multiple characters appear in a limited series or "special event." These events seem to be more and more popular, with many superhero-based publishers building an entire year's publication schedule around them. The graphic novels that collect these events can drive librarians to distraction, as the story arc can be spread across multiple books by multiple authors. For example, the *House of M* event in 2005 had far reaching implications for some of Marvel's most popular characters, including the X-Men and Wolverine, but the story spread across twelve trade paperback collections. Your collection development policy may want to mention event series. For example, one library might have a policy of purchasing the "main" graphic novel of an event or crossover series and some auxiliary titles, depending on the popularity of the featured character. So in the *House of M* event, *House of M* and *World of M Featuring Wolverine* might be purchased, but not *House of M: Avengers.* Much like the voracious manga fans mentioned above, interlibrary loan should be a well used service for the superhero completist.

Ratings

Some collection development policies specifically mention age ratings. When deciding if your policy should include a section on age ratings, you need to understand the age ratings found on most graphic novels. The age recommendations assigned to graphic novels are helpful, but they can be a source of confusion as well. Most graphic novel publishers label their books with some sort of rating on the cover. The simplest one is the "Mature Readers" designation, used by many American publishers, which indicates that the title is meant for an adult audience. However, many publishers will go one step further and indicate for what age group the title is intended.

Most librarians and bookstores heartily approved when TOKYOPOP began putting age ratings on their manga titles, so other publishers followed suit. However, many librarians have not considered the origin of the ratings and what they mean. Because of the ubiquity of the Motion Picture Association of America's rating system (G, PG, PG-13, R, NC-17), most assume that graphic novels have a similar rating system, and a similar process to assign the rating. In fact, nothing could be further from the truth.

In order for a film to receive an MPAA rating, the film in question is submitted to the MPAA, where a full-time ratings board evaluates it. The board then uses a pre-agreed upon set of criteria that considers theme, violence, language, nudity, sensuality, drug abuse, and other elements to determine the rating the film receives.[1] This procedure is independent of the actual creation of the film, and there are appeals processes and other structures in place, if the creators disagree with the assigned rating.[2]

By contrast, a much more subjective process determines the age ratings found on graphic novels. Each publisher develops their own age recommendation system, and the application of these age recommendations is up to the editorial staff. There is no independent oversight, no set of formal criteria, and the creators of the work may be involved in the assignment of the rating as well.

Age recommendations are self-assigned by the publisher, usually by the editor of the title. Even if a publisher has a set of criteria used by all editors, those criteria can be applied differently by different people. This leads to the wide variance in age recommendations, even among titles produced by a single publisher. For example, TOKYOPOP rates the series *Sorcerer Hunters* by Satoru Akahori "older teen." Rightly so, since this manga fantasy series delves into sadomasochistic humor. TOKYOPOP also rates two of their boys' love titles, *Gravitation* and *Eerie Queerie!* as being older teen. Did either of these series explicitly portray sexuality? No more so than some of TOKYOPOP's teen rated heterosexual romance series like *Mars, Peach Girl,* or *Kare Kano.* So it appears that TOKYOPOP rates nudity and homosexual sexuality for older ages, but they do not consistently apply the adult or older teen rating to titles with sexual content. Typically, violence is not a cause for alarm for many patrons, unless the portrayal is excessive, as in the series *Battle Royale,* which earned a whopping 18+ rating. Yet, librarians have voiced concern over the excessive violence in the teen-rated *Demon Ororon.* This series has the king of hell fighting demons, devils, and anyone else standing in his way. While the violence is unrealistic, it still surprised many that it was only rated 'T' for teen.

Adding to the confusion about age ratings on graphic novels is the lack of information about the age recommendations criteria or even information about the ratings themselves. Some publishers, such as DC Comics, do not have a formal ratings system, choosing only to assign some comics with the "Mature Readers" designation. Others, such as Marvel, have very complete systems with several age categories. Some, like Oni Press, split the difference and use a handful of age categories. Some publishers make their age criteria available on their web sites or in auxiliary publications, but most do not. Even librarians with a great deal of time to devote to collection development find that tracking down the information about age recommendations is both time consuming and tedious.

Manga series have a unique issue with age recommendations. Many manga are long running series, with some running to dozens of volumes. Often, an American manga distributor will begin publishing a title before the entire run of the series is translated to English or before the series has been completed in Japan. Therefore, a series that receives a Teen, 13+ rating, for the first three volumes may later warrant a 16+ rating, Older Teen, for the remainder of the series. Two examples of this type of change in rating are the TOKYOPOP series *Love Hina* and VIZ's series *Nana*. *Love Hina* by Ken Akamatsu originally was assigned a T or Teen rating, but TOKYOPOP changed the rating to an older teen rating a few volumes into the series to address the sexual comedy nature of the story. VIZ's series was rated Older Teen until the eighth volume when a pregnancy plotline became prominent.

While it is not the end of the world when a series change ratings, issues can arise. First, a librarian may not be aware of the change unless notified. Publishers usually do not announce changes in ratings; therefore, unless a librarian is actively following the series, he or she may not even know that the rating has changed. Once aware of the rating change, the librarian will have to decide if the library is going to continue collecting the series. With limited budgets for ordering graphic novels, it can be extremely frustrating to find that a series to which you have committed funds and that has developed a readership may no longer be appropriate for your teen collection. If the librarian chooses not to continue a series, he or she will have to be prepared for patrons requesting later volumes in the series. One solution is to move a reclassified series to the adult area.

A similar issue may arise in American graphic novels, particularly those featuring a long- running character. It is not unusual for a publisher to create a more mature take on a beloved character, either to allow creators more artistic freedom, or to increase the character's popularity. These graphic novels will carry a higher age rating than the other collections featuring the character. For example, the X-Men trade collections are most usually rated T, or appropriate for teen readers, by Marvel. However, the *X-Men Noir* collection, which collects a pulp inspired, hard-boiled take on the X-Men, carries a

Parental Advisory rating. Spotting these collections before they make it to your teen collection can be problematic, particularly if you are using standing order plans.

When it comes to manga, some titles may have been edited to adjust the age ratings. For example, the young main character in *Dragon Ball* has underwear drawn on him, because sometimes he doesn't wear any! While this series' nudity was depicted for comedic purposes and was not meant to titillate the reader, another series made adjustments to make sexualized nudity more appropriate for the Teen rating. The CMX release of a heavily edited volume of *Tenjho Tenge* by Oh! Great (pen name of Ogure Ito) caused fans to campaign on the Internet for an uncensored version. This action manga originally had its fair share of nudity, fan service (scenes in anime or panels in manga that have mild erotic content and have nothing to do with the plot), and sex. So why did CMX add underwear and steam in appropriate places, zoom into art to avoid breast shots, and redraw skirts to hide panties? CMX says that they do not feel comfortable placing age recommendations on their material, so they request the rating from the Japanese publishers. CMX does not carry an older teen rating like other publishing companies. While CMX does cover up much of the nudity, the reader still very easily imagines it. The manga series would have been better served with an older teen rating, especially since the audience of the series is older teens and adults. Unfortunately, the rating changes for series in progress or creative editing by publishing companies uncomfortable with applying subjective ratings means that librarians are going to have to take an extra step to see if teen rated materials are appropriate for their collection. Luckily, many manga series have a strong fan base by the time they're released in America, so librarians can research on the Internet and find basic information from fan sites.

Ratings can serve as a useful guideline for purchasing an unknown title. Librarians need to be aware of them, particularly since the rating is often published on the cover of a graphic novel, making it instantly visible to the public. However, because of the issues and limitations of graphic novel ratings, the authors believe it is preferable that a policy does not clearly define a library's collection on ratings alone. If your policy is crafted to disallow older teen titles from teen graphic novel collections, as many libraries do, this does a disservice to older teens within the community, and may severely limit the types of materials you buy. For example, most manga that have homosexual themes are rated at least "older teen"—even if it is innocent in its artwork and storyline. Additionally many popular and award winning

American graphic novels are published in "mature readers" imprints. If a policy includes a discussion on ratings, it should not exclude graphic novels due to their rating, but instead state that mature readers or "OT" graphic novels will be given closer evaluation before being added to the collection.

Age ratings also often conflict with an issue we discussed earlier in this chapter: popularity. Many of the most popular graphic novel titles, and those most requested by teens, may not be designated appropriate for a teen audience. For example, many teens request the purchase of *Johnny the Homicidal Maniac (JTHM)* by Jhonen Vasquez. *JTHM* is the story of a deeply disturbed psychotic, who kills both to maintain a sense of peace and to keep a demonic wall in his house forever bathed in fresh blood. *JTHM* contains some serious discussions of the nature of violence and entertainment. It is also very funny, though in an extremely disturbing way. It is probably this skewed sense of humor, together with Vasquez's distinctly stark artwork, that creates its teen appeal. However, violence, profanity, and other adult content kept this title out of the teen collection at Glendale (AZ) Public Library, despite the howls of outraged teens.

Another example is a recent request by a young teen boy for more *ecchi*, light erotic material, in our teen collection. This particular request brought chuckles to the librarians, since the teen considered manga titles like *Ranma ½* by Rumiko Takahashi to be *ecchi* because it depicted nudity. However, if the young man was informed about *ecchi*, he would realize that these materials would not be appropriate for a teen collection—even humorous ones like *Futaba-kun Changes* by Hiroshi Aro due to to its excessive nudity and sexualization of the characters.

Also keep in mind that the visual nature of graphic novels intensifies content that may be edgy, but still deemed acceptable in a prose novel. For example, the novel *Battle Royale* by Koushun Takami is violent, but not so much that the novel would be inappropriate for teens. With the addition of illustrations in the graphic novel adaptation, the violence is intensified and causes the series to be rated 'M' for mature.

Challenges

Your collection development policy should also address the issue of challenges. Many librarians are hesitant to add graphic novels to their collections because they fear challenges from the community. While it is a fallacy that graphic novels elicit instant challenges, there have been many high-profile challenges to graphic novels in libraries. Your collection development policy needs to speak to this possibility. This may be as simple as referencing the already existing library policy regarding challenges, or it may involve something more complex. Graphic novels present a unique question in regards to challenges, since they are such a visual medium. Sexuality, nudity, and to a lesser extent, violence, in graphic novels are much more apparent, because you can "see" it in front of you, instead of reading about it. If your library has a policy for challenges to other visual media, such as DVDs, you may wish to look to it for clues on how to handle challenges to the visual content of graphic novels. If your library does not have a policy for dealing with visual materials, you may find yourself on your own.

Discussions regarding visual materials and age appropriateness can quickly devolve into parodies of themselves—i.e. showing a nude woman's silhouette is acceptable for a teen collection, but artwork with nipples is not. Artwork depicting decapitation is okay, but artwork of a disembowelment is not. A formula some librarians find useful in determining if a book is too objectionable for a teen area is to count the total number of panels in a book, and the total number of objectionable panels. This will give the librarian a rough estimate of how much of the book may be considered objectionable. Other librarians look to the guidelines laid down by the Motion Picture Association of America to determine age appropriateness. Ultimately, it falls to you as the purchasing librarian to determine what is acceptable for your community, and to be prepared to defend a graphic novel should a challenge arise.

Deselection

Finally, your collection development policy should include a discussion of deselection criteria, or when you will remove a graphic novel from your collection. One issue to consider, when thinking about deselection criteria, is the physical condition of the item. Some of these issues are obvious and do not need to be addressed, such as missing pages or ruined bindings. Other issues may not be so cut and dried.

For an example, at Glendale (AZ) Public Library, one patron has taken on the role of "secret censor." This is a patron who checks out graphic novels, almost exclusively DC and Marvel titles, and then uses a black marker to cross out any curse words, references to God, or other salty language. This patron also will color in any cleavage showing on female characters, and has been known to lengthen hemlines with her marker. Emma Frost, the leader of the *Astonishing X-Men,* went from wearing a white corset and white knee-high boots to sporting a neck-to-toe black cat suit. Perhaps most perplexing, the censor will also draw black miniskirts on male characters, most notably Superman, to cover up their "maleness." These titles are still readable, although hopelessly altered. Should they be removed from the collection? A solid collection development policy should address situations like this.

A well thought out graphic novel collection development policy will allow you to set clear goals for your collection, as well as give you the opportunity to articulate your philosophy on graphic novels. It will also help you clearly state to staff and patrons why graphic novels belong in your library. This can be of invaluable assistance, should you meet with resistance to a graphic novel collection from the public or other library staff.

Overcoming Staff Resistance

We are veterans of presentations about graphic novels in libraries. We have talked to librarians, in groups large and small, local and national, about some of the unique aspects of graphic novels, and the benefits of adding graphic novels to libraries. In every presentation, it seems, there is one "special" librarian in attendance—the librarian who is only there because he or she was coerced, the one who believes that all comic books are trash, the one who refuses to add them to the library's collection no matter what. There comes a moment, in every presentation, where she shares her opinions with the group—loudly, and with great emphasis. The authors, after many experiences with this kind of librarian (who can be of any gender, age or race) have come to welcome this "bunhead" input, because

---

The Graphic Novels in Libraries Listserv
GNLIB-L

This e-mail listserv began in 1999 to connect librarians working with graphic novels with one another. There are more than 700 subscribers. To subscribe, send a blank e-mail message to GNLIB-L-subscribe@yahoogroups.com. You can also read it online on Yahoo Groups website: *http://groups.yahoo.com/group/GNLIB-L/.*

it gives the other members of the group a taste of what they may face when trying to introduce graphic novels to their home libraries.

Before we proceed, let it be said that many librarians are wholehearted boosters of the graphic novel format. Indeed, librarians translated some of the first fansubs of anime. The Graphic Novels in Libraries listserv, GNLIB-L, is swollen with the ranks of die-hard comics lovers, some of whom have been fans since childhood. At every anime, manga, and comic convention, you will find more than a few librarians wandering about, sometimes in costume. But, despite all the evidence of the benefits of graphic novels, despite the tremendous popularity of the materials, there are still librarians and other library staff who object to the inclusion of graphic novels in the library. In a survey done by the authors, more than 47 percent of challenges to graphic novels came from library staff, particularly cataloging staff. This is a disturbing statistic and one that has serious implications for librarians seeking to add graphic novels to their collections.

There are a number of ways to educate staff about the benefits of graphic novels. Perhaps the most obvious of these are formal presentations. There are librarians around the country who are willing to come and speak to library staff about comics and manga; the GNLIB-L listserv and the Young Adult Library Services Association are excellent resources for finding these librarians. The authors have done several small-scale presentations for individual libraries. If you are active in your state or regional library association, consider requesting a program on graphic novels as part of the conference programming. These presentations are an effective way to reach large groups of interested librarians in the topic.

If librarians and staff are truly hostile to graphic novels, or perhaps just apathetic to the format, it can be challenging or downright impossible to get them to attend a presentation. For these staff members, in the experience of the authors, the most effective way to overcome their resistance to the format is to be a constant, unapologetic, relentless, and immovable cheerleader for the materials. At the Glendale (AZ) Public Library (GPL), graphic novels are included on almost every booklist that is produced by the staff and they are included in every display. In addition, every book order includes at least one graphic novel, and we talk up the new titles we have read and enjoyed to other staff members. By being enthusiastic, and sharing that enthusiasm with your co-workers, you will find that they may be more open to the idea of graphic novels than you might think.

For example, the Main branch at GPL held weekly manga screenings during the summer, featuring the first season of the *Ranma ½* television show. Unfortunately, just before the program was set to begin, the programmer came down with influenza, and the program was overseen by another teen staff member, Sue. When the organizer of the program returned three weeks later, Sue raved that *Ranma* was really, really funny and that she was enjoying watching it—and she had no intention of giving up the program. Sensing an opportunity to recruit another to the comic's side, the programmer relinquished control of the anime screenings, and provided Sue with some suggestions of books and magazines that she might enjoy. Sue has become a comics and manga fan, to the point of carrying an issue of *Shojo Beat* to the salon with her, because she liked the character's haircut in *Nana*!

Sue was already open to the idea of graphic novels and manga, and was willing to read and discover more about these materials. While they might not be outwardly hostile, some staff members just might not be interested in the materials. This is natural; everyone has different reading tastes (Merideth, for example, only reads historical fiction when she has no other alternative. Kristin dislikes hard science fiction, and actively avoids it). But because graphic novels are so popular, an apathetic librarian can sometimes make it hard for teens to find the material they want. For proof, we provide this conversation, overheard at the Youth Reference desk at GPL:

Teen: "I'm looking for *Fruits Basket*"

Library Staff Member 1: "You want books on fruit baskets?"

Teen: "No, *Fruits Basket*."

Library Staff Member 2: "You mean like gift baskets?"

Teen: "NO, *Fruits Basket*."

LSM1: "Well, we have books on basket making."

LSM2: "And we might have books on gift baskets. But fruit baskets is kind of an odd search term. Maybe we can find some information on the Internet."

Teen: "No, I want *Fruits Basket*!"

LSM1: "Sweetie, I'm telling you, we don't have anything on fruit baskets."

Teen: "It's a comic book."

LSM1 and LSM2: "Oh! – (yelling to staff workroom) MERIDETH!"

As this conversation demonstrates, the odd titles, interweaving series, and other comics jargon (Also overheard: "*Shojo*? Do you mean Show Low?") can be confusing for staff that are not familiar with the lingo of comics and manga. One way of overcoming this is to provide "cheat sheets" for staff that list popular comics and manga titles, with brief summaries, and hints for finding them in the catalog or on the shelf. A sample "cheat sheet" can be found following this chapter. This reassures staff that they will not have to keep up with dozens of titles in order to serve the public.

What about those staff who are not just disinterested, but downright hostile to graphic novels, an attitude that cannot be won over with passionate book talks and genre lists? It seems that there is least one staff person at every library who considers comics to be fluff at best and downright degenerate at the very worst. More often than not, these staff members will make a concentrated effort to keep graphic novels off the shelf, particularly those titles they find offensive, usually because of sexuality or nudity.

If you are in a situation where a staff member has challenged a title, determine if your library has a separate policy for dealing with internal challenges, or if they are handled in the same manner as patron challenges. Libraries handle challenges differently and you need to follow your library's policy. Generally, we recommend locating reviews of the challenged title, if they are available. Scour the Internet and online catalogs for other libraries that hold the title, and see where they place the materials. The GNLIB-L listserv is again a great resource, as other librarians may know of reviews you are unaware of, or may be able to offer testimonials about challenged titles. The Comic Book Legal Fund and the American Library Association's Office of Intellectual Freedom will also be able to assist in challenges—whether they come from staff or patrons.

To the uninitiated, the world of graphic novels, particularly manga, can be a scary place, filled with creepy, big-eyed girls in sailor suits, giant robots, glowing crystals and impossibly over-muscled men who dress-up in tights, while laughing maniacally. Some staff members are confused by the format, but are willing to learn. Others are disinterested, and a select few are strongly opposed to the inclusion of graphic novels in the library collection. By being a proponent of the format, providing help for confused staff members, and by being prepared to defend your choices to naysayers, your graphic novel collection can grow and thrive.

---

1   "What Do the Ratings Mean? " *Ratings.* Motion Picture Association of America, 2005. Web. *http://www.mpaa.org/ ratings/what-each-rating-means.* (18 Jun 2010)

Glendale Public Library's Graphic Novel Cheat Sheet

Important Notes: Most graphic novels come up under a keyword search,

not a title browse or title keyword!

* Denotes a manga (Japanese comic) title. Authors and illustrators are in **bold.**

100 Bullets by Brian Azzarello. A crime/conspiracy drama featuring a mysterious agent, a suitcase and 100 untraceable bullets. Very sharp writing; the series has completed and is housed in the Adult GN collection. Each volume has an individual title. Do a keyword search to find them all in the catalog. (A/YA)

A Distant Soil by Colleen Doran. A sci-fi series with heavy fantasy overtones, this is the story of a young girl who is born the heir to an alien religious dynasty. Often recommended for teens, it does have some controversial plot elements (homosexuality, pedophilia). A love it or hate it title. Each volume has an individual title. Do a keyword search to find them all in the catalog. (S, A/YA)

Ai Yazawa. A manga artist known for her hip, fashionable, and lanky characters. Best known work is *Nana*.

Akira. Set in a futuristic Tokyo, a motorcycle gang butts heads against a government operation dealing with supernatural powers. Anime movie available. Six volumes total. (S A/YA)

Akira Toriyama. The manga artist of the long-running *Dragon Ball* series.

Alan Moore. A comics god, Moore has written a number of highly respected maxi-series including *From Hell, Watchmen,* and *V for Vendetta.* A few very popular film adaptations have made him more visible to teens. All Moore titles will be found in the Adult GN collection.

Alex Ross. An illustrator celebrated for his photo-realistic style, Ross's artwork is often featured on covers. Using acrylic painting techniques instead of traditional pen and ink, Ross has developed a series of posters and other materials for both Marvel and DC. If you're lucky, he'll come up under additional authors.

Alice 19th. Shojo series by Yu Watase that deals with Alice and her ability to awaken the power of words. Seven volumes total. Each volume has an individual title. Do a title keyword search to find them all in the catalog. (J, S)

Amulet. A fantasy/adventure title by Kazu Kibuishi. Good for kids who are looking for something after *Bone.* Two volumes with more on the way.

*Angelic Layer. Shonen title by CLAMP. Misaki, a new kid in Tokyo, controls a doll and has battles with other dolls. Five volumes total. (All Ages)

*Apocalypse Meow. Historical Fiction set in Vietnam War with anthropomorphic characters. Gritty violence and language. Three volumes total. (S, A/YA)

Art Spiegelman. Art Spiegelman is the Pulitzer Prize-winning creator of *Maus,* and a feature of the alternative comics scene. He is currently publishing the Toon Books early reader comics. All of his work is in the Adult GN section.

*Astro Boy. A classic series about a boy robot who watches out for humanity. Anime series is available. Two words—not one. (All Ages)

Astro City. A more realistic look at superheroes in fantastic linked stories set in the utopist Astro City. Some of the best writing and artwork in comics. These are housed in the Adult GN collection, more for interest level than appropriateness. Each volume has an individual title. Do a keyword search to find them all (J, S, A/YA)

*Azumanga Daioh. A hilarious series about Japanese high school life and friendship told in individual four-panel comic strips. Anime series is available. Four volumes total. (J, S)

*Banana Fish. Weird title for a crime drama manga set in New York in the '80s. Some boys' love undertones. (S, A/YA)

*Basara. Fantasy where a girl pretends to be her dead brother who was claimed to be the "Child of Destiny"—the one who will bring peace to the country and overthrow the current empire. Romance with hidden identities. Lots of volumes (J, S)

Batgirl. A really outstanding series. *Batman* spinoff, part of the DC Universe. Each volume has an individual title. Shelved by Series. Do a keyword search to find them all in the catalog. Related titles: *Birds of Prey, Batman.* (J, S, A/YA)

*Battle Angel Alita. Science fiction series about Alita, a cyborg with little memory. Stories focus on her quest to find her past and what it means to be human. Nine volumes total for the first series. (S)

*Battle Royale. Series that is essentially *Lord of the Flies* meets *Survivor,* with guns and explosives.

Translation is bad. Lots of violence. The prose novel is highly recommended for older teens. (A/YA)

Brian Michael Bendis. A prolific and popular comics writer, who works for both mainstream and independent presses. Best known for *Ultimate Spider-Man* (Marvel) and *Powers* (Image) but has pretty much taken over Marvel's entire line.

Big O. In a world of amnesiacs, Roger Smith is a negotiator who almost always ends up using his giant robot to end negotiations. The animated series was very popular on Cartoon Network and is available. (All Ages)

Birds of Prey. A female crime-fighting team featuring a paraplegic librarian and a power deprived superhero. Much cooler than it sounds. A *Batman* spin-off; part of the DC Universe. Shelved by series. Each volume has an individual title. Do a keyword search to find them all in the catalog. Related Titles: *Nightwing, Green Arrow* (J, S, A/YA)

Blade of the Immortal. Historical fiction samurai series starring Manji, a swordsman who is immortal until he kills 1,000 bad guys. Beautiful pencil work in this violent series. Slow moving pace though. Each volume has a separate title, so do a keyword search for this series. (S, A/YA)

Bleach. Shonen action title. Contemporary teen sees spirits and becomes a soul reaper to send them to their afterlife. Volumes have individual titles. Do a keyword search to find them. (J, S)

Bone by Jeff Smith. Three cousins, driven from their home, get lost in a beautiful but mysterious valley and caught up in an epic war. A fantastic *Lord of the Rings* type story with cute cartoon characters. The library no longer owns the black and white originals, but the color reprints are housed in Youth GN. (All Ages)

Books of Magic by Neil Gaiman, spin-off series by John Reiber. Story of Tim Hunter, a boy who will become the world's greatest magician. Like a hard-core Harry Potter. Housed in the Adult GN collection. Each volume has an individual title. Do a keyword search to find them all in the catalog. Related Works: *Books of Fairie.* (S, A/YA)

Boys Be. Short stories all about guys and love, includes some actual good tips for guys. Can be read out of order. (S, A/YA)

Boys over Flowers. Also called Hana Yori Dango. Poor girl gets into elite private school and ends up on the bad side of the four male student leaders. Romance *shojo* title. (J, S)

Brain Powered. *Mecha* series. If a teen liked *Gundam,* give them this. Four volumes total. (J, S)

Buddha. The story of Siddhartha, the prince who became Buddha. written by Osamu Tezuka. Some non-titillating nudity. Do a keyword search for Buddha and Tezuka. (S, A/YA)

Buffy the Vampire Slayer. The "8th season" of the defunct TV show is being published in comics. Each volume has an individual title. Do a keyword search to find them all shelved under series title. The *Spike* and *Angel* comics are also under the series title *Buffy.* (J, S, A/YA)

Buronson. Also known as Sho Fumimura, a manga writer who has collaborated with Ryoichi Ikegami (*Sanctuary*) and Kentaro Miura (*Japan*).

Captain America. Steve Rogers got shot up with super-solider serum, won WWII for our side, then fell out of a plane, and was frozen for fifty years. Now he's back. Never a big mover, these will get way more popular because a really hot actor, Chris Evans, was cast in the movie. Each volume has an individual title. Do a keyword search to find them all in the catalog.

Cardcaptor Sakura. A girl has to capture all the magical cards before they can wreak havoc. There are some hints of homosexual feelings. An edited colorized anime graphic novel series of this story is called *Cardcaptors.* Twelve volumes total. (All Ages)

Castle in the Sky. A series created by taking screenshots from the anime movie. Four volumes total. The movie is available. (All Ages)

Catwoman. Socialite by day, cat burglar by night, full time ambivalent love interest of Bruce Wayne. Shelved under series title. Each volume has an individual title. Do a keyword search to find them all in the catalog. (S, A/YA)

Ceres, Celestial Legend. Aya has the spirit and power of Ceres, a celestial maiden stuck on earth, living inside her seeking revenge on her family. Created by Yu Watase. This *shojo* series has fantasy, romance, and good art rolled up in one. Each volume has a separate title in the catalog; do a keyword search. (S, A/YA)

Chobits. Created by CLAMP. Science fiction about persocoms—personal humanoid robots—and the men who love them. The story delves into a discussion of what it means to be human. Some risqué humor. Eight volumes total. (S, A/YA)

CLAMP. A manga team of four women, Nanase Okawa, Mokona Apapa, Mikku Nekoi, and Satsuki

Igarashi. Due to their unique style, one can immediately tell if something is by CLAMP or not. Their work includes: *Chobits, Magic Knight Rayearth,* and *X.* They work very similarly to American comic creative teams. Their Web site is in Japanese.

CLAMP School Detectives. By the popular CLAMP artists. Elementary boys solve mysteries for distressed women. Cute fluff. Three volumes total. (All Ages)

Confidential Confessions. Realistic short stories about Japanese teens that can be read in any order. (S, A/YA)

D.N. Angel. Fourteen-year-old Daisuke is burdened with the family curse. Whenever he sees his crush, he turns into master thief Dark Mousy. You must put in the period or a space in the title in order to find it in the catalog. (M, J)

Daredevil. A blind superhero with extra-sensory powers who's an attorney by day. Related Titles: *Elektra.* Those by Frank Miller are shelved in Adult GN, the rest are in Teen. Shelved by series title. Each volume has an individual title. Do a keyword search to find them all in the catalog. The age level varies by individual author, but most are J or S with a few in A/YA.

Deadpool. A Wolverine spinoff about a mercenary; made popular because Ryan Reynolds plays him in the movie. We don't have many of these, but what we do have is in Teen GN. Each volume has an individual title. Do a keyword search to find them all in the catalog.

Demon Ororon. Chiaki, a half-human, half-angel girl, heals the injured king of hell, Ororon. In return, he grants her a wish, and she asks that he never leave her. Thus begins the doomed romance of an angel and and a demon. Violent, but hip artwork. Four volumes. (S, A/YA)

Dragon Ball. Goku and his friends search for the seven dragon balls to have a wish granted. Martial arts action. Perverted old man as a side character. *Dragon Ball Z* continues the story after five years. You must search with dragon and ball as separate words. (M, J)

Elfquest. Elves struggle to survive in a hostile world. Fun, but not subtle at all. Some violence and sexuality in later volumes. Each volume has an individual title. Do a keyword search to find them all in the catalog. (S, A/YA)

Essential Spider-Man. Black and white reprints of original Silver Age Spider-Man from the 1960s. (J, S, A/YA)

Essential X-Men. Reprints of original Chris Claremont written X-Men comics. (J, S, A/YA).

*Excel Saga. A kooky comedy about world domination. Anime is available. (J, S)

Fables. Fairy tale characters live incognito lives in a NYC apartment complex. Awesome, awesome, awesome; but not for younger kids. Housed in the Adult GN collection. Each volume has an individual title. Do a keyword search to find them all (A/YA)

*Flame of Recca. The adventures of Recca, a teenage ninja with the power to control fire. (J, S)

Frank Miller. A prolific and hard to classify writer and artist. Thanks to film adaptations of *Sin City* and *300*, he's even more popular than ever. All Miller (including Batman) is shelved in the Adult GN collection.

*Fruits Basket. Tohru Honda lives with the Sohma family, a family burdened with the curse of the Chinese zodiac. When one is hugged by a member of the opposite sex, the or she turn into a zodiac animal. Anime is available. (J, S)

*Full Metal Panic. Mecha comedy about an undercover teen military agent and the high school student he protects. Anime is available. (J, S)

*Fushigi Yugi. Also called *Mysterious Play*. Miaka is literally sucked into a book that places her in Ancient China as the Priestess of Suzaku. Some details of a rape are discussed. For a title search use *Mysterious Play*. (J, S)

*Gadget. Shuichi, electronics junkie, and his friend Manami search out the alien admirers who gave Manami an electronic gift. Cute squashed character designs. (All Ages)

Garth Ennis. A popular comics writer, who gained attention for his *Preacher* series. We don't own a lot of his material; it's a little hardcore for us. What we do have will be in the Adult GN collection.

GloomCookie. Goth soap opera set in the San Francisco club scene. Only popular with a certain type of teen; but very well done. Gets kind of icky in places. (J, S)

Grant Morrison. Morrison is highly regarded as one of the most original and inventive writers in the comics medium. His work is spread between teen and adult.

Greg Rucka. A writer who's taken on some of the most iconic characters in comics, including Wonder Woman, Wolverine, Superman, and Batman. He also writes prose crime fiction, so be sure to limit to graphic fiction. His work is spread between Teen and Adult.

Green Arrow. A wealthy, liberal vigilante who uses bows and arrows. If you like *Batman,* you'll like this. Part of the DC Universe. Shelved by series title. Each volume has an individual title. Do a keyword search to find them all in the catalog. (S, A/YA)

Green Lantern. Series about a team of universal policeman who protect Earth, and other planets, from extra-terrestrial threats. There are several Green Lanterns, with Hal Jordan being the most famous. Expect these to get more popular as Ryan Reynolds is playing him in the movie. Shelved by series title. Each volume has an individual title. Do a keyword search to find them all in the catalog. Part of the DC Universe. (J, S)

*GTO. Great Teacher Onizuka. Ex- biker becomes a teacher using tough love to bring his students around. Some perverted comedy ensues. (S, A/YA)

*Gundam. Multiple series—all different storylines, but all focus on the mecha that are piloted in the series. Anime is available. Series titles: *Mobile Suit Gundam Wing, Mobile Suit Gundam 0079* and *Mobile Suit Gundam Seed.* (Ranges from All Ages up to S)

*Gunsmith Cats. Rally and "Minnie" May are bounty hunters in Chicago in this great action series. There is nudity. Each volume has an individual title. Do a keyword search to find them all in the catalog. Anime is available. (S, A/YA)

*Hana-Kimi. Girl cross-dresses to attend an all-guys school to be closer to her favorite athlete, a high jumper. Title needs the hyphen or space to be found in the catalog. (J, S)

*Hellsing. Hellsing, an organization that fights supernatural evil, has specialized soldiers and weaponry—including Alucard, a vampire. Hip artwork with a fun horror story. Anime is available. (S)

Hopeless Savages. Punk rock icons Dirk Hopeless and Nikki Savage settle down in the 'burbs to raise a family. One of Merideth's favorites. Each volume has an individual title. Do a keyword search to find them all in the catalog. (J, S, A/YA)

*Imadoki. Tanpopo is a weed in the elite school where everyone is a type of flower, but she's determined to make friends with the leader of the school, Koki. A drama by Yu Watase. A nice gardening theme and includes a realistic portrayal of teen pregnancy. Five volumes total. Each volume has an individual title. Do a keyword search to find them all in the catalog. (J, S)

Incredible Hulk. Science nerd is transformed into mindless, gigantic, green monster when angered;

thanks to driving too close to a nuclear test. Many of these TPBs are just terrible. Shelved by series title. Each volume has an individual title. Do a keyword search to find them all in the catalog. (J, S, A/YA)

Initial D. Street car racing in the mountains. (J, S)

InuYasha. Also called *Feudal Fairy Tale.* By the famous artist, Rumiko Takahashi. Kagome falls into a dry well and ends up in feudal Japan. Paired with half-demon InuYasha, they must gather the pieces of the Shikon Jewel. For a title search use *Feudal Fairy Tale.* Anime movie is available. (J, S)

Iron Man. Tony Stark: alcoholic billionaire with a super-suit of armor. Movie version is way more charming than the comics version (comics Tony has been a real jerk lately). Can be found in Youth and Teen GN collections. Shelved by series title. Each volume has an individual title. Do a keyword search to find them all in the catalog.

JLA or *Justice League.* Heroes of the DC Universe working together. Superman, Batman, Wonder Woman, etc. Lots of different artists and writers. Shelved by series title. Each volume has an individual title. Do a keyword search to find them all in the catalog. (J, S)

Justice League Adventures. Based on the Cartoon Network series, *Justice League.* (All Ages)

Juvenile Orion. Also called *Aquarian Age.* A girl and five teen boys fight to stop a war that has waged for thousands of years between humans, angels, demons, wizards, and aliens. Pretty boys prevail in this series. Five volumes total. (J, S)

Kare Kano. Also called *His and Her Circumstances.* Yukino appears to be the perfect student, except it's all an act. Soiichiro is the real deal. Romance in a comedy-drama kind of way. Anime is available. (J, S)

Kindaichi Case Files. Mysteries that can be read in any order. (S)

Kodocha. Also called *Sana's Stage.* Sana, a child actress, tries to fix everyone's lives. Ten volumes total. (M, J, S)

Lone Wolf and Cub. Historical fiction samurai. Violent and some nudity. Shelved in Adult GN collection. (S, A/YA)

Love Hina. Keitaro, a student trying to get into Tokyo University, becomes the manager of the girl's dorm. A sex comedy ensues. Fourteen volumes total. Anime is available. Shelved in Adult GN collection. (S, A/YA)

Magic Knight Rayearth. Three girls are transported to Cephiro, a fantasy world built upon wishes. Six volumes total. Anime is available. (All Ages)

Maison Ikkoku. Yusaku Godai is in love with his apartment manager, the young widowed Kyoko. A mature romance written by the famous Rumiko Takahashi. Fourteen volumes total. Each volume has an individual title. Do a keyword search to find them all in the catalog. (J, S, A/YA)

Marmalade Boy. Romance between girl and her step brother. Eight volumes total. (J, S)

Mars. Good girl falls for the "bad" boy in school. There is sex, but handled delicately. Fifteen volumes total. For a title search use "*Mars Volume*" to bring up all the titles. (J, S)

Naruto. Ninja story. Very popular with girls and guys alike. Each volume has an individual title. Do a keyword search to find them all in the catalog. (J, S)

Nausicaa of the Valley of the Wind. Nausicaa is a princess fighting to keep peace as other kingdoms begin to war over the last of the world's natural resources. A good meaty read. Four volumes total. Anime movie is available. (J, S)

Neil Gaiman. You know him. He won the Newbery. He also writes comics. *Sandman* is the best known. He has prose and comics scattered throughout Youth, Teen and Adult. Be sure to limit your search. Or ask Merideth, because she's read them all.

Neon Genesis Evangelion. Mecha piloted by teens fight against "Angels" that once caused a worldwide catastrophe. The pivotal series was first an anime then a manga series. The anime is available. (J, S)

Nightwing. The original Robin, Dick Grayson, all grown up and on his own. A guilty pleasure for many female comics readers. *Batman* spinoff; part of the DC Universe. Shelved by series title. Each volume has an individual title. Do a keyword search to find them all in the catalog. Related titles: *Batgirl, Birds of Prey, The Outsiders.* (J, S, A/YA)

Oh My Goddess! Keiichi accidentally dialed a Goddess Helpline when ordering take out. He's granted a wish and when he jokes that he wants the goddess to stay forever, she stays. Each volume has an individual title. Do a keyword search to pull up all of them. (J, S)

One Piece. Monkey D. Luffy, a "rubberman," and his comedic adventures in his quest to become the Pirate King. Each volume has an individual title. Do a keyword search to find them all in the catalog. (J, S)

The Outsiders. Second generation superheroes and former kid sidekicks band together after the dissolution of the Teen Titans and take a more active role in hunting down criminals. Could be better than it is. Shelved by series title. Related Titles: *New Teen Titans.* (J, S, A/YA)

*Peach Girl. High school drama. Momo and her relationships with Toji and Sae, her best friend who is more of an enemy than friend. The series continues in *Peach Girl Change of Heart.* (J, S)

*Petshop of Horrors. Each volume is four short stories dealing with the unique pets that Count D sells. This series can be read out of order, but there is an underlying story continuing slightly throughout. (S)

*Planetes. Space story about the garbage men who pick up space exploration's trash. Thoughtful and moving. (S)

Powers. "Capes and crime." Police procedural starring detectives who investigate crimes dealing with superheroes. Good writing and a unique art style. Shelved in Adult GN collection. Each volume has an individual title. Do a keyword search to find them all in the catalog. (A/YA)

Preacher. A preacher bonded physically and spiritually infused with an otherworldly being, his ex-girlfriend, and an alcoholic vampire go on a search for God— to kick his butt. Fantastic writing, but deeply blasphemous, and every "adult" element you can think of. Shelved in Adult GN collection. Each volume has an individual title. Do a keyword search to find them all in the catalog. (A/YA)

Punisher. Former Special Forces member, seeking vengeance for the death of his family and a host of other stuff, turns into hyper-violent vigilante. Light on dialog, heavy on violence. The most requested are mature readers titles. Each volume has an individual title. Do a keyword search to find them all in the catalog. (J, S, A/YA)

*Ranma ½. Ranma Saotome changes into a girl when splashed with cold water. Nudity and a lot of different fiancés prevail in this wacky martial arts sex comedy. Anime is available. (S)

Robert Kirkman. Creator of popular horror comic *The Walking Dead.* Has also done work for Marvel. His work is spread between Teen and Adult GN.

Robin. A title featuring Batman's junior partner. *Batman* spinoff; part of the DC Universe. Shelved by series title. Each volume has an individual title. Do a keyword search to find them all in the catalog. (J, S, A/YA)

Rurouni Kenshin. Historical fiction about the wandering Kenshin, a swordsman with a backwards blade sword. Each volume has an individual title. Do a keyword search to find them all in the catalog. Anime is available. (S)

Runaways. The children of super-villains run away from home to keep from joining the family business. A lot better than it sounds. Shelved by series title. (J, S)

The Sandman. A fantastic dark fantasy series that is probably the most acclaimed work of graphic storytelling ever. Housed in the Adult GN collection. Each volume has an individual title. Do a keyword search to find them all in the catalog. Related Titles: *The Sandman Presents; Death: The High Cost of Living; Death: The Time of Your Life.* (S, A/YA)

Sin City. Dark noir crime stories set in a fictional locale. Graphic in every sense of that word. Basis for the film. Shelved in Adult GN collection. Each volume has an individual title. Do a keyword search to find them all in the catalog. (A/YA)

Spawn. A former solider is re-animated as a servant of Hell. Tremendously popular. Deeply icky. (S, A/YA)

Spider-Man. Nerd gets bitten by radioactive spider; nerd acquires superpowers. Nerd fights crime in a red and blue costume; nerd marries supermodel. The series that launched a thousand spin-offs. We hold *Spider-Man* titles in Youth, Teen and Adult, make sure to limit your search. When searching for Spider-Man, *you must hyphenate!* (M, J, S, rating depends on series)

Star Wars: Clone Wars Adventures. Star Wars tie-in based on the Cartoon Network animated series. (All Ages)

Star Wars: Clone Wars. Comic-form stories set in between Episode II and Episode III. Not to be confused with *Clone Wars Adventures.* (J, S, A/YA)

Teen Titans Go! Comics adaptation of the anime-like TV series. The comics are aimed slightly younger than the TV show. These books have a fantastic writer, J. Torres. Shelved by series title. Each volume has an individual title. Do a keyword search to find them all in the catalog. (All Ages)

Teen Titans. A bunch of sidekicks and younger superheroes form their own crime fighting team. Not to be confused with *Teen Titans Go!* Related titles: *New Teen Titans, The Outsiders.* Shelved by series title. Each volume has an individual title. Do a keyword search to find them all in the catalog. (J, S, A/YA)

Tenchi Muyo. Tenchi and his house guests, Ryoko, a demon, Ayeka, an alien princess, Washu, a mad scientist and more! Each volume has a title. Do a keyword search to find them all in the catalog. (J, S)

Tokyo Mew Mew. Magical girls who are infused with the powers of extinct animals. Very popular with elementary aged girls (All Ages).

Transmetropolitan. Adventures of a tattooed, chain-smoking, gun-toting journalist in a dystopic future. Shelved in the Adult GN collection. Each volume has an individual title. Do a keyword search to find them all in the catalog. For mature readers. (A/YA)

A Treasury of Victorian Murder. Fictionalizations of famous 19th century murders. All compiled and illustrated by Rick Geary. An acquired taste. Each volume has an individual title. ,. (J, S, A/YA)

Trigun. Vash the Stampede is a wanted man for destroying a town. Science fiction and spaghetti western rolled up into one story. Story continues in *Trigun Maximum.* Each volume has an individual title. Do a keyword search to find them all in the catalog. (J, S)

Tsubasa. A CLAMP crossover that takes old CLAMP characters and places them in new situations. Very popular. (J, S)

Ultimate Spider-Man. A "reimagining" of the classic character, placing him in a contemporary setting and completely restarting his storyline. Part of the *Ultimates* universe; but unlike most things in the *Ultimates* universe, these are actually good. Each volume has an individual title. Do a keyword search to find them all (J, S, A/YA)

Ultimate X-Men. A "reimagining" of the classic superhero team, set in a contemporary time period, and completely restarting their continuity. Part of the *Ultimates* universe. (J, S, A/YA)

Ultimates. The Hulk, Nick Fury, Giant-Man, the Wasp, Iron Man, Thor, and Captain America form a superhero team. Reads even worse than it sounds and full of already dated pop culture references. However, this looks to be the basis of the *Avengers* movie. Part of the *Ultimates* universe. Each volume has an individual title. Do a keyword search to find them all in the catalog. (J, S, A/YA)

Vagabond. Historical fiction story about Miyamoto Musashi. Very violent and has nudity. Also recommended is the novel *Musashi* that the series was based on. Mature teens. (A/YA)

W Juliet. Guy dresses as girl in high school. If he can graduate as a girl, then he can become an actor. Good *shojo* drama. (J, S)

The Walking Dead. Zombie survival story. Easily the most requested mature readers comic we own. Shelved in the Adult GN collection. Each volume has an individual title. Do a keyword search to find them all in the catalog.

Wolverine. Highly popular spin-off character from the X-Men; now star of his own series. Originally short and hairy; he now looks like Hugh Jackman. Lots of action, lots of violence. Writing and artwork quality varies. Wolverine roams all over the collection, with titles in youth, teen and adult. Be sure to limit your search! Shelved by series title. Each volume has an individual title. Do a keyword search to find them all in the catalog. (J, S, A/YA)

Wonder Woman. A princess with near godlike powers, raised in a sheltered matriarchal society, comes to Man's world to act as a champion and protector. Many authors, many artists, many variations in quality. Merideth is a big fan of the newest volumes written by Simone. Jodi Piccoult took a pass at this series; it wasn't very good, but we get asked for it quite a bit. Each volume has an individual title. Do a keyword search to find them all in the catalog. (J, S, A/YA)

X-Men. Classic story of a team of super-powered mutants in a society that refuses to accept them. Series titles include *X-Men, New X-Men, Uncanny X-Men, X-Force, X-Factor, Exiles, Weapon X,* and *New Mutants. New X-Men* by Morrison and *Astonishing X-Men* by Whedon are the most frequently asked for. X-Men are housed in youth, teen, and adult. Be sure to limit your search! Shelved by series title "X-Men" Each volume has an individual title. Do a keyword search to find them all in the catalog. (J, S, A/YA)

Y: The Last Man. Everything with a Y chromosome is wiped off the face of the earth except for Yorrick Brown and his pet monkey. A fascinating dystopic sci-fi story. Shelved in the Adult GN collection. (A/YA)

Yotsuba&! The mixed-up adventures of new girl in town, elementary school aged Yotsuba. She's completely clueless, and that's what makes this series so hilarious and charming. (All Ages)

Yu Yu Hakusho. After dying unexpectedly, Yusuke is given a chance at life again as a spirit detective. Each volume has an individual title. Do a keyword search to find them all in the catalog. (J, S)

Yu-Gi-Oh! A little older than the target audience of the anime series, but the kids watching the show are reading the books too. More appropriate for older elementary aged kids (fourth or fifth grade). Make sure to have the hyphens or spaces or else they won't show up! (M, J)

Evaluating a Graphic Novel for Purchase

Evaluating a graphic novel is a different experience than evaluating a prose novel. Graphic novels are collaborations between imagery and text. The review criteria applied to them must include evaluating the synergy between these elements. Beyond evaluating a graphic novel for its innate quality, how "good" or "bad" the book is, it is also necessary to evaluate based on the title's popularity, the library's current collection, the reputation and quality of the creators, and the physical attributes of the book itself.

Popularity

Taking these issues one by one, perhaps the most important issue for a teen audience is popularity. Graphic novels are popular with teen readers, but some are more popular than others. When evaluating a graphic novel for purchase, keep in mind the demand for the material. Look for titles already owned that feature a similar topic or theme, or feature the same characters, and check how well they circulate. Also, research the demand for other titles by the author, artist, or creative team.

Popularity is critical when one considers the expense of an item. Compared to other teen materials, graphic novels tend to be more costly. With its potential popularity in mind, consider a graphic novel's worth versus its expense. For example, *1985* by Mark Millar and Tommy Lee Edwards is a a well-written, well-reviewed book by respected creators, and a 2010 Great Graphic Novels for Teens selection. However, if vintage superheroes and 1980s nostalgia don't fly with your teens, accolades may not be enough to offset the book's $20.00 price tag. This is especially true when two less-well received, but more popular, manga or digest titles could be purchased with the same funds. Expense versus worth should also be considered with series titles. A manga series may have multiple volumes—some number more than thirty! When starting a manga series, keep in mind the expense factor for continuing the series.

While depth is a goal for any library collection, remember that graphic novels are a popular culture medium. Sacrificing one's budget to maintain a well-rounded collection that does not circulate will not benefit the library or the patrons. No matter how well reviewed, well written, or well drawn a book is, if no one is reading it, you might as well not own it. Since it would be impossible for one library to buy all of the graphic novels in print, or even all of the graphic novels requested by patrons, it may be necessary to employ a more lateral thought process while building your collection. It is possible to achieve a balanced collection on a system level, while housing particular materials at different locations. Take, for example, the collection at the Glendale (AZ) Public Library. At the main branch, the teen graphic novel collection was started with older teens in mind. It was created at a time when few manga titles were available and emphasized American comic titles. Later, when the Foothills Branch created their teen graphic novel collection, they chose to emphasize manga and aimed the collection at a wider age group. The smallest branch in the Glendale System, the Velma Teague Branch, houses American and Japanese titles, but due to space concerns, focuses on only the most popular titles and holds a much smaller collection than the other two branches. At separate branches the collections are vastly different, but as a whole, the library system has a well-rounded collection.

The last issue to keep in mind when thinking of a graphic novel's potential popularity is age appropriateness. This issue is especially important for children's and teens' librarians, for whom age-appropriateness is a constant concern and a potential battle. We discussed age ratings and popularity in an earlier chapter, but it bears repeating: Graphic novel age ratings are decided subjectively, with the criteria varying widely from publisher to publisher. In other words, a Teen rating from Oni Press does not equal a Teen rating from Marvel, which does not equal a Teen rating from TOKYOPOP. Being aware of the age ratings on a book and how that will impact potential readership, is crucial.

Current Collection

The second factor when evaluating a graphic novel is to keep in mind your current collection, and how well the title under consideration fits in with what you already own. A collection that focuses on *shonen* manga might benefit from the addition of sports titles like *Whistle* by Daisuke Higuchi, but the addition of a more *shojo* title, like *Crimson Hero* by Mitsuba Takanashi, would be an odd fit. Also, consider if the title is a sequel, a prequel, or depends heavily on other material.

If the title is part of a series, then consider where it falls in that series, particularly when purchasing manga. Most manga titles are multi-volume series. In the majority of manga, it is important to read these volumes in order. Story arcs will flow from volume to volume. One arc may wrap up, but another might begin in the same volume. Volume seven of *The Prince of Tennis* by Takeshi Konomi would not be a smart buy for a library that does not already own the first six volumes.

As above, we encourage you to think laterally about your collection, and consider building a collection on a facility or system scale. Hotly requested titles that pack too high of an age rating for a teen collection could find shelf space in an adult collection. A library whose patrons love manga but hates superheroes could find the situation reversed at the branch across town. Collaborating to build your collection across departments or across facilities can stretch your money and tailor the collection to the tastes of your site.

Creators

The reputation or the importance of the creators should also be considered when evaluating a graphic novel. Graphic novels are truly a collaborative medium, in which any number of people are involved in the creation and distribution of a book. However, certain creators or publishers will display certain characteristics throughout their works. For example, VIZ has several imprints: Shojo Beat, Shonen Jump, Kids, and Signature. These imprints alert the reader to the type of story they are getting. Similarly, American publishers are often associated with a particular type of story. Slave Labor Graphics is well known for publishing materials that appeal to a "Goth" crowd, while DC Comics' mature readers line, VERTIGO, is most often associated with dark, adult fantasy.

Individual creators can also have distinctive aspects to their work. Mark Millar, a Scottish comic book writer, creates gritty superheroes in real-world settings. Rumiko Takahashi, a Japanese manga artist, is famous for her action comedies which have a hint of romance to increase the appeal to her female readership. To compare comic creators to filmmakers, a savvy movie-goer will get a sense of an artist's style after seeing a few films. Michael Bay makes splashy action movies, Diablo Cody's characters have a unique style of speech, and Michael Moore makes liberal-leaning documentaries. Many creators and publishers are the same way. The reputation of a creator or publisher is something learned, as one becomes more familiar with the medium. Once you become familiar with a publisher or creator's style, then you can know what to expect from their works.

Awards

One way to quickly research the reputation or significance of the graphic novel is to search the comics industry awards. Not well known outside the comics industry, these awards are selected by adults "in the know." The following list gives information about some of the most important of these industry awards.

Comics Buyer's Guide Fan Awards. Also known as the CBG awards, these are awards selected by readers of the *Comics Buyer's Guide*. The winners in ten different categories are then published in *CBG*. The official Web site of the *Comics Buyer's Guide* is *http://www.cbgxtra.com/*, and information about the awards can be found at *http://users.rcn.com/aardy/comics/awards/cbg.shtml*.

Diamond Gem Awards. The Gem Awards are given out by Diamond Comics Distributors to publishers and manufacturers in the comics industry. Nominees are selected by a panel of Diamond industry professionals from all products shipped during a given year and then voted on by the most critical segment that serves the comic book public—comic book specialty retailers across the U.S. and abroad. The Web site, *http://www.diamondcomics.com/gemawards* has information about the award and past winners.

The Glyph Awards. Awarded to the best in comics made by, for, and about people of color, the Glyphs are given out at the East Coast Black Age of Comics Con. More information about the Glyph Awards is avaliable at *http://ecbacc.com/wordpress/*.

The Harvey Kurtzman Awards. The Harvey Awards are awarded in more than twenty categories at the Museum of Comics and Cartoon Art Festival Weekend. Unlike the Eisner awards, the Harvey's are both nominated by and selected by the full body of comic book professionals. For information on the award and past winners, visit the official Web site at *http://www.harveyawards.org*.

The Ignatz Awards. Named for Ignatz, the mouse in the classic comic strip "Krazy Kat" by George Herriman, this award recognizes outstanding achievement in comics and cartooning. Awarded at the Small Press Expo, the nominees are selected by a five-member panel of artists and voted on by the attendees of SPX. More information is avalable on the official Web site *http://www.spxpo.com/?page_id=22*.

Japan Media Arts Festival Manga Award. The Japan Media Arts Festival has created a category for excellence in manga that is held in high esteem in Japan. More information and previous winners are on the official Web site *http://plaza.bunka.go.jp/english/festival.html*.

Kodansha Manga Awards. In Japan, Kodansha publishing has created an award for manga published by Kodansha in four categories: children's, *shojo*, *shonen*, and general manga. The official website is in Japanese, but for information and previous winners in English, try *http://users.rcn.com/aardy/comics/awards/kodansha.shtml*.

National Cartoonists Society Awards. These are the oldest awards associated with American cartoons, commonly known as the "The Reubens." Excellence in the fields of newspaper strips, newspaper panels, TV animation, feature animation, newspaper illustration, gag cartoons, book illustration, greeting cards, comic books, magazine feature/magazine illustration, and editorial cartoons, are chosen by the members of the National Cartoonists Society. The website of the National Cartoonists Society is *http://www.reuben.org.*

Shogakukan Manga Award. A Japanese award sponsored by Shogakukan Publishing for excellence in children's, *shojo, shonen,* and general manga, with a focus on Shogakukan titles. Again, the official site is in Japanese only, but information and winners are located at *http://users.rcn.com/aardy/comics/awards/shogakukan.shtml.*

Tezuka Osamu Bunka-sho (Osamu Tezuka Cultural Prizes). Sponsored by the Asahi newspaper, the Grand Prize award is given annually for manga published in Japan the previous year. Other prizes are awarded, but not necessarily every year. The public makes nominations, but the voting is only by a panel of judges. The official Web site is in Japanese: *http://www.asahi.com/tezuka/kiroku.html,* but this Web site *http://www.hahnlibrary.net/comics/awards/tezuka* has a listing of previous winners and a little more information about the award.

The Will Eisner Comics Industry Awards. The best known of the comics awards, and arguably the most prestigious, the Eisners award publications and creators of the previous year in more than two dozen categories. A panel of comics industry professionals chooses the nominees; voting is open to members of the comics industry community. The awards are given out at Comic-Con International San Diego in July or August of each year. For a brief history of the award, FAQs, and a complete list of winners, go to: *http://www.comiccon.org/cci/cci_eisnersfaq.shtml*

YALSA's Great Graphic Novels for Teens. The Young Adult Library Services Association (YALSA) created an annual booklist inaugurated in 2007. This list aims to find the best graphic novels for teens published within the previous sixteen months and is announced every January at the Midwinter Conference of the American Library Association (ALA). The list is created through nominations and then is vetted by a committee of school and public librarians who are members of YALSA. For more information, go to *http://www.ala.org/ala/yalsa/booklistsawards/greatgraphicnovelsforteens/gn.htm.*

As we said earlier, many librarians are not aware that these awards exist, particularly in the case of the manga awards. While looking for award-winning graphic novels, there are a few items to keep in mind. One is that an adult audience is choosing the winners, therefore "award-winning" does not translate into "library-friendly," and many of these titles are intended for mature readers. Another issue, unique to the Japan-based manga awards, is that not all of the manga titles that have won awards have been translated and released in the United States.

Physical Attributes

The physical attributes such as print quality, paper quality, and the ability to withstand multiple uses are important features to consider when previewing a graphic novel. Print quality, or the quality of the reproduction of the artwork, is of special significance. Is it possible to see details in the artwork, or does it look unnecessarily muddy? If the artwork was originally published in color and now is being reproduced in black and white, as with the *Essential* line from Marvel, was the artwork modified for the new format, or is it obvious that the artwork was merely replicated without color? If the artwork was reduced from its original size, as in the *Elfquest* series from DC, did the integrity of the artwork survive the reduction, or is it now cluttered and difficult to read? In a manga series, consider the translation of background noises or other onomatopoeia. Do these translations distract from the original artwork? If the artwork is not duplicated properly, or if it is improperly formatted for a layout change, whole dimensions of meaning and substance could be lost.

Paper quality is an issue of particular importance when purchasing graphic novels, because paper quality is directly linked to the lifespan of the binding. Many manga publishers use a heavier weight paper than most trade paperback publishers. This puts stress on the bindings, causing large sections of the book to fall out. Other manga publishers go to the opposite extreme and use very thin paper that will not stand up to multiple users. On the American side of the ledger, there are many anecdotal accounts of the slick paper warping and falling out of the bindings, as well as with thicker graphic novels, pages simply fall out. Consider if the book will stand up to multiple uses. Because of their popularity, you can expect graphic novels, particularly manga, to circulate much faster and much more often than other teen materials. What you buy must endure multiple usages in a short time period. Look at other titles in your collection from the same publisher: How did those titles hold up? Did they fall apart after few uses, or are they "built to last"?

For example, some titles in the collection at Glendale (AZ) Public Library have circulated over one hundred times without needing mending; by contrast, some of the CineManga titles from TOKYOPOP fell apart before being processed for checkout. At Glendale (AZ) Public Library, before mending a graphic novel, we mark how many times it had circulated before needing repair. In three years of mending graphic novels, the average number of circulations before a graphic novel needed mending was thirty-three.

Graphic Novel Quality

Finally, graphic novels are subject to the same criteria as prose works—with a few twists. The elements of writing, such as originality of the work, realistic or well-developed characters, well-written believable dialogue, pacing, and an engrossing plot, are all important parts of the text portion of a graphic novel. However, when evaluating a graphic novel, be careful to avoid the trap that many librarians fall into: focusing exclusively on the textural elements of the graphic novel, while giving short shift to the artwork.

Many librarians feel more comfortable evaluating text, since evaluating artwork can be subjective. One reviewer may love the moody, atmospheric, collage interpretations of Dave McKean, while another may consider them cluttered and confusing. Gene Yang's clean, cartoony style may work for some, but others may find it lacking in detail and realism. Nonetheless, there are a few criteria that can be applied to all graphic novel art, regardless of style.

Note the panel layout of the artwork. Are your eyes pulled from panel to panel? Or is it necessary to rely on textual information, or even directional arrows, to keep the flow of the panels? Good artwork will move the eye and carry the reader from panel to panel, page to page. Consider the dramatic impact of the artwork. Does the artist's style mesh well with the story being told? For example, renowned superhero artist Jim Lee teamed with gritty writer Frank Miller for an alternate take on Batman in

All Star Batman and Robin. Lee illustrated Miller's tale of a near psychotic Batman in his typical style: cleanly drawn, fan-friendly presentation with lots of candy-bright colors and curvaceous women. His character designs work against Miller's tone, and critics and fans argued loudly about whether this was a deliberate choice or a bad pairing of artist and author.

When appropriate, you should also take into consideration the work of the colorist and letterer. Do the colors work with the artwork and the overall feel of the book? For example, the monstrous superhero *Spawn* originally featured a very bright, cartoony color palette, one that was quite at odds with the dark tale of obsession and revenge. Is the lettering readable? Are different fonts used for different characters, and does this add to the book, or is it just confusing? To cite a classic example, in the *Sandman* series by Neil Gaiman, the lead character Morpheus's dialogue is lettered using white text on a black background. This was done to give the character a unique "voice" but was executed over the objections of the letterer, Todd Klein.[1] Whether or not it succeeded is a question of taste. Colors, layout, and lettering: All of these elements work together to create a graphic novel or manga and need to be evaluated.

The ability of the art to convey information is vital in graphic novels. Elements of the narrative, such as the emotional state of the characters or location changes, are conveyed via the artwork. If the characters never change expression, or if the backgrounds are static, then the reader must guess at these vital plot elements. Readers should not have to read "Back in the Batcave" to know that Batman is in the Batcave. The artwork should plainly show it. Particularly in manga, nonverbal cues such as character expressions and other panel art relay much of the story. For example, in the *Kindaichi Case Files* series by Yozaburo Kanari and Fumiya Sato, the ultimate mystery solution is conveyed through the artwork. In order to be successful, artwork must transmit information convincingly.

Graphic novels depend on the synergy between image and text; the two must be considered in unison to give a graphic novel a fair and complete evaluation. The two must work together and match in tone. One should not duplicate information conveyed by the other. Though there is no official term for this synergy, we have chosen to call it "flow." Text and art with flow create a final product that is utterly dependent on the two elements working together. Flow is the ultimate goal of any graphic novel, and the final criteria for its evaluation.

Reviews

Though a hands-on evaluation of a graphic novel will give a librarian a more accurate evaluation of the material, librarians will not have the ability to preview every title they consider for purchase. Bookstores and comics specialty stores are good resources for hands-on evaluations; however, this is not practical if you are buying a large number of titles. Otherwise, librarians must depend on reviews, and should know what to look for in a quality graphic novel review. When looking at reviews, a librarian needs to consider what the benefits and drawbacks are to different types of graphic novel reviews. In this section, we address fan-written reviews and professional library journal reviews.

Fan Reviews

To begin, we will discuss the fan reviews found online or in magazines. It is something of a misnomer to call some of these reviews "fan" reviews, since some are written by professional reviewers for a personal Web site or Webzine. However, for lack of a better term, we will stick with fan reviews. Also, the vast majority of reviews to be found on the web are not written by professional reviewers.

Fan reviewers are generally knowledgeable about the given topic. With series, many reviewers will take into account how the particular volume plays into the series as a whole. Fan reviewers are more enthusiastic in their reviews, whether positively or negatively. Online reviewers publish more frequently and in a timelier manner than professional reviews, and there are a much greater number of fan reviewers.

The fan reviews sound great so far, but they do have drawbacks. With little editorial oversight, you will find badly written reviews and ones that nitpick over very small issues. One major drawback is that reviewers can allow personal biases to seep into their reviews and outweigh critical commentary. Although it may not be readily apparent, bias can be built into a review because many fan reviewers critique what they would already read as fans. This means that they already have an affinity for the title they are reviewing. Fan reviews tend to focus on recent graphic novels, so if you are looking for an older title, you might find it difficult to locate material. The biggest drawback for librarians using

Reliable Fan and Comic Critics Reviews

Unsure of what fan sites to trust? Here are a few the authors like.

Comics Worth Reading. http://comicsworthreading.com/. Go here for professional quality reviews coordinated by longtime critic Johanna Draper Carlson.

Eye on Comics. http://www.eyeoncomics.com. Reviews and commentary on graphic novels, comic books, the comics industry, and other pop culture related to comics by longtime online comics critic Don MacPherson, formerly of *The Fourth Rail,* Fandom.com's *Comics Newsarama,* and *Psycomic.*

GirlWonder.org. http://www.girl-wonder.org. Because capes aren't just for boys, this Web site dedicated to "fighting misogyny in comics, the comics industry, and comics fandom," features thoughtful reviews and recommendations.

Graphic Novel Reporter. http://www.graphicnovelreporter.com. Part of the Book Reporter Network, this site features reviews and interviews with creators, as well as preview pages and news items.

Manga.About.com. http://manga.about.com/. Deb Aoki's manga blog is one of the top places to keep current on manga news, reviews, and graphic novels.

Manga Blog. http://www.mangablog.net/. This site touts itself as an "ongoing conversation about manga," which is completely true, but it also combs through many, many fan review blogs to help keep its blog readers abreast on all things manga.

Manga Maniacs. http://www.mangamaniacs.org. While this site is no longer updated, it has a wealth of information about manga titles published before 2003. Of the titles they do have, the reviews are in depth and come with a rating scale and a note on objectionable material at the bottom of the review.

Manga Recon. http://www.popcultureshock.com/manga/. This site features reviews, news, and commentary on manga.

Read About Comics. http://www.readaboutcomics.com. This blog, which bills itself as "where to find what's really good," features reviews of comics and manga from Greg McElhatton, a professional writer and critic.

Sequential Tart. http://www.sequentialtart.com. Sequential Tart is a monthly webzine written by women and dedicated to exploring the comics industry. Look for reviews, as well as interviews with creators, artists, writers, movers and shakers in the industry, including current, up and coming, and past greats. In addition to comics, they provide articles and interviews on popular culture, including movie and book reviews. A section of genre reading lists is of particular interest to librarians and teachers.

fan reviews is that these reviews are aimed at other fans and do not take into consideration the needs of libraries. Consequently, there may be no mention of content concerns, such as violence, gore, and nudity. In addition, the review may not tell if the title is a good starting point for people interested in beginning to collect the series.

Professional Library Journal Reviews

In comparison to the fan reviews, the professional library journal reviews still have a long way to go. While some journals have reviewed graphic novels for a number of years, many journals have only gotten serious about the format in the last few years. The best parts of a library journal review are that they have editorial oversight and they make the reader aware of content and collection issues.

The biggest drawback is that there are simply not enough reviews. Given the colossal number of graphic novels produced each month, it would be impossible for a single journal, one not devoted exclusively to graphic novels, to cover them all. Many quality graphic materials go unreviewed, small press titles in particular. It is much more difficult to find a review of a graphic novel published by a non-mainstream publisher. However, since many journals have decided to make articles and columns about graphic novels a regular feature, small presses may get better coverage in these publications.

While journals try to publish reviews in a timely manner, most graphic novels are a few months to a year old when reviewed. As many librarians can attest, teen readers are clamoring for the newest graphic novels before they are even available. While timeliness will always be an issue for print journals, this is becoming less of an issue as more graphic novel publishers send out advance copies to journals. In addition, the ever-multiplying number of graphic novel columnists, both online and in print, help to inform about new titles. As fans of the format, these columnists know what is "new and hot" and can bring it to the attention of readers faster than regular reviewers can.

Particularly with manga, a review of volume one of a multiple volume series is difficult, since the first volume may just set the stage for the series. At the same time, if a library journal reviews volume five of the same series, it may be incomprehensible without reviewing the previous four volumes. Again, the timeliness issue arises, if the library journal chooses to hold off a series review until there are multiple volumes. Multi-volume series often receive better coverage in articles and columns than in regular reviews.

With the vast amount of graphic novels available to purchase, it is imperative to weed out the bad titles from the good ones. However, many times professional reviews fail in this regard, because negative reviews of graphic novels are more difficult to find than negative reviews of novels and nonfiction.

Reliable Library Journals

These professional journals consistently provide quality reviews on graphic novels.

Booklist. http://booklistonline.com/. In addition to regular reviews in their review section, *Booklist* highlights graphic novels annually in the Spring "Spotlight on Graphic Novels" feature.

Library Journal. http://www.libraryjournal.com/. Steve Raiteri and Martha Cornog write regular graphic novel reviews. In addition, *LJ's* online only "Xpress Reviews" regularly feature graphic novels.

Library Media Connection. http://www.linworth.com/lmc/. This school media center journal has been publishing graphic novel reviews for six-plus years. The reviews are mostly quality level, but when the reviewer does not recommend a title, there is little detail as to why.

Publisher Weekly. http://www.publishersweekly.com/. In addition to great reviews, *PW* provides a weekly email column called *PW Comics Week* with reviews, panel previews, and news items.

School Library Journal. http://www.schoollibraryjournal.com/. Graphic novel reviews are included in the monthly reviews in the print journal, and online the "Good Comics for Kids" blog features additional reviews and items of interests.

Voices of Youth Advocates. http://www.voya.com. *VOYA* has "Graphically Speaking" a regular graphic novel column written by library consultant, Kat Kan. In addition to the column, reviews of graphic novels can be found throughout the review section of the journal.

Perhaps this is because the format is so popular that anything would move off the shelf, as many graphic novel readers, particularly teens, could care less about the reviewers' opinions. It is also possible that library journals try to seek out only the finest of the graphic novel publishing field and are less concerned with mediocre or bad material. Whatever the reason, it is just as important to know what titles stink as well as what titles rock.

The state of professional librarian graphic novel reviews is not as dire as this may sound. As more and more libraries accept that graphic novels are a legitimate part of a reputable library collection, the review sources most commonly used by librarians are following suit. Many journals have excellent reviews of all types of graphic materials. A good library journal reviewer will discuss the art and text, content issues, the appeal of the book, and similar or related works. What a librarian collecting graphic novels should do is determine which reviewers are well informed about graphic novels and consider that knowledge when reading reviews—whether professional or fan reviews—and take to heart the issues surrounding all reviews, regardless of who is writing them.

Other Review Sources

Outside of fan reviews published on the Web or reviews found in journals for librarians, there are a few other review sources for graphic novels and manga. As graphic novels continue to penetrate the mainstream marketplace, you can find reviews of graphic novels mixed in with those of other print materials in conventional publications. Graphic novel reviews can be found in mainstream magazines, newspapers, and blogs dedicated to culture both high (*The New York Review of Books*) and low (*Entertainment Weekly*). Often, the reviews of graphic novels and manga in mainstream publications are not a regularly occurring feature; therefore, eagle-eyed librarians must constantly be on the lookout for them.

Another review source for graphic novels are magazines created for fans of the format. *Protoculture Addicts, Wizard,* and *Comics Buyer's Guide* are just a few examples of this type of publication. Often, the reviews in these magazines are short on evaluative content and long on description, but they are an excellent gauge of what is new in the marketplace and usually feature the titles your patrons will be asking for soon.

Of course, with the massive increase of graphic novels being published, libraries will not have enough funding to buy everything—perhaps not even everything requested by the patrons. Remember that most graphic novels are for leisure reading and personal enjoyment, not education or self-improvement. Keeping in mind graphic novels' potential popularity, the library's current collection, and the reputation of the creators will help librarians select the best graphic novels—whether by previewing graphic novels at a bookstore or local comic shop, or reading reviews. Savvy librarians should utilize all the tools at their disposal.

---

1   Klein, Todd. "Neil Gaiman/Sandman." *Todd Klein: Lettering-Logos-Design.* N.p., n.d. Web. 6 Apr. 2010.

Purchasing Options

While there are many options for where to purchase graphic novels, each has their own pros and cons. The options we will be discussing are comic specialty stores, chain and online bookstores, library book jobbers/distributors, and buying direct from the publisher or the comic distributor, Diamond.

Comic Specialty Stores

Before we begin our discussion, let us add a disclaimer: Every comic specialty store is different. The information provided here is a generalization. The authors have had both very positive and very negative experiences in working with comic specialty stores, for purchasing and library programming. Your results may vary with a comic specialty store, depending on the owners and the store.

The major benefit to purchasing graphic novels from a local store is that comic specialty store staff and owners are very knowledgeable about comics and graphic novels. Since comics and related merchandise is their only business, they are better able to stay abreast of new titles, changes in creative teams, age ratings, and other comics information that may slip by a harried librarian. However, be aware that a comic store staff's knowledge may skew towards a specific type of comics. For example, one storeowner may know a massive amount about superheroes, but not much about manga. Another store may be the reverse. But in either case, they will know what is selling in your community. Even if you do not plan to buy from your local comics specialty store, a conversation with the staff may be helpful. In the authors' experience, most comic specialty storeowners are happy to share their knowledge and expertise with the local librarians and are excited about getting more people to read comics and graphic novels, regardless of where those comics are being purchased.

Another benefit to comic specialty stores is their access to materials. While libraries may have to special order some titles, particularly small press material, comic stores have better access to materials and often have them on hand. Most stores will allow you to look through their graphic novels, though some do shrink-wrap or bag their merchandise. Get permission from the staff before opening the bags to flip through the graphic novels in question.

There are possible drawbacks to using comic specialty stores. The biggest concern is a lack of awareness of library needs. This drawback can be overcome through discussions between the librarian and the owner. This may seem like an obvious solution, but we have seen libraries taken advantage of by stores. In one instance, the librarians set up monthly orders with a comic store to provide popular graphic novels to the library. Without knowledge of graphic novels, the librarians trusted the opinions of the store staff. However, the store took advantage of the situation by supplying the library with back stock material, graphic novels that had not sold well. Also, some of the titles the comic specialty store staff selected, although popular, were inappropriate choices for the age group the library catered to. However, once the librarians became more educated about graphic novels, the librarians and the comic store staff discussed the issues, fixed some problems, and began a mutually satisfying relationship.

What one should learn from this cautionary tale is simple: A librarian must have a full discussion with the comic store staff, if the specialty store staff will be selecting the graphic novels for the library. Both parties must learn about each other in order for the arrangement to work. For example, Wednesdays are busy for comic stores, since new titles arrive that day. Instead of visiting on busy days, librarians should schedule appointments on days that are less hectic for the comic store staff.

Librarians will need to educate the store staff about the library's specific needs. For example, if your library collection does not allow nudity regardless of context, then make sure that the store staff knows this. Non-sexual nudity can be found in many titles aimed at teenagers, particularly in manga. Since this type of nudity is so prevalent, many comic store staff members may not even be aware of it anymore or realize that it may be a problem for libraries.

Another potential drawback to comic specialty stores is that they do not provide additional processing or have access to MARC records. Comic stores may give discounts on the library's purchases, but the amount of the discount varies from store to store. We found that our book jobbers give us much better discounts than our local comic stores, though we have heard of stores giving out great discounts to libraries.

Chain Bookstores

Another place to purchase graphic novels is national chain bookstores. Chain bookstores like Barnes & Noble or Borders have many of the same benefits and drawbacks as the comic specialty stores. Their major drawback is supply, since many of the stores only supply the most popular or recent titles. Small press titles are almost non-existent in chain bookstores. For beginners, chain bookstores are usually a good place to familiarize oneself with the newer and popular titles. Overall, buying only from a chain bookstore will not allow for depth in your collection.

Online stores, whether a bookstore like Amazon.com, a comic store like Mile High Comics (*http://www.milehighcomics.com*), or an anime store like Right Stuf International (*http://www.rightstuf.com*), typically function much like a chain bookstore with the same limitations but fewer advantages. One may get a better discount online than at a chain store, but you will not be able to view the material beforehand, and returning material is more of a hassle.

Book Jobbers

Librarians are familiar with using book jobbers/distributors to purchase material. We do it every day for other library material. So why do so many people not use them for graphic novels? The number one reason is that for years the vendors hardly had any graphic novels worth buying. However, in the past several years, that has changed dramatically. Today, at least five vendors offer standing order plans for graphic novels in different age ranges.

These vendors cater directly to libraries. They are already aware of our needs. They offer discounts, depending on your library's contract, and offer extra services like MARC records and pre-processing to help catalog graphic novels. The majority of vendors include reviews and citations, and their MLS-accredited staff can create core lists for your library. The major drawbacks are that the librarians cannot review the material easily beforehand, small press titles can be difficult to obtain through these vendors, and returns may be complicated—especially if your library has pre-processing done through your vendor.

Diamond Comic Distributors

Diamond Comic Distributors is a name that comes up often in the world of comic books and graphic novels. Diamond is the largest comic book distributor serving North America. They have exclusive arrangements with most major U.S. comic book publishers, and they transport materials from the publishers to the retailers. Diamond is also the parent company of Diamond Select Toys and Diamond Book Distributors. Diamond is a major force in the comic book industry, as they are the only means retailers have to access materials. Diamond also sells directly to libraries, offering a discount and the assistance of their staff.

Getting materials from Diamond has one big advantage: They have almost everything. Just about every comic book and graphic novel publisher makes their products available through Diamond. It doesn't matter if the company in question is mainstream or independent, a small press or large press, or where they are located. If they sell comics, Diamond probably has their materials. In recent months, a handful of publishers, most notably Marvel Comics, have left Diamond for other book distributors. It is too early to say if this is a trend or anomaly among graphic novel publishers, and for the time being, Diamond is still the go-to distributor for most companies.

The drawback to ordering directly from Diamond is that their discount may not be as generous as those from book jobbers. Also, Diamond does not offer any processing of materials. Finally, ordering from Diamond is a more convoluted process than that of most book jobbers or online vendors.

Buying Directly from the Publisher

Another option is to purchase directly from the publisher. Most graphic novel publishers have Web sites and catalogs that they are more than willing to share with librarians. This option is particularly useful, if you are focusing on smaller press titles. However, buying directly from the publisher can quickly eat up budgets, as there is no standard discount, and shipping costs can accumulate quickly.

There is no "wrong" place to buy graphic novels. It all depends on your library's needs and which option can deliver those needs best. Many libraries may choose to use a variety of these options.

Resources

With so much material being produced in the graphic novel field, it is imperative that librarians have some type of guide to new releases and small press titles; otherwise, it would be impossible to keep up. There are several options available to librarians to keep abreast of new releases, each with positive and negative aspects. In this next section, we will walk through different ordering resources that will help you when investigating graphic novel titles.

Diamond *Previews*

When discussing ordering comics and graphic novels, it is necessary to first mention the gold standard for the field, Diamond *Previews*. *Previews* is a monthly catalog published by Diamond Comic Distributors for use by the direct market, i.e. comic specialty stores. Every month, the *Previews* catalog lists thousands of items available through comic book retailers. If it is comics or graphic novel-related, it will most likely be found in Diamond Previews. It is too soon to tell how changes in the book distribution market, such as Marvel comics leaving Diamond Book Distributors, will impact Diamond *Previews*. At this time, there is no better place to see the entire graphic novel universe in one place.

This inclusiveness is the great strength and the great weakness of using *Previews* to order for libraries. *Previews* does include information on every graphic novel being published, small and independent presses included, three months ahead of the actual publication date. This is very useful if you are trying to stay ahead of the curve and keep up with the latest releases in the field. However, because it does include *everything*, *Previews* is often a phone book-size catalog that can terrify those new to the field of graphic novels. Furthermore, while pornographic or "Adult" comics are featured in a separate issue of *Previews*, enough salacious material slips in to make reading *Previews* an occasionally blush-worthy experience. In fact, Merideth was almost ejected from the bus on her morning commute, by a driver who took exception to some of the featured art. Despite these drawbacks, *Previews* is the single best source of information on upcoming small press and independent titles. *Previews* can be purchased at your local comic specialty store, or you can subscribe either directly through Diamond or EBSCO. An important note: A subscription through EBSCO costs about $175 a year and through Diamond about $150 a year. But single issues purchased in a comics store cost only about $5.00 a month.

Another issue to be aware of is that it does not limit itself to print materials. While *Previews* does list upcoming graphic novels, manga and comics, it also lists comics-related merchandise. Some of this material may be related to libraries, such as art books, novelizations, and prose works about comics, but most of it is "swag"—items such as push dolls, Zippo lighters, maquettes, action figures, t-shirts, trash cans, limited edition and signed books, and everything else you can imagine sticking a comic book character on. While it can be cool to see what is being produced in the comics merchandising field, it can also be frustrating to wade through page after page of non-book material. The merchandise pages are dangerous for another reason: Both of the authors have fallen prey to merchandise they did not know existed, and now can't possibly live without.

Another drawback: *Previews* does not typically include the ISBNs of the titles; instead, it uses the Diamond Comic Distributors' numbers. If purchasing through Diamond, then this is no problem, but other vendors may not have the title in their system yet or not have the exact title. This makes for some frustration on the librarians' part, because they will need to track down the ISBN from another source.

Diamond *Bookshelf*

Some of the problems presented for librarians using Diamond *Previews,* have been solved by a sister publication, Diamond *Bookshelf. Bookshelf* is a publication produced specifically for librarians and only covers graphic novel materials. Weeding out the single issues, merchandise, and other materials that are featured in *Previews, Bookshelf* is a much more compact volume. Of special interest to librarians, the Diamond *Bookshelf* Web site (*http://bookshelf.diamondcomics.com/*) includes book reviews.

The main drawback to using Diamond *Bookshelf* for ordering is the way in which it is organized. *Bookshelf* uses genre and age classifications to organize titles; this can make looking for a specific title very frustrating. Also, as we have discussed, age ratings on graphic novels are very subjective, and some of the age recommendations made by Diamond will not work for libraries in conservative communities. However, for librarians new to the format, or those who are uncomfortable with the massive *Previews, Bookshelf* is a good resource.

The New Comic Book Release List

Aside from the Diamond Products, there are other options for librarians looking for updates on new releases. The New Comic Book Release List, available online at *http://www.comiclist.com/,* provides a weekly list of comics and graphic novel releases. The New Comic Book Release List is notable primarily for its ease of use; the weekly format is much more comprehensible than the phone book-like *Previews.* Like Diamond *Previews,* it doesn't provide evaluative content, but the Web site does link to a number of graphic novel review Web sites. If you are aware of its limitations, the New Comics Release List is an extremely convenient way to stay on top of most graphic novel publishing.

IcV2.com

This website, available at *www.icv2.com,* stands for Internal Correspondence version 2. This pop culture Web site provides bestseller lists from Bookscan, the bookstores, Diamond Indexes, and the comics

Publisher Web Sites

Aardvark-Vanaheim. A Canadian comic book company most known for publishing Dave Sim's *Cerebus.* Aardvark-Vanaheim has no official Web site.

Abstract Studios. *http://www.abstractstudiocomics.com.* Home of Terry Moore's comics *Strangers in Paradise* and *Echo.*

AdHouse Books. *http://www.adhousebooks.com/books/books.html.* A boutique publishing house. Their most well-known property is *Johnny Hiro.*

Antarctic Press. *http://www.antarctic-press.com.* An American manga publisher, best known for featuring the work of Rod Espinosa.

Arcana Studios. *http://www.arcanacomics.com. Kade* is the flagship title of this multi-media content studio.

Archaia Comics. *http://www.archaia.com.* An independent publisher and critical darling, this company produces the acclaimed *Mouse Guard, Gunnerkrigg Court,* and *Artesia.*

Archie Comics. *http://www.archiecomics.com.* The gang from Riverdale is still at it after all these years. *Sabrina the Teenage Witch* and *Josie and the Pussycats* can also be found here.

Aspen Comics. *http://www.aspencomics.com.* Publishing house featuring the work of writer/artist Michael Turner.

Avatar Press. *http://www.avatarpress.com.* A prolific publisher featuring work from Alan Moore, Warren Ellis, Garth Ennis, George R.R. Martin, Christos Gage, David Lapham, and more.

Bandai Entertainment. *http://www.bandai-ent.com.* This toy manufacturer and anime company also publishes manga, including *Code Geass* and *Eureka Seven.*

Bongo Comics. This company, publisher of the *Simpsons* and *Futurama* comics, has no official Web site.

Boom! Studios. *http://www.boom-studios.net.* This independent publisher has gotten a lot of attention for their licensed properties, particularly those from Disney and Pixar.

Dark Horse Comics. *http://www.darkhorse.com/.* An American publisher with both original and licensed properties, Dark Horse features American comics and manga. Aside from their regular site, Dark Horse features a site just for librarians, *http://libraries.darkhorse.com/,* with reviews, a backlist catalog, and catalog sorted by age rating.

DC Comics. *http://www.dccomics.com.* The official *DC* Comics web page. Plenty of information about all their titles including Batman, Superman and the Justice League.

--Vertigo Comics. *http://www.dccomics.com/vertigo.* An imprint of DC Comics that features "Mature Readers" materials, often with a horror or supernatural theme. Recently, Vertigo has been expanding into crime and noir graphic novels.

--Wildstorm Comics. *http://www.dccomics.com/wildstorm.* A subsidiary imprint of DC Comics, Wildstorm publishes American comics as well as independently created content and licensed properties.

Del Ray. *http://www.randomhouse.com/delrey/.* The publisher has recently gotten into the business of publishing graphic novels and manga, including *Negima!* and *Kitchen Princess.*

Devil's Due Publishing. *http://www.devilsdue.net.* Comic book publishers, carrying original, creator-owned and licensed properties including G.I. Joe and Dungeons and Dragons.

Publisher Web Sites *(continued)*

Digital Manga Publishing. *http://www.dmpbooks.com. Trigun, Hellsing* and *Antique Bakery* are only a few of the titles from this diverse manga publisher.

Fantagraphics. *http://www.fantagraphics.com.* An independent publisher of graphic novels, featuring the work of artists such as R. Crumb, Peter Bagge, Gilbert and Jaime Hernandez, Dan Clowes, Joe Sacco, and Chris Ware.

First Second. *http://www.firstsecondbooks.com.* A critically acclaimed, award winning publisher of graphic novels for teens and youth.

IDW Publishing. *http://www.idwpublishing.com.* This company currently publishes a wide range of comic books and graphic novels including titles based on *Angel, Doctor Who, GI Joe, Star Trek, Terminator: Salvation,* and *Transformers.* Their original comics include work by Peter David and Joe Hill.

Image Comics. *http://www.imagecomics.com/.* A creator-owned publishing house, best known for featuring the work of Robert Kirkman and Todd McFarlane.

Top Cow. *http://www.topcow.com/Site/comics.html.* A partner studio of Image Comics, known for *Witchblade* and *The Darkness.*

Marvel Comics. *http://marvel.com/.* The House of Ideas featuring X-Men, Iron Man, the Avengers, and the Incredible Hulk.

NBM. *http://www.nbmpub.com.* An independent, general interest publisher, NBM features comics from creators around North America and Europe.

Oni Press. *http://www.onipress.com.* A general interest publisher, best known for *Scott Pilgrim, Courtney Crumrin* and *Queen and Country.*

Papercutz. *http://www.papercutz.com.* This imprint of NBM focuses on materials for ages eight to fourteen. Papercutz publishes Nancy Drew and Hardy Boys graphic novels, and a variety of licensed properties.

SLG Publishing. *http://www.slgcomics.com.* Formerly Slave Labor Graphics, this is a diverse publisher with a number of licensed properties, plus the work of Evan Dorkin, Andi Watson, and Jhonen Vasquez.

Amaze Ink. The all-ages imprint of SLG Publishing.

TOKYOPOP. *http://www.tokyopop.com. The largest North American manga* publisher, TOKYOPOP's titles include *Fruits Basket, Loveless, Princess Ai, D.N.Angel, .hack,* and many more.

Top Shelf. *http://www.topshelfcomix.com.* Although it's gotten the most press for being the new home of Alan Moore, Top Shelf is an independent publisher featuring the work of American and European creators.

UDON Entertainment. *http://www.udoncomics.com.* A publisher of manga and art books, as well as English of Korean manhwa titles.

VIZ Media. *http://www.viz.com.* This manga publishing powerhouse includes the *Shonen Jump* monthly manga anthology and numerous anime properties.

Yen Press. *http://www.yenpress.us.* The manga publishing arm of Hachette Book Group, Yen Press is producing the *Twilight* graphic novel.

specialty stores, giving a larger scope to the comics and graphic novel market. They also have quarterly top graphic novel properties broken down into different categories such as manga, kids and tweens, superhero, fiction and reality, etc.

New York Times Graphic Books Best Sellers List

While the *New York Times* best sellers lists are a well known staple in library land, many never realized that they had started a graphic books list in 2009. Called Graphic Books to encompass illustrated prose, nonfiction titles, and fictional graphic novels, the list is broken down into three categories: hardcover, softcover, and manga. The easiest way to access the list on the New York Times web site is to start at the Best Sellers site: *www.nytimes.com/pages/books/bestseller/* then click into the Graphic Books list.

Vendor Catalogs or Supplements

Other options for librarians are vendor catalogs or supplements that focus specifically on graphic novels and manga. Currently BWI, Baker & Taylor, and Ingram all produce graphic novels supplements for librarians. These supplements come out quarterly to annually and are generally sent to the acquisitions or collection development staff. If you do not receive this automatically, you may need to request a copy from your vendor. These supplements focus on upcoming titles and may include: core lists for collection development; reviews of featured titles; interviews with creators; or other items of interest. While these supplements can be useful in learning what titles are available from your vendor, you should be aware that publishers pay to be included in these supplements, which may skew the editorial content.

Publishers' Web Sites

Finally, when looking for information on new graphic novels, remember that you can always go straight to the source. Publishers' Web sites will always contain a list of graphic novels currently in print, and unlike the resources listed above, will include older materials. Many of these Web sites will include sample pages or artwork samples, which allow librarians to get a feel for the book before purchasing. The downside to using publisher Web sites as an ordering resource is that, of course, there are many publishers of graphic novels, and it is incredibly time consuming to search them all.

Because graphic novels are newbies in the world of libraries, finding a place to purchase them can be frustrating. Comic specialty stores and chain bookstores, both online and brick and mortar, can be a good resource for finding knowledgeable staff and a large number of titles; however, purchasing through them might be more expensive and time consuming than using an established library vendor. Large distributors such as Baker & Taylor or Ingram might not have the same diversity of materials as a comics specialty store. There are several options for staying current in the world of graphic novels, some of which are created specifically for a library market. By finding which vendors and information sources work best for you and your library, you can create a top-notch graphic novel collection.

Mending

When graphic novels and manga first made their way into libraries, librarians complained loudly over the poor quality of the books' bindings. *Sailor Moon* and other early manga titles had bindings that fell apart almost instantaneously. Glossy reprints of superhero comics from DC and Marvel had pages that would warp and fall out. Those days are over. For the most part, the graphic novel publishers listened to librarians and worked hard to make their publications' bindings more durable. But graphic novels still will fall apart, just like any other book. In this chapter, we look at some solutions for extending the life of your graphic novels and manga, as well as steps to take once the book has begun to fall apart.

Binding Issues

In a conversation with Oni Press Editor in Chief James Lucas Jones, we discussed the possible causes of binding weaknesses. In many cases, the culprit is the glue. Back in the early days, manga and graphic novels were purchased by collectors. These collectors would "baby" their books, treating them gently and with respect. However, this is not true of most library patrons. Many comics' publishers were not aware of the stresses being put on their books by an eager public. Listening to the howls of outraged librarians, most graphic novel publishers are now using stronger glues to bind their products.

The weight of the paper and inking may be other factors. The glossier and heavier the paper, the weaker the binding becomes. Let's take, for example, TOKYOPOP's cine-manga graphic novel line and VIZ's ani-manga line, which are notorious for falling apart. The authors themselves have mended many, many books from these imprints. While tracking their mending, the authors discovered that the average number of circulations before an ani-manga book fell apart was ten. Why? Heavy paper and the colored ink, combined with weak glue, contribute to binding failure.

A slightly less obvious culprit in binding breakage is the storage of the books—not just in the library after it has been purchased, but before the purchase as well. While the books are stored for shipping or purchase, they may not be kept in a climate controlled area. Both high heat and low temperatures can weaken bindings. Storage after the book has been added to the library's collection can also cause binding failure. In the Southwest, where temperatures often hit the triple digits, an hour or two in the car can cause significant damage to print materials. Also, as every librarian knows, patrons can be very cavalier about the library's materials, leaving books in bathrooms, cramming them into overfull backpacks, and tossing them around. All of this abuse can lead to binding issues.

However, the number one reason graphic novels appear to fall apart quicker than other books is that graphic novels just circulate faster and go through the hands of readers more quickly than a regular novel. When evaluating the longevity of your graphic novels, think in terms of circulation numbers instead of the number of months you've owned the book. Graphic novels circulate fast and hard, with some going back out as soon as they've been returned. So, although it may seem that graphic novels fall apart sooner than other materials, it just may be that they circulate more frequently in a smaller time frame.

The chart below is taken from circulation statistics at the Glendale Public Library. In it, we list the average number of circulations before mending from a variety of graphic novel publishers. This chart illustrates that graphic novels typically circulate twenty to twenty-five times before needing mending. In the authors' experience, this is comparable with a mass-market paperback's durability.

Mending

Mending can add more circulations and extend the shelf life of these products. Some mending options are time consuming and expensive, but others are easily accomplished. It is up to you to decide how much work is needed to save a book from being withdrawn.

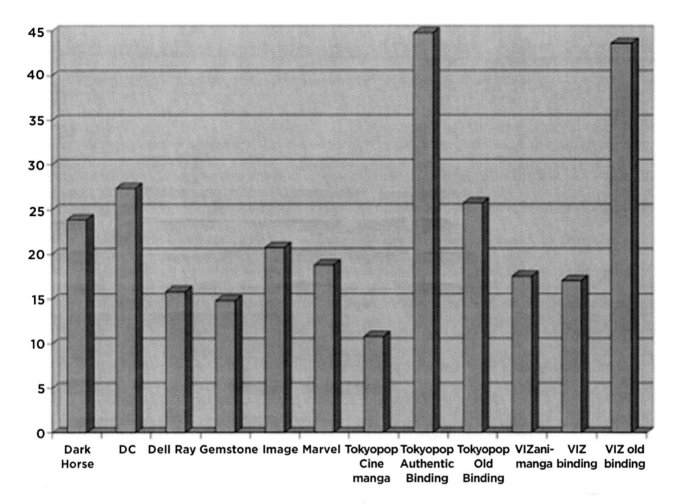

Average Circulations before Mending by Publisher

Processing

Some mending options are preventative measures, which should be implemented before the book is put into circulation. The easiest and most helpful measure is using book tape to secure the first and last pages to the covers. These pages are the weakest links in bindings, and the book tape helps them become more stable. A stable binding is a happy binding!

To protect the cover from wear and tear, use a laminate cover. This preventative measure can be done in-house or as part of processing offered by your book jobber. We have found that the cold laminate protects the cover and causes less stress on the bindings than the heavier laminate Kapco covers.

In-Library Fixes

After a graphic novel has circulated and fallen apart, there are several mending options to consider. Whatever option you choose, it is important to note that a mistake can ruin the book, so take care. In many libraries, mending is a task that falls to volunteers or members of the processing staff. In our experience, it pays to make sure that the people who mend are well-trained and appreciate graphic novels. An inattentive or apathetic mender can make catastrophic mistakes in your graphic novel. For instance, some volunteers have mended graphic novels with pages out of order and sometimes even upside down!

A relatively easy and inexpensive mending option is to re-glue the pages that have fallen out. Tapping the pages back into place with a thin layer of book glue will keep the book in circulation longer. Re-gluing can be done for individual pages as well as whole sections. This method of repair is not as time-consuming as some of the other options.

Comb binding, stapling, velobinding, and spiral binding are different variations of an in-house rebinding process. Each requires supplies and/or special equipment that may be expensive, and require extensive staff or volunteer training to accomplish. Each of these options may diminish the artwork, depending on how much gutter space is left between the pages. But if mended correctly, these methods may allow the graphic novel to last for several more circulations. At Glendale (AZ) Public Library, we have used both comb binding and velobinding to repair graphic novels. The process is simple, though time intensive.

To comb bind or velobind a book, you must begin by taking apart the book, a process that sounds simpler than it actually is. Although the binding may have failed, it rarely fails completely, and separating pages is a deliberate and tedious process. Using a velobinder or comb binding machine, staff or trained volunteers punch holes in the gutter space of the pages and add a new binding. The comb binding method allows the reader to open the pages fully, but is more unattractive, particularly in standard spine-out shelving. While comb binding will extend the life of your graphic novels and manga, expect a dip in the circulation on titles that have been mended this way, since the books are less appealing to browsing patrons. Velobinding allows the book to appear in fine condition on the shelf, but it doesn't allow for fully opened pages, which can frustrate patrons.

Rebinding and Prebinding

The last mending option is to send the book to a professional rebinder. Many times this rebinding will be more expensive than it would be to re-purchase the item. Rebinding has also become known as prebinding, since book jobbers offer these books as original purchases. These prebound books tend to be more expensive, sometimes double or triple the price of the original graphic novel. Often, the book is less aesthetically pleasing once it has been prebound, and teens are less likely to pick them up. Also, only a fraction of graphic novels are available prebound, although more are being added to jobbers' lists every day. Although expensive, some of the book jobbers do offer a lifetime guarantee on these prebound books. We are philosophically opposed to prebinding services, because we feel that it removes the publisher's responsibility for improving the bindings of the graphic novels. In informal conversations about bindings with the authors, more than one publisher's representative have shrugged and suggested prebinding as the solution for complaints about ineffective original bindings.

Ultimately, it is up to the librarians to determine what method of mending will work best for their library and collection. While it is easier and sometimes cheaper to re-order a graphic novel, book budgets are becoming tighter with every passing year, and titles do go out of print, so it may prove useful to know what mending options are available.

Programming with Graphic Novels

Teen librarians have more than a casual interest in programming. Finding programs that will attract teens to the library and keep them coming back is always a challenge. Luckily, graphic novels and manga are an easy collection connection for programming. In this chapter, we will discuss both passive and active programming built around graphic novels and manga.

Active Programs

Anime Screenings/Anime Festival

Although it's not really discussed in this book, anime and manga go hand in hand. Anime can be thought of as manga's animated counterpart. Many popular manga series have a companion anime and vice versa. In fact, it is not uncommon for the same characters and basic plot to be featured in a manga, anime, and tie-in video game. Most manga fans are also rabid consumers of anime.

Because of its popularity among teens, anime programming has become a staple in libraries in the past few years. One of the most attractive aspects of showing anime in the library is that libraries are not typically charged a screening fee. Some anime companies, most notably Funimation, have "anime club" programs that will send libraries free screening DVDs. Those companies that do charge a screening fee, such as Disney/Buena Vista, may be covered by a blanket film license. Whether free or covered as part of a larger license, anime screenings are a low-cost program for many libraries.

Suggested Anime Titles

Additional titles can be found in the *VOYA* articles at the end of this chapter.

Afro Samurai	*Full Metal Panic*	*Pumpkin Scissors*
Air Gear	*Gankutsuou: The Count of*	*RahXephon*
Angelic Layer	*Monte Cristo*	*RESERVoir CHRoNiCLE*
Argentosoma	*Gokusen*	*Tsubasa*
Azumanga Daioh	*Gunslinger Girl*	*Saiyuki*
Beck (Mongolian Chop	*Hikaru no Go*	*Scrapped Princess*
Squad)	*Howl's Moving Castle*	*Shura no Toki*
Black Cat	*Kodocha*	*Steamboy*
Bleach	*Le Chevalier D'Eon*	*Sugar, a Little Snow Fairy*
Boys Be	*Lupin III Movie Collections*	*Tactics*
Boys over Flowers	*Mushi-shi*	*Tekkon Kinkreet*
Castle in the Sky	*My-Hime*	*Tokyo Godfathers*
The Cat Returns	*One Piece*	*Twelve Kingdoms*
Chrono Crusade	*Ouran High School Host Club*	*Vexille*
Comic Party	*Peacemaker*	*Wallflower*
Doki Doki School Hours	*Peach Girl*	*Whisper of the Heart*
Dragon Drive	*Planetes*	*xxxHolic*
Fruits Basket	*Prince of Tennis*	

Anime programming can be as easy as showing an anime film occasionally, or more intensive, like an facilitating an anime club that meets on a regular basis. At Glendale Public Library (GPL) we have featured a number of successful anime screenings. Typically, over the summer, we show installments of an ongoing series, such as *Fullmetal Alchemist* or *Ouran High School Host Club,* every week. This is a good stragegy, because it keeps teens coming back to the library to find out "what happens next." The downside is that teens who miss a week or two might be lost if the series has a particularly complicated plot. Another way to host anime screenings is to show stand alone anime movies, sometimes called OVAs (Original Video Animations). These stand alone films require less of a time commitment from both staff and patrons, and can be less intimidating to the casual fan.

An even more time intensive form of anime programming is hosting an anime festival. Festivals typically take up a full day of anime screenings and activities. Merideth and Kristin have created festivals for a number of years. Each one is different and invigorating. Teens love them and look forward to them all year long. In past festivals, we have included *cosplay* (fan speak for costume contests in which teens dress up as a character), Japanese taste tests, anime bingo, name that tune/character, and trivia contests. While all of these programs have their fans, the taste tests are particularly popular. We have provided "fake" and candy sushi, sweet bean paste buns, melon soda, mochi, and the perennial favorite, Pocky (a pretzel stick dipped in various flavored coatings, chocolate in particular).

Anime festivals are an excellent chance to get teen patrons and volunteers involved in library programming. Merideth relies on her teen advisory group to assist at the anime festivals. Merideth likes to give her anime festivals a theme, a single thought line that shapes the festival. In the past she's hosted festivals with the theme "Secrets and Spaceships" (sci-fi and fantasy anime), "Curses!" (anime featuring a cursed character), and "Ninjas v. Pirates v. Zombies." Members of the anime screening group and the teen advisory board selected these themes, as well as suggesting anime to fit each theme. On the day of the event, teen volunteers host a trivia quiz for festival attendees and act as judges during cosplay and contests. Other teen volunteer tasks include publicizing the event at local schools, either by handing out flyers or getting information to the school newspapers. Although terrifying to contemplate, daunting to plan, and exhausting to oversee, anime festivals can be a big draw for the library and fun for staff and patrons. See "The Anime-ted Library" by Kristin Fletcher-Spear and Kat Kan (a *VOYA* online only article originally available in April 2005) at the end of this chapter.

Costume or Cosplay Parties

Costume parties are a popular programming option, especially in October. Costume parties can be held as a separate program or as a part of a bigger event. Themes add extra fun for these parties. A library could host an all manga costume party, a superheroes-themed party, or a fantasy themed party. Graphic novels and manga lend themselves to costume parties, because so many of the characters wear recognizable or bizarre outfits. The authors never fail to be astounded at the lengths that teens will go to recreate the costume of their favorite character, even if it means enduring

Photo credit: Karen Reed

"**Kristin cosplaying as Sana's mom from** *Kodocha: Sana's Stage*. **She has also cosplayed as Cardcaptor Sakura, Witch Hunter Robin, and** *Gokusen's* **Kumiko.**

a restricting kimono for hours (Sakura, from *Cardcaptor Sakura*), wearing a straight jacket for a prolonged period (*Johnny the Homicidal Maniac*), or painting themselves head to toe in red body paint (*Hell-Girl*).

The highlight of many comic and anime conventions is the masquerade or costume contest. Even those who don't dress up look forward to seeing the costumes and skits presented by others. If you are planning an all day festival or "mini-con" at your library, make sure to include a cosplay contest as an element. When planning a cosplay contest or costume party, make sure that you set some rules for those participating. The authors' favorite rule is "No costume is no costume" which discourages those who think scanty equals cool. This rule also extends to liquid latex and body paint-derived costumes. You might also want to include a rule that all costumes must be original work and that no "store bought" costumes are allowed. Also, find out if there is a local convention group or costuming association who may be willing to come in and teach a workshop about creating budget-minded costumes, or who would be willing to act as judges for a cosplay workshop. This partnership can benefit both the library and the other groups, as they can market their convention or organization events to the teens.

Comic Book Trivia

This fun trivia program is easy to do. Writing trivia questions can be time intensive, but there are plenty of Web sites and books like *Anime Trivia Quizbook* by Ryan Omega to help you out. A "quick and dirty" game board can be made out of sheet protectors and foam core board, or the technologically savvy can download a PowerPoint template for a *Jeopardy*® style board. Played like the television show *Jeopardy*®, librarians can select random teens to be contestants or arrange for groups to play as a team. If only a handful of teens get to play, make sure the audience gets a chance at questions for prizes to keep their attention on the game. A few suggested categories are Secret Identities; Comics into Movies and TV; Team-ups; Villains; Who am I?; and Lingo/Jargon. More anime trivia questions are available at the end of this chapter.

Sample Trivia Questions

More trivia questions can be found after this chapter.

1. Five characters—four male, one female—have worn Robin's uniform. Can you name them all? (Answer: Dick Grayson, Jason Todd, Tim Drake, Stephanie Brown and Damian Wayne)
2. In *Princess Mononoke*, the spirits of the forests are called what? (Answer: Kodoma)
3. In *Watchmen* by Alan Moore, what main character is named after a psychological test? (Answer: Rorschach)
4. Superman entrusted a piece of kryptonite to a fellow superhero in case he ever got out of control. Who did he give it to? (Answer: Batman)
5. What is the name of the metal that covers Wolverine's skeleton? (Answer: adamantium)
6. What must Manji in *The Blade of the Immortal* do in order to regain his mortality? (Answer: kill 1,000 evil men)

Author or Artist Visits

Author visits are another way to use your graphic novel collection to program for teens. It never fails to amaze us where graphic novel creators can be found. That quiet woman who sits next to you on the bus could be a comic artist. The bald guy who brings his kids to storytime may be a possible comics writer. Your local comic book store is a great resource for locating creators who live in your area. As part of Teen Read Week 2002, science fiction, fantasy, and comic book author Michael Stackpole came to GPL to speak and sign materials. His appearance drew both teens and adults who were eager to discuss his work on the *Star Wars* comics, his original fantasy work, and other topics. (See "A Week of Graphic Pandemonium" at the end of this chapter.)

Also as part of Teen Read Week 2002, Phoenix-area creators Phil Mateer and Mike Banks came to the library and taught workshops on writing and drawing for comics. In the scripting workshop, Phil Mateer went over the basics of scripting for comics and explained how comics writing is both similar and different from writing prose. For aspiring artists, *Blind Mice* creator Mike Banks held a drawing workshop, reviewed portfolios, gave teens an idea of what comic book publishers look for in an artist, and explained how to present their work effectively.

By bringing a "real live" creator to your library, you can show teens who are also interested in creating that working in the comics industry is an attainable goal. Many comic book creators are happy to come and speak about their experiences with creating comics, working in the comics industry, and other unique aspects of graphic novel creation.

Create Your Own Comic Book

This program can be managed in many different ways. One of the easiest versions of this program is simply providing supplies and the space for teens to work on their own comic art projects. Make sure to offer to bind their comic at the end of the process or put their work on display in the teen area. GPL did this version one summer. Over the course of ten weeks, teens worked on their projects, helped one another with various opinions and aid, and met teens who had similar interests. At the end of the summer, their art was displayed in a library art show and then in the Quaranteen (teen) area of the library.

This program can be more instructive if partnered with a guest presenter on the topic. Local comic bookstores and art schools are great partnering resources for presenters. Working with guest presenters can be a one-time event or a reoccurring program depending upon your partnership and budget.

A fabulous book on this topic is *Manga High* by Michael Bitz. The book details a four- year study of an after-school comic book club in New York City, in which high school students created their own comics. Bitz includes guidelines on how to replicate the project.

Graphic Novel Discussions

Holding graphic novel discussion groups can incorporate graphic novels into programming that may already exist at your library. If you already host a teen book discussion group, try adding a graphic novel to your slate of books. Manga, with a lower price point and a wide variety of genres to choose from, is an especially good choice for pre-existing discussion groups. Also, try looking at independent American publishers such as Oni, Papercutz, and Fantagraphics for non-superhero teen appropriate books. "Susan's Book Club" at GPL held its inaugural meeting with a discussion of *Othello* by Satomi

Ikezawa. Other book clubs, aimed at tweens and teens, have incorporated graphic novels into their recurring discussions. Sample discussion questions for graphic novel book discussions can be found at the end of this chapter.

Another option is to host a discussion group that is devoted entirely to graphic novels and manga. This can be a difficult program from a financial standpoint, because graphic novels and manga are more expensive than the mass market paperbacks used for most teen discussion groups. Many libraries around the country have used grant money to fund graphic novel discussion groups, or worked with their state libraries to develop a consolidated program such as the California Center for the Book's "Comix.@$#!" program. A more economical option is held at GPL's Velma Teague Branch, where teens are invited to read independently and then come together at the library to share their opinions about what they have read. This style leads teens to booktalking titles, so make sure to teach them how not to reveal spoilers. It also leads to less consolidated discussion, as nobody is reading the same thing, but it takes a financial burden off the library.

Mini-Con

Comics fandom centers around cons or conventions, where fans can meet, interact with creators, and celebrate their hobby. At such shows, vendors sell comics, manga, anime, and related merchandise. Fantasy and science fiction books and related merchandise are also offered for sale. Gaming is also represented in all its forms—video games, roleplaying, tabletop, and more. Anime is shown along with science fiction, fantasy, and superhero films. If you are looking for a large scale program, you could always host a mini-con at your library. Invite local comic book and

"Members of the 2002-2003 Teen Library Council at Glendale Public Library at the Teen Read Week Mini-Con. As you can see, we attracted all sorts of visitors."

collectable stores to set up booths at your library. Contact local creators and invite them to speak. Set up film screenings and gaming events. But beware: Mini-cons are not for the faint of heart, as they are time-consuming to plan and can attract large crowds. However, mini-cons are great opportunities to showcase cooperation between the library and the community. They also do a great deal to raise the profile of the library among comics and manga fans.

As part of Teen Read Week 2002, the GPL invited local used bookstores and comic specialty stores to set up tables on the front lawn of the library and sell their merchandise. Michael Stackpole came and gave a speech, signed books, and generally added to the fun of the event. In conjunction with a local comic specialty store, teens competed in a *Yu-Gi-Oh* tournament. To add "color," members of the local 501st Stormtrooper Division, the Dune Sea Garrison, were present in costume. Many people who had never been to the library before discovered us on that day. More than one person came up to the librarians or teen volunteers assisting at the event and asked about other library programs. (See "A Week of Graphic Pandemonium" at the end of this chapter.)

Passive Programming

Passive programming is not passive for the librarian. Just like active programs, passive programs can be both time consuming and labor intensive to produce. However activities such as surveys, trivia, and other contests, can be done without the active assistance of a librarian.

Character Design Contest

This contest requires teens to design, draw, and name their own comic book characters. If you expect many entries, create separate categories for age ranges or genres of the characters. For more teen participation, have the teen library council members judge the contest. If possible, reward the participants with prizes for best entries and display the artwork in the teen area. To turn this passive program into an active program, make contact with your local comic book store or local art school and ask them to lead a caricature drawing or "creating a comic book" program.

Photo credit: Kristin Fletcher-Spear

Displays

Displays are a fantastic way to encourage interest in your collection. Using discarded graphic novels, one can easily create eye-catching posters for displays of any topic. You can create a display entirely of graphic novels or just include graphic format material in your regular displays.

Name that Character Contest

This is a stand-alone contest held in the library. Cut out images of various characters and put them on a poster board with an entry form beside it for participants to fill in their answers. Put the entries with the most correct number of answers into a drawing for a prize. After the contest is over, make sure to post the answers up in the teen area. A "romantic" variation on this contest is Match the Super-Couple, where pictures of famous comic couples—such as Sailor Moon and Tuxedo Mask, Cyclops and Jean Grey, or Oracle and Nightwing—are posted, and teens must decide who belongs with whom. This is a fun contest to do around Valentine's Day. Another good visual display is "Who is that Masked Man or Woman?" Pictures of actors are posted, and participants must match the actor with the superhero they played on screen.

Superhero Death Match

Who would win in a battle between Superman and Batman? How about between Goku and Yugi? These are the types of questions that a Superhero Death Match asks its participants. This survey has no wrong answers, since the responses are purely subjective, but if the answers are entered in a raffle, it's another opportunity to get teens involved in the library. Make sure to compile and post the results for teens to see what everyone thought. This is a fun program to play during Free Comic Book Day. Everyone who completes the form receives a comic book and gets entered into a raffle prize drawing. See our Superhero Death Match Poll at the end of this chapter.

Trivia Contest/Web Hunt

Passive trivia contests or Web hunts make for a fun passive program. Simply make a sheet of trivia questions and hand it out to teen patrons or leave it in your teen area. In conjunction with Free Comic Book Day, GPL offered a passive Trivia Contest. Teens were encouraged to go online to find the answers to the questions. The grand prize was a gift certificate to a local comic specialty store. Other ideas on this theme include a Superhero Aliases tests (match the alias with the superhero), a variation on the couples display mentioned above, or a Web hunt that specifically targets Free Comic Book Day.

Once you start thinking about graphic novels with a programming eye, you'll find it easier to come up with a variety of programming ideas. We hope that this section will be a starting point for you to explore the fun of programming around graphic novels.

Anime Trivia Questions

Game 1   Cartoon Network   100
In the ninja series, *Naruto*, what is Naruto's ultimate goal?
To become the Hokage of the Leaf Village

Game 1   Cartoon Network   200
This hair-brained TV show has a bald villain who wants everyone shaved.
Bobobo-bo Bo-Bobo

Game 1   Cartoon Network   300
In the *Dragon Ball Z* world, how many times can you be revived by the earth dragon balls?
One time

Game 1   Cartoon Network   400
What anime was produced as a joint venture between Production I.G. and Cartoon Network?
IGPX

Game 1   Cartoon Network   500
What anime was first featured on Adult Swim?
Cowboy Bebop

Game 1   Miyazaki   100
Hayao Miyazaki is a cofounder of what famous studio?
Studio Ghibli

Game 1   Miyazaki   200
In *Princess Mononoke* what are the friendly forest spirits called?
Kodamas

Game 1   Miyazaki   300
In Japan, the name of the movie was *Laputa*, but in the overseas release was called this.
Castle in the Sky

Game 1   Miyazaki   400
Name the only Miyazaki movie in which the story originally came from a Miyazaki manga.
Nausicaa of the Valley of the Wind

Game 1   Miyazaki   500
The Ghibli film, *Tales from Earthsea*, was directed by a family member of Miyazaki. What is the relation?
His son, Goro Miyazaki

Game 1   Before it was Anime   100
In the US, it was called *Robotech*, but what was it known in Japan?
Take any of these 3 answers: *Super Dimensional Fortress Macross*; *Super Dimension Calvary Southern Cross*; *Genesis Climber Mospeada*

Game 1   Before it was Anime   200
This anime was a novel by Diana Wynne Jones.
Howl's Moving Castle

Game 1   Before it was Anime   300
What major manga storyline was not included in the *Rurouni Kenshin* TV series?
Revenge Arc or Jinch arc

Game 1   Before it was Anime   400
Where did the story idea for the anime series, *12 Kingdom*, come from?
A trilogy novel series

Game 1   Before it was Anime   500
Nadia: The Secret of Blue Water was loosely inspired by what classic novel?
20,000 Leagues under the Sea by Jules Verne

Game 1   Shojo   100
Who is Momo's best friend and bitter enemy in

Peach Girl?
Sae

Game 1   Shojo   200
This Boys' Love anime focuses on the
relationship between a writer and a singer.
Gravitation

Game 1   Shojo   300
What is the name of the book that transports
Miaka in *Fushigi Yugi?*
Universe of the Four Gods

Game 1   Shojo   400
This anime is about a girl who fights back
against the elite bullies at her high school.
Boys over Flowers

Game 1   Shojo   500
In this anime, Sora leaves Japan to join a circus.
Kaleido Star

Game 1   Final Question
Animal Pals
In *Ranma ½*, who turns into a duck?
Mousse

Game 2   Shonen   100
This action movie portrayed Yomiko Readman
as a secret agent who can control paper.
R.O.D.

Game 2   Shonen   200
Which two limbs are missing from Edward
Elric's body?
Right arm, left leg

Game 2   Shonen   300
In *Case Closed*, Jimmy picks his "Conan" name
in honor of what famous author?
Sir Arthur Conan Doyle

Game 2   Shonen   400
This series was touted as what Harry Potter
would be if a Japanese created it—complete with
fan service.
Negima

Game 2   Shonen   500
In what anime does the main character join the
Shinsengumi to exact revenge for his parents'
murders?
Peacemaker

Game 2   Who am I?   100
My name means strawberry in Japanese. My
claim to fame is that I can see dead people.
Ichigo from *Bleach*

Game 2   Who am I   200
I'm a teacher with a yakuza past.
Kumiko from *Gokusen*

Game 2   Who am I   300
I'm the cat in the family, so I always try to fight
with the rat in the family.
Kyo from *Fruits Basket*

Game 2   Who am I   400
I am a vampire who calls a human my master.
Alucard from *Hellsing*

Game 2   Who am I   500
I am possessed by a ghost who seeks "The Divine
Move"
Hikaru from *Hikaru no Go*

Game 2   Rumiko Takahashi   100
What is Takahashi's longest running manga to
date?
InuYasha

Game 2   Rumiko Takahashi   200
InuYasha and Kagome are collecting pieces of

what jewel?
Shikon no Tama or Jewel of the four souls

Game 2   Rumiko Takahashi   300
In what cursed spring did Ranma fall into?
"Spring of the Drowned Girl"

Game 2   Rumiko Takahashi   400
In *Maison Ikkoku*, what job does Godai finally
get that allows himself the security of marrying
the landlady?
Preschool teacher

Game 2   Rumiko Takahashi   500
Takahashi studied manga art under what famous
comic artist who is best known for his manga
Lone Wolf and Cub?
Kazuo Koike

Game 2   Sidekicks   100
Sakura's guardian of the Clow Cards.
Kero-chan or Kerberos from *Cardcaptor Sakura*

Game 2   Sidekicks   200
Sister Rosette's partner.
Chronos from *Chronos Crusade*

Game 2   Sidekicks   300
The blue-nosed reindeer doctor.
Tony Tony Chopper from *One Piece*

Game 2   Sidekicks   400
The back of his shirt means "evil" and was
originally hired to kill the *Battosai*.
Sanosuke Sagara from *Rurouni Kenshin*

Game 2   Sidekicks   500
His name is Yuya, but Gal-pal Ran always calls
him this.
#2 from *Super Gals*

Game 2   Final Question
Gankutsuou is a futuristic revision of what
famous French novel?
The Count of Monte Cristo by Alexander Dumas

Game 3   Sports   100
Tennis show on Cartoon Network.
The Prince of Tennis

Game 3   Sports   200
Manga about a girl who will do anything to play
volleyball.
Crimson Hero

Game 3   Sports   300
An Anime about girls who want to start a
competitive baseball team at their school.
Princess Nine

Game 3   Sports   400
Car Racing anime series with a techno music
soundtrack.
Initial D

Game 3   Sports   500
Oh Great!'s sports anime that combines an
extreme sport and flying.
Air Gear

Game 3   CLAMP   100
What world are Umi, Fuu, and Hikaru
transported to in *Magic Knight Rayearth*?
Cephiro

Game 3   CLAMP   200
What is the name of Misaki's doll in *Angelic Layer*?
Hikaru

Game 3   CLAMP   300
This series is a crossover that uses old CLAMP
characters in new stories.
Tsubasa RESERVoir CHRoNiCLE

Game 3   CLAMP   400
This four volume manga has an angel living with a human.
Wish

Game 3   CLAMP   500
This series was CLAMP's professional debut work.
RG Veda

Game 3   People   100
I am the creator of TV shows *Serial Experiment Lain, Haibane Renmei,* and *Technolyze.*
Yoshitoshi Abe

Game 3   People   200
I am the manga-ka of anime like *Ceres, A Celestial Legend* and *Fushigi Yugi.*
Yu Watase

Game 3   People   300
I am the director of anime shows like *Excel Saga* and *Nerima Daikon Brothers.* I play the character Nabeshin in both series.
Shinichi Watanabe

Game 3   People   400
I am the wealthiest manga-ka in Japan. My latest manga will be around 50 volumes once they find all the shikon shards.
Rumiko Takahashi

Game 3   People   500
I am a famous Japanese voice actress doing character voices like Ranma Saotome, Faye Valentine, and Rei Ayanami. I also have sung anime theme songs like *Slayers* and *Love Hina,* and I had an advice column in *NewType Magazine.*
Megumi Hayashibara

Game 3   Live Action   100
This fighting video game has been a manga, an anime, and a live action movie.
Street Fighter

Game 3   Live Action   200
This Korean action film has a prequel manwha (comic). It was also on MTV in a dubbed version with voice acting done by Snoop Dogg and Outkast.
Volcano High

Game 3   Live action   300
This classic car racing anime was remade into a live action film in 2008.
Speed Racer

Game 3   Live Action   400
This Japanese film features Shinigami and Light, the human who has the Shinigami's notebook.
Deathnote

Game 3   Live Action   500
This film features two characters with the same name--in fact it's the name of the movie too!
Nana

Game 3   Final Question: Classics
What was the first anime TV series shown on US television?
Astro Boy

Teen Comic Trivia Challenge!

Answer these questions. Feel free to use the Web to find your answers.
Return it to the Youth Desk to enter the drawing for the $25 gift certificate to Atomic Comics!

Who played Deadpool in the *Wolverine* movie?

A . Ryan Reynolds

B. Liev Schreiber

C. William Shatner

D. Taylor Lautner

Who created the Marvel Universe?

A. Joe Shuster and Terry Siegel

B. Erik Larsen, Jim Lee, Rob Liefeld, Todd McFarlane, Whilce Portacio, Marc Silvestri, and Jim Valentino.

C. Stan Lee and Jack Kirby

D. Will Eisner

An Otaku is:

A. A type of Japanese animation

B. A person obsessed with anime

C. A Pokemon

D. Yummy with wasabi

Wonder Woman was born on what island?

A. Greece

B. Amazonia

C. Hawaii

D. Greenland – it's an is-land, you know.

Who is the man without fear?

A. Superman

B. Batman

C. Daredevil

D. Flash

Madoka from *Kimagure Orange Road*, Miki Karou from *Revolutionary Girl Utena*, and Kei from *Marmalade Boy* all play what instrument?

A. Violin

B. Kazoo

C. Piano

D. Cello

Who is Oliver Queen?

A. Green Lantern

B. Green Arrow

C. Queen of Swords

D. Dr. Octopuss

How are Son Goku and Son Gohan in *Dragonball Z* related?

A. Brothers

B. Cousins

C. Father and son

D. Cow and Dairymaid

Which of these Graphic Novels are non-fiction (true) books?

A. *Persepolis* by Marjane Satrapi

B. *Maus* by Art Speigelman

C. *The Photographer* by Emmanuel Guibert

D. All of the Above

Who is the director of the *Iron Man* movies?

A. Jon Favreau

B. Christopher Nolan

C. Brian Singer

D. Nobody, it's a documentary. They just filmed what actually happened!

How many Gundams (in *Gundam Wing*) were there?

A. 3

B. 2

C. 5

D. 4

Jean Grey turned into:
  A. Marvel Girl
  B. Dark Phoenix
  C. Retro Girl
  D. Dust (when she died)

Which of these characters is not a member of the Astonishing X-men?
  A. Emma Frost
  B. Wolverine
  C. Shadow Cat
  D. Sabertooth

The word anime is borrowed from what language?
  A. French
  B. English
  C. Italian
  D. It's Japanese, doofus!

Which of these Graphic Novels features almost every character in the DC universe?
  A. Howard the Duck
  B. JLA Earth 2
  C. Infinite Crisis
  D. Civil War

Dick Grayson, the original Robin, grew up to become:
  A. Darkwing Duck
  B. Nightwing
  C. The Oracle
  D. He died, so he didn't grow up at all.

What are "mecha" in manga and anime?
  A. Androids
  B. Mechanics
  C. Giant Robots
  D. There's no such thing as mecha; you librarians made it up.

Who invented the graphic novel?

  A. Todd McFarlene
  B. Will Eisner
  C. Joss Weadon
  D. Stan Lee

Umi is a character in what manga series?
  A. Neon Genesis Evanglion
  B. Marmalade Boy
  C. Magic Knight Rayearth
  D. Every manga has a character named Umi.

Which one of these publishers prints manga?
  A. Viz
  B. Udon
  C. Tokyo Pop
  D. Duh, all of them.

A Freebie: What's your favorite comic, manga, or anime? _____

Your Name: _____
Your Age: _____
Your Phone #: _____

Superhero Death Match Poll

Circle who you think who would win these matches
and be entered into a raffle for a comic-related prize!

Who would win in a match?

Superman or Batman?
Pokemon or Digimon?
Wonder Woman or Rogue?
Sailor Moon or Card Captor Sakura?
Spider-Man or Daredevil?
Gundam or Macross?
The Incredible Hulk or The Thing?
Green Lantern or Green Arrow?
Yusuke (from YuYu Hakusho) or Goku (from DBZ)?
The Tick or Space Ghost?
X-Men or Justice League of America?
Robin or Supergirl?
Poison Ivy or Harley Quinn?
Tuxedo Mask or Tamahome (from Fushigi Yugi)?
The Joker or Two-Face?
Wolverine or Spider-Man?
Aquaman or Storm?
Catwoman or Black Cat?
Nick Fury or Batman?
The Flash or Cyclops?

Return completed forms to the Youth Reference Desk.

Name:_____

Age:_____

Phone:_____
Drawing will be held on Saturday, May 4th.
Winners will be notified by phone.
Ages 12-18.

Discussion Questions for Graphic Novels

These questions are adapted from book discussion groups at the Glendale Public Library. They are a good starting point for a general discussion of a graphic novel. However, just like prose books, each graphic novel is unique, and these questions should be "tweaked" accordingly.

1. Who was the protagonist of the book? Was it the main character, or someone different?

2. Who was the antagonist? Why were they opposed to the protagonist?

3. What story is the author trying to tell? Why do you think she wanted to tell this story?

4. Why do you think the author chose to tell this story in a graphic format? Do you think this was a good choice? Would the story work as well, or better, in a prose format?

5. What was the setting of the book? Did the artwork convey the setting well?

6. Discuss the character designs; are they realistic? Cartoony? Do you think they worked with or against the story being told?

7. What do you think of the art featured in the book? Do you think it meshed well with the story?

8. What about the colors used? Did the color enhance or detract from the story?

9. Who do you think the audience is for this book? Do you think that is the audience the author/artist was reaching for?

10. What other thoughts do you have about the work? Would you recommend it to a friend? A classmate? Your parents?

THE anime-ted LIBRARY

KRISTIN FLETCHER-SPEAR ◄
AND KAT KAN

Two and a half years after our first article, *Showing Anime in the Library* (**VOYA** April 2002), it's high time for an update! Librarians have used our tips to create some great programs for the teens at their libraries. We want to highlight those programs, give a suggested list of newer anime titles, and provide an updated contact list of anime studios to make anime programming one of the easiest events you can stage.

LIBRARY ANIME/MANGA PROGRAMS

After our e-mail request soliciting examples of how librarians are using anime with teens, we received the following great examples. We also include our own.

ANIME SCREENING PROGRAMS

Kristin's Anime Afternoons at the Foothills Branch Library in Glendale, Arizona, use the three anime companies' screening programs to provide materials for her teens in addition to Kristin's own collection. During the school year, Anime Afternoons meets once a month, culminating in an all-day festival in May. During the summer, the group meets once a week. So lots of anime is needed!

Each company's screening program is a little different, but joining them is free. Bandai Entertainment's **Anime Addict** program provides a free DVD each month during the school year to clubs who then fill out a survey on the Anime Addict Web site to let Bandai know what teens think. Occasionally Kristin receives a more mature title than she would consider showing her teens, but Bandai understands that not every DVD is appropriate for every club.

Funimation's **Operation Anime** also provides one free DVD a month from their selected titles. Member librarians simply request the title that they would like to screen from the Operation Anime Web site. Funimation sends the DVD and surveys about a week before the performance date. Although their e-mail communications sometimes arrive late, they really do receive the requests! The one extra step necessary with Operation Anime is to find the age ratings on a different Web site. For some reason, Operation Anime does not include age levels in their information about an offered title.

ADV's **Anime ADVocate** program just began in December 2004. It appears that their plan is to send out a compilation DVD of first episodes each month and request that the librarian fill out a survey on the Anime ADVocate's Web site. They also have a monthly newsletter with anime information as well as an insider's interview with American voice actors.

How have other libraries presented Bandai's programs? These libraries use Bandai's Anime Addicts:

- Morris Area Public Library in Morris, Illinois, uses the program run by anime distributor Bandai. The anime club meets on the third Saturday of the month to view anime, have refreshments, rate the anime for Bandai, and socialize. Young Adult Coordinator Lois Feldman also works to get screening permissions from other anime distributors to meet her teens' requests. Twelve to fourteen "hardcore" members gather every month.

- Venus Rowland at the Finney County Public Library in Garden City, Kansas, signed up her library's Anime Club. The club has twenty-five members, and eighteen to twenty usually meet every month; ages range from eight to thirty-six years old, but most members are teens.

- Cuyahoga County Public Library's Club Otaku at the Brooklyn Branch in Ohio meets to watch anime, play anime-related video games, do drawing sessions, and help YA librarian Mike Pawuk review manga for the library. Meetings draw from ten to twenty-five members.

- The Cesar Chavez Central Branch of the Stockton-San Joaquin County Public Library in California has created an Anime Addicts Club. Librarian Eva Volin previews each anime sent by Bandai to be able to discuss and rate them with the teens who attend.

- At the Aurora Central Branch of the Aurora Public Library in Colorado, librarian Megan S. F. Ellis started an Anime Club in the summer of 2004, and reports that her monthly audiences number up to twenty-two, with ages ranging from ten to nineteen. The teen response has been so strong that registration is filled several months in advance. She is thinking about starting a graphic novel discussion group for the teens who can't get into the Anime Club.

OTHER SCREENING PROGRAMS

- The East Greenbush Community Library in Greene County, Ohio, hosts Quest Anime, a teen group that organized itself. The youth services librarian helps the group obtain screening permissions and attends some of their meetings. Librarian Steve Raiteri, who is a graphic novels expert and reviewer and also maintains a great Web site, sometimes provides anime for the teens to watch.

- Teen librarian Barbara Lundt and children's librarian Kelly Verheyden at Madison Public Library in Wisconsin work together to run a biweekly anime program. Attendance ranges from thirty to forty at each program, and ages range from ten to seventy years old, with most attendees in their teens and twenties. Sometimes Lundt and Verheyden will show "mature" titles such as *Jin-Roh* and *Vampire Hunter D*. All attendees under age sixteen must have a signed parental permission slip. They sometimes hold all-day events on Saturdays. To help the library, Lundt also tries to get the attendees to rate the anime they show on a scale from 1 to a high of 10.

- At the Brandywine Hundred Library in Wilmington, Delaware, Teen Librarian Melissa Rabey started showing anime in May 2004. She screens anime on Saturdays, taking teen requests for what to show. She provides snacks and brings a selection of manga and how-to-draw books to the screenings for teens to check out.

- After attending several workshops that encouraged anime clubs, Ruhama Kordatzky at Burlington Public Library in Wisconsin just started an anime club in late September 2004. Initial response from the local teens is very enthusiastic, and Kordatzky has noticed some teens who hadn't used the library before. Now they are viewing anime and discussing manga and their own drawings in their monthly meetings.

ANIME REVIEW GROUPS AND OTHER TEEN PARTICIPATION

- Jane Halsall and her colleagues at McHenry Public Library in McHenry, Illinois, started a teen Anime Review Board more than three years ago when they discovered that most anime were not rated. Halsall contacted high school art teachers to recommend students to help preview anime titles for the library. Over the years, the teens on the ARB have enjoyed watching anime with others of the same mind; Halsall describes the screening sessions as "like nothing so much as Mystery Science Theater 3000" (an old television series that showed old movies to a misfit crew making sarcastic comments about the movie). The library holds a Comic-con every year during Teen Read Week, and the ARB has a booth to screen anime.

- Reference Librarian Victoria Vogel started the Japanese Anime Advisory Board for the Dayton Metro Library system in Ohio in November 2002. There are currently ten to fifteen members on the board, ranging in age from twelve to twenty years old. All participants under the age of eighteen must have a signed parental permission form because the group reviews some anime that have the equivalent of PG-13 and R ratings. The library reimburses Vogel for the DVDs that she purchases, and the teens discuss the anime after screening to rate it for quality of animation, plot, quality of dubbing, subtitles, and fight scenes. They then use the MPAA ratings (PG, PG-13, R) to assign an overall rating. The teens also help plan additional activities, such as anime movie marathons and cosplay events (costumed play, dressing up as anime characters). Most of them do other volunteer work in the library and help plan other YA programs as well.

- Haney Mussa, Youth Services Librarian at the Albion Branch of the Toronto Public Library, believes that her AnimeShon Club is the only anime program in Canadian public libraries as of November 2004. She runs the club with the AnimeShon Teen Advisory Board (ATAB), whose first screening in May 2004 attracted seventy-six teens. The ATAB selects the anime and organizes other events such as their "supreme otaku contests," also lining up guest speakers. Mussa handles screening permissions, record keeping, and equipment, "playing devil's advocate" in the discussion sessions. The ATAB grew out of the Youth Advisory Board that already existed when Mussa started her job in February 2004; three teens from YAG started ATAB, and then five more teens joined. The group meets monthly to discuss programming and event ideas.

- The Cape Coral Anime Club at Cape Coral-Lee County Public Library in Florida started in August 2004, mostly because of the efforts of high school senior Erin Timberlake. The biweekly meetings see attendance of thirty-five to fifty-five members, who are ranked in seniority (Minions, People, and Underlings) based on their contributions to club activities. The members take care of everything during the meetings. Since they're not too far away from Orlando, the club has also engaged in fundraising activities so that they could attend the Orlando MegaCon in February 2005. Young adult librarian Keith Schuerman assists with screening permissions, snacks, and the fundraisers, which have included car washes, bake sales, and garage sales. The club members have also come up with programming ideas for the library and have helped with suggestions for collection development. Schuerman reports that one of the teens remarked "You know, it doesn't even feel like I'm in the library any more . . . this is cool!"

ANIME AND MANGA

- The Manga Mania club at Allen County Public Library in Ft. Wayne, Indiana, started at the request of a teen in June 2002; its beginnings were described in Kat Kan's article, *Really Getting Graphic* (**VOYA** October 2002). The club has continued to flourish with the guidance of Young Adults' Services Manager Mari Hardacre. Currently about twenty teens meet monthly to share their drawings, discuss manga and anime, and watch anime. When the main library moved to temporary quarters in Fall 2002, the regular monthly Anime Festivals, which Kat started in 2001, halted for a while. In 2004, Young Adult Services began using the Silent Reading Room for occasional programs and have held a couple of Anime Festivals. Manga Mania gamers branched off to form Game Knights, a group that meets monthly to play video games and Magic, a collectible card game. Manga Maniacs' artwork adorns the teen art wall in Young Adults' Services and appears in the online gallery at ACPL's teen Web site.

- Teen Services Librarian Nathalie Demers at the Wilmington Memorial Library in Massachusetts started a Teen Comics Club about two years ago. The club meets every three weeks, with attendance ranging from nine to twenty-five middle school and high school teens. This informal group invites guest speakers, watches anime, draws manga and comics, plays Yu-Gi-Oh and Magic, and gets "first dibs" on the new manga and anime titles coming into the library collection.

- Ximena Miranda, children's librarian at Allentown Public Library in Pennsylvania, started the Otaku Club in April 2003. Her first six-week program was geared to fifth and sixth graders, who ended up being more interested in playing Yu-Gi-Oh. For the next six-week session, she opened the program to twelve- to fifteen-year-olds. The members read manga, watched anime, and brainstormed ideas to produce their own manga. The most recent incarnation of the Otaku Club started in September 2004 and met every Friday afternoon for an hour. Miranda, who also has a degree in Fine Arts, guided the group of mostly boys through basic exercises in comic design and inking. A new session started in January 2005.

- Gretchen Ipock works at Sellers Library (or Upper Darby Township and Sellers Free Memorial Public Libraries in Pennsylvania) and reports that Sarah Ryan, a library employee who is an illustration student at Moore College of Art and is passionate about anime and manga, runs an after-school drop-in cartooning club once a week during the school year for sixth through twelfth graders. More than twenty teens show up every week, after first going home to change into their "artist black" for the meetings. During the summer, Ryan runs a six-week session in which teens create their own comic book, from character development through binding.

SUGGESTED ANIME

After hearing from librarians across the nation, you'll want to pick up some great anime to watch with your teens! Organized by genre, here are some titles that we and our teens have particularly enjoyed.

ACTION/ADVENTURE

Initial D (Tokyopop)
The first five episodes of this car-racing anime series is the first story line and race. This series is great for discussing Japanese teen culture and has fantastic use of computer-generated illustrations and techno music. Unfortunately Tokyopop has broken it down into two DVDs. For ages 13 and up. The manga is also available.

Jubei Chan the Ninja Girl: Secret of the Lovely Eyepatch (Bandai)
When the famous samurai Yagyu Jubei was dying, he asked his disciple to find his successor. After 300 years of searching, he finds Jiyu, an eighth grade girl who has no desire to wear the Lovely Eyepatch. This thirteen-episode series is funny and full of satire on the samurai films. The first DVD is a good stopping point, but the whole series can be viewed in two sessions as Kristin's teens did. For ages 13 and up.

Read or Die, Original Animated Video (Manga)
Yomiko Readman is a schoolteacher with a real jones for books—she drags a suitcase full of them everywhere. She is also "Agent Paper" for Section A of Library Special Operations. Someone is re-creating historical people through their DNA and using them to steal valuable old books. Yomiko, using her special powers over paper, must prevent the thefts. This miniseries is heavy on the action with a little violence. For ages 13 and up.

Read or Die the TV series (Geneon)

Michelle, Maggie, and Nina are the Paper Sisters—they can create weapons and battle with paper. Hired to protect author Nenene, they travel to Tokyo with her and learn of her obsession to find her teacher, Yomiko Readman, who disappeared years ago. This series starts out slowly but builds up suspense and picks up the action by the second disk. For ages 13 and up.

Tsukikage Ran: Carried by the Wind (Bandai)

This thirteen-episode series follows the wanderings of female samurai, Ran, and her not-so trustworthy sidekick, Meow of the Iron Cat Fist. This Japanese sword drama is easy for anime screenings because the episodes stand alone. For ages 13 and up.

COMEDY

Azumanga Daioh (ADV Films)

High school hijinks abound in Miss Yukari's homeroom class, where the teacher is ditzier than the students! This comedy shows what Japanese high school is like (athletic festivals, cultural festivals, and plenty of after-school clubs), while provoking laughter. The short episodes make it easy to show in an anime program. For ages 13 and up. The manga is also available.

Excel Saga (ADV Films)

Excel is one of the very few members of ACROSS, an organization determined to take over the world, one city at a time. This series is hilarious and pokes fun at many different anime and manga stereotypes. Although this title is rated 17 and up, Kristin thinks the rating applies to the last episode, which is very over the top. The first DVD is fine to show teens with its exaggerated violence (i.e., the main character, Excel, dies several times in the first episode and gets back up; and her partner,

Hyatt, continually dies through illnesses.) The manga is also available.

Super Gal (ADV Films)

Watch out Shibuya, here come the gals! Three friends, Ran, Miyu, and Aya, live, shop, and play in the Shibuya area of Tokyo. This hilarious look at the Kogal (for a good definition, see http://explanation-guide.info/meaning/Kogal.html) *lifestyle is a hit with Kristin's teens. ADV rates this series 15 and up. The manga is also available.*

DRAMA

Fruits Basket (Funimation)

Orphaned Tohru Honda is befriended by the Sohma family, who take the homeless girl into their household. She stumbles upon their secret— when hugged by a member of the opposite gender, the Sohmas change into animals of the Chinese zodiac. But Kyo turns into a cat, which makes him an outcast. Can Tohru help the Sohmas and Kyo deal with their curse? For ages 13 and up. The manga is also available.

Princess Nine (ADV Films)

Nine girls from an all-girls school team up to take on the boys in baseball. This series is great for a feel-good experience. The DVDs include a lot of fun extras like how to Cook Oden noodles. For ages 12 and up.

Tokyo Godfathers (Columbia Tri-Star)

On Christmas Eve in Tokyo, three homeless people find an abandoned baby girl, and they team up to solve her mystery and find her parents. Along the way, they each learn to face their future. Kat's son considers this film his favorite Christmas movie. For ages 13 and up.

HORROR

Descendents of Darkness (Central Park Media)
Afterlife supernatural detectives work to stop vampires and the like from preying on living humans. The first three episodes provide a complete story arc. This title has been requested by Kristin's teen girls because it has the pretty boys and shonen ai undertones. For ages 13 and up. The manga is also available.

Witch Hunter Robin (Bandai)
The Japanese team of a special organization, STN-J, hunts witches who abuse their supernatural powers. The most powerful member of the team is Robin, a teen girl who is able to control flames. This series is episodic in nature until around the thirteenth installment, after which the episodes continue into one another. The series is good for the gothic teens. For ages 13 and up.

MECHA

Mobile Suit Gundam Seed (Bandai)
War has been going on between the Earth Alliance and the Coordinators' (genetically enhanced humans) ZAFT forces. Then the ZAFT attack a neutral colony to capture the Alliance's new secret weapons—Gundams, gigantic fighting robots controlled by a human pilot. Teenage civilian Kira ends up being the only one capable of operating a Gundam to help the Alliance, but as a Coordinator, to do so means betraying his people. These Gundams are new but have the same mecha action as in previous series. For ages 13 and up. The manga is also available.

Robotech Remastered (ADV Films)
This classic mecha anime is back, restored to its original anime form. A giant alien spacecraft crash lands on a war-torn Earth, and the people unite to deal with the new technology. Humans then must face the alien race when it comes to reclaim its spacecraft and seems determined to destroy anything in its way. The SDF-1, as an Earth fortress, must go into space to defend the planet. For ages 13 and up.

MYSTERY

Case Closed (Funimation)
Brilliant teenage detective Shin'ichi Kudo is poisoned by men in black who want to kill him. Instead he shrinks in size to look like a first grader again. Taking refuge with his high school friend Ran and her private detective father (who don't know his real identity) and using the name Conan Edogawa, Shin'ichi helps them solve cases and searches for the men in black in hopes of finding an antidote. After the first disk, the series will not repeat anything already shown on Cartoon Network's Adult Swim, and all the names will be Westernized. For ages 13 and up. The manga is also available.

ROMANCE

His and Her Circumstances (Right Stuf International)
Yukino wants to be adored. She works hard to be perfect and to get that admiration. Now beginning her high school career, she thinks that she will be #1—until she meets Arima. From that very moment, she hates Arima and wants to beat him. He is the real thing—perfect without even trying. The first two episodes are hilarious and a great introduction to this fun series. For ages 13 and up. The manga is also available.

Kimagure Orange Road (AnimEigo)
In a three-way romance series whose main boy has paranormal powers, Kyosuke is in love with Madoka, but her best friend, Hikaru, is in love with Kyosuke! This sweet series has hints of comedy and science fiction as Kyosuke's

powers sometimes get the best of him! For ages 13 and up.

Marmalade Boy (Tokyopop)

Miki just wants a normal family, but it's pretty difficult when her parents divorce and swap partners with another couple, with all four living under the same roof! Immediately against the preposterous relationships, Miki hopes that she can find some solace in her friendships at school, but her new stepbrother, Yuu, transfers to her school. Soon she discovers that life with four parents might not be so bad, especially when she realizes that she could have feelings for the dashingly handsome Yuu. For ages 13 and up. The manga is also available.

SCIENCE FICTION/FANTASY

Inu-Yasha: Affections Touching Across Time (VIZ)

Most will have heard of the titular half-demon and his partner Kagome thanks to the Cartoon Network, but the movie is a great one-time program screening option. Essentially a stand-alone long episode, this movie has action and romance. For ages 13 and up.

Voices of a Distant Star (ADV Films)

This thirty-minute show was created by one man and is incredibly moving and beautiful. When Mikako volunteers to fight in an outer-space battle against aliens, she must leave behind her love. With cell-phone text messages as her only means of communicating with him, she goes farther into space, and as the distance between them grows larger, the time between messages increases as well. For ages 13 and up.

Geisters (Anime Crash)

On an Earth devastated by an asteroid impact that has created a dangerous new life form called Siliconians, the Geisters are an elite force designed to protect humanity. Humanity itself is sharply divided, however, and the Geisters are caught in the middle. Lots of action keeps interest, while the political machinations will spark thought. For ages 13 and up.

Wolf's Rain (Bandai)

In the future, the world has become inhospitable, and wolves have been extinct for a century. But one man, Quent, believing that the wolves still exist and are evil, hunts them. Meanwhile the wolves have learned to take human form as a disguise and seek Paradise even as they struggle to stay alive. Lots of action and some violence. For ages 13 and up. The manga is also available.

ANIME CONTACT LIST

Why should you get screening permission from the anime studios? Beyond the issues of copyright infringement, Japanese licensors require screening requests to be on file.

ADV Films, Inc.

Rod Peters
5750 Bintliff Drive, Suite 217
Houston, TX 77036-2123
Phone: (713) 341-7100
Fax: (713) 341-7199
E-mail: rpeters@advfilms.com
http://www.advfilms.com

Information needed: E-mail Rod with the title and date you would like to show. He will check to see that ADV is allowed to grant permissions and then will send a screening agreement for the librarian to sign and return. Keep a photocopy for your own records. For the Anime ADVocates program, you must register at their Web site at http://www.advfilms.com/advocates/index.asp. This new program offers monthly DVDs to libraries with anime clubs whose attendance is at least 15 teens.

AN Entertainment

Krystyn Jones

Creative and Marketing Director

13929 Lynmar Boulevard

Tampa, FL 33626

Phone: (813) 925-1116

Fax: (813) 925-1247

E-mail: krystyn@an-entertainment.com

http://www.an-entertainment.com

Information needed: When requesting titles, please remember that AN Entertainment can only give permissions for the anime titles that they distribute and not for the anime titles that they sell through their retail division, AnimeNation. E-mail Krystyn with the anime title, date of screening, and the name and location of the library.

Anime Crash

James Veronico

Vice President of Sales and Marketing

The Crash Media Group, Inc.

244 West 54th Street, 9th floor

New York, NY 10019

Phone: (212) 757-0700

Fax: (212) 765-1987

E-mail: info@crashcinema.com

http://www.animecrash.com

Information needed: Formerly an anime retail chain, Anime Crash is now the newest distribution company in anime production. Send an e-mail with the anime title, date of screening, name of the library, and the location of screening. James will respond with approval or refusal. E-mail is preferred.

AnimEigo

Anita Thomas

P. O. Box 989

Wilmington, NC 28402-0989

Phone: (910) 251-1850

Fax: (910) 763-2376

E-mail: miyu@animeigo.com

http://www.animeigo.com

Information needed: E-mail Anita with the anime title, episode number, date of the screening, and the name and location of the library. Anita then will check to assure that they are able to grant permission and get back to the librarian. E-mail is preferred.

Bandai Entertainment

Fan Support

P. O. Box 6054

Cypress, CA 90630

E-mail: fansupport@bandai-ent.com

http://www.bandai-ent.com

http://www.animeaddict.org

Information needed: E-mail Fan Support to ask permission to screen specific titles. Include the title, the date of the showing, and a declaration that the screening will be free and that no illegal taping will be allowed. The fan support department of Bandai will respond quickly to your e-mail. You must register at *http://www.animeaddict. org* for the Anime Addict program that provides regular screening opportunities for anime clubs. Registration is free, and every four to six weeks, except during the summer, they send a DVD for viewing and some flyers or other freebies. In return, your teens must fill out a survey on their Web site. Kristin usually puts the survey into a Microsoft Word document and photocopies it for the teens. She inputs the information in the actual survey because teens are unlikely to remember to go the Web site. The twenty-plus-member requirement is not required for libraries.

Central Park Media

John O'Donnell

Managing Director

250 West 57th Street, Suite 317

New York, NY 10107

Phone: (212) 977-7456, ext. 201

Fax: (212) 977-8709

E-mail: jod@teamcpm.com

http://www.centralparkmedia.com

Information needed: Send an e-mail to John with the anime title, date of screening, name of the library, and location of screening, and state that the program will be free to the public. John will e-mail back approval or refusal. To see what anime titles CPM offers, go to their Web site for their catalog.

Funimation

Sophie McNutt

6851 N.E. Loop 820, Suite 247

Fort Worth, TX 76180

Phone: (817) 788-0627

Fax: (817) 788-0628

E-mail: Sophie.mcnutt@funimation.com

http://www.funimation.com

http://www.operationanime.com

Information needed: E-mail Sophie with the anime title, date of showing, and the address where the screening will be held. Sophie will e-mail permission or decline. For Operation Anime, Funimation's monthly screenings for anime clubs, you must register at *http://www.operationanime. com*. It is free and you can request one DVD per month to show your anime club. The Web site says that clubs must have twenty or more members, but they might waive that requirement for libraries. The librarian signs in to the Web site to request one of the available titles. Sophie will send you the DVD, some flyers, and a questionnaire for the viewers to answer after they have watched the DVD. In return, the teens get to take home a coupon for 40 percent off the DVD they just watched from Funimation's online store. It's painless, and unlike Bandai's Anime Addict, you choose the titles that are shipped.

Geneon Entertainment

Stephen Tang

2265 East 220th Street

Long Beach, CA 90810

Phone: (310) 952-2606

Fax: (310) 952-2142

E-mail: stephen.tang@geneon-ent.com

http://www.geneonanimation.com

Information needed: Under new ownership, this company was formerly Pioneer Entertainment. Contact Stephen either by phone or e-mail for permissions. He needs the basic information: title and volume number, date of screening, address of the screening location, and a statement that the show will be free. Make sure that he has your e-mail and snail mail contact information because he will send out a screening agreement form to you via both. The snail-mail agreement must be signed and returned for their records. Kristin loves Geneon's titles, but Stephen is difficult to contact. Once you get in touch with him, though, the permission is easily attainable.

Manga Entertainment

Unable to contact in time for the article. For their information, contact Kristin.

Media Blasters

John Carchietta

519 8th Avenue, 15th Floor

New York, NY 10018

Phone: (212) 868-0991

E-mail: johnc@media-blasters.com

http://www.media-blasters.com

Information needed: Send an e-mail to John with the title, the date of the screening, where it will be shown, and that it is free to attend. Although the screening is free, John still needs to be asked but gives permission immediately.

Right Stuf International

Screening Permissions

P. O. Box 71309

Des Moines, IA 50325

Phone: (800) 338-6827

http://www.rightstuf.com

Information needed: According to the Web site, you should send a letter to the above address stating that admission will not be charged for the showing itself and that illegal copying of the show will not occur, and include the title of the show you want to screen. You will also need to state that you inform viewers where they can purchase the program, either from a local outlet or directly from The Right Stuf.

Synch-Point (Broccoli International USA)
Shizuki Yamashita
Director of Operations
12211 West Washington Boulevard, Suite 110
Los Angeles, CA 90066
Phone: (310) 313-1850
Fax: (310) 313-2850
E-mail: producer@synch-point.com
http://www.bro-usa.com

Information needed: Please e-mail Shizuki with title, date, organization name, location, contact information (mailing address and e-mail), expected attendance, and mention that it is a free screening. Synch-Point and Broccoli can provide promotional items and prize donations if contacted at least four weeks in advance.

Tokyopop
Grace Sun
Events Manager
5900 Wilshire Boulevard, Suite 2000
Los Angeles, CA 90036
Phone: (323) 692-6700
Fax: (323) 692-6701
E-mail: graces@toykyopop.com
www.tokyopop.com

Information needed: Please e-mail Grace with the anime title and date of the screening, and state that the showing will be free to the public. Grace will get back to you about the permissions.
Urban Vision Entertainment

5120 West Goldleaf Circle, Suite 280
Los Angeles, CA 90056
E-mail: info@urban-vision.com
www.urban-vision.com

Information needed: According to the Urban Vision Web site, you should send an e-mail with the title; the name of your organization and your affiliation with a school, library, or convention if applicable; your name and contact information; dates and location of the screening; and whether you will be charging an admission fee.

VIZ, LLC
P. O. Box 77010
San Francisco, CA 77010
Phone: (415) 546-7073
Fax: (415) 546-7086
http://www.viz.com/about/contact/viewings.php

Information needed: Go to the above Web site and fill out the .pdf file. It must be signed and mailed or faxed to VIZ. If there are no problems with the screening, the form will be signed and returned to you. Viz is in the process of changing their format, but this information is current.

Kat Kan, **VOYA***'s* Graphically Speaking *columnist, has been watching anime since she was seven years old; currently she lives and works in Panama City, Florida, where she is a freelance library consultant and selector specializing in graphic novels and manga. She is also a judge for the 2005 Will Eisner Comics Industry Awards, the first librarian in that position.*

VOYA *reviewer Kristin Fletcher-Spear watched anime as a teen without realizing it was anime. She was formally introduced to anime during her first date with her now husband. She works at the Foothills Branch Library in Glendale, Arizona where she is a teen librarian. She can be contacted at kfletcher-spear@glendaleaz.com.*

A WEEK OF
Graphic
Pandemonium

MERIDETH JENSON-BENJAMIN

WHAT: Get Graphic @ Glendale Public Library, a week-long series of comics-related events to celebrate Teen Read Week 2002

WHERE: Glendale Public Library in Glendale, Arizona

WHO: Five separate events plus a mini-con drew more than 350 teens to the library in one week—along with some parents.

WHEN: Teen Read Week, October 13–19, 2002

HOW: Planned by the Teen Library Council and two youth services librarians, Merideth Jenson-Benjamin and Kathy Pastores, with lots of brainstorming, planning, letters and phone calls, and the generous help of members of the local comics community, an entire week filled with teen events related to graphic novels and comics included an art contest, an Instant Winner program, comics scripting and illustration workshops, an anime screening, a Yu-Gi-Oh! Tournament, a mini comics convention, and a visit from science fiction author Michael Stackpole.

Because graphic novels are the most popular part of Glendale Public Library's young adult collection, the 2002 Teen Read Week theme, Get Graphic @ Your Library, made both the Teen Library Council (TLC) and the young adult

staff, myself and Kathy Pastores, excited about programming possibilities.

After countless brainstorming sessions, we decided that the library would focus on a whole week of programming about the creation and consumption of graphic novels and comic books. Both writing and art would be featured. Some program suggestions were more feasible than others. Ideas included anime screenings, an after-hours masquerade and dance, workshops on comics art and animation, a comic-themed mural on the library windows, and a novel writing contest. Having several talented artists among our teen patrons, we YA librarians decided to hold a character design contest, and also resurrect Instant Winners, a program that was popular during the summer. We designated eighty books from the teen collection as instant winners in the circulation system. When a teen checked out one of these books, she or he would instantly win a prize. A generous donation from the publisher, Tokyo Pop, allowed us to give graphic novels as prizes. To end Teen Read Week, the TLC wanted to "go out with a bang" (in the words of one council member) as the library hosted a mini-convention featuring comics stores selling merchandise, and a local science fiction author as a speaker.

It was the most ambitious program that we had ever attempted. To begin, I made a list of comics retailers in the Phoenix metro area, writing letters inviting them to take part in the mini-con. Having determined that Michael Stackpole, author of several science fiction series books, was a local resident, I began searching for his contact information. The process of trying to find both comics stores and Michael Stackpole proved challenging. Many stores listed on the Internet *(http://www.the-master-list.com)* and in the Yellow Pages were defunct or had undergone name or location changes. Michael Stackpole was even more elusive. His agent and publisher did not reply to my requests. Thanks to several members of the GNLIB-L listserv, I finally reached him and invited him to speak. With plans moving along for the mini-con, Kathy and I turned our attention to the other events of the week.

Our search for presenters was easier because several members of the local comics/science fiction community had already reached out to the library. Mike Banks, owner of Samurai Comics, had dropped by during one of the library's anime screenings to offer his services. He gave invaluable assistance in planning events and acting as a liaison with other comics creators. Mike volunteered to teach an illustration workshop and portfolio review, and he contacted artist/creator Eric Mengel to assist him. Phil Mateer heard about our events through Mike, and volunteered to teach a comic-scripting workshop. Members of the 501st Stormtroopers had also offered to appear at a library event. TLC members Matt Neff, Scott Lloyd, Levi Overstreet, Tom Arnold, and Amy Arnold promised to make events run smoothly by helping to set up and break down the mini-con.

We finally had a firm schedule of events:

• Get Graphic: Teen Read Week Character Design Contest: Teens submitted original comic book characters in three categories: manga-inspired, fantasy, and superheroes. The Teen Library Council judged the entries. The first prize was a gift certificate to a local comic book store. More than twenty teens entered the contest.

• Anime for Okatu and Typical Teens: At a showing of the anime film *Slayers* in Japanese with English subtitles, refreshments were provided, and a discussion followed the film. Ten teens attended.

• Comics Scripting Workshop: Philip Mateer, an English professor at Glendale Community College, presented a workshop on writing for comic books. Fifteen teens and parents attended.

• Comics Illustration Workshop and Portfolio Review: Mike Banks, co-owner of Samurai Comics, and Eric Mengel, creator of Blind Mice comics, presented a workshop on the basics of drawing for comics. Teens were encouraged to bring in original artwork for a portfolio review. Fifteen teens attended.

• Yu-Gi-Oh! Tournament: Moryha Banks, co-owner of Samurai comics, presented a Yu-Gi-Oh! Card Game Tournament. The library paid the $5 fee for each participant. Teens who took part in the tournament received a tournament game card pack. Twenty-four teens participated.

• Comics Pandemonium Mini-Con: Two events filled the day.

1. Comics Stores: Five comic book stores from around the Phoenix metro area set up shop on the library's front lawn to offer comics, paperback books, and other merchandise for sale. All attendees received free comic books. To add color to the festivities, members of the local 501st Stormtrooper Legion, the Dune Sea Garrison, came in full costume. Approximately two hundred people participated.

2. Author Speaker: *Star Wars*® and *Battletech*® author Michael Stackpole was the keynote

speaker of the Pandemonium Mini-Con. His one-hour address dealt with ways for young writers to get published, his writing process, and the intricacies of writing series fiction. He answered questions for 45 minutes after his speech, and stayed for a book signing. More than 80 people attended the lecture, with 23 staying for the book signing. Overall, the events were very successful. Library information officer Diane Nevil sent press releases for all events to the local media, and we received coverage in the newspapers.

Teen and Participant Comments

"Awesome! The free comic books were sweet!"—Bill, age 13.

"Michael Stackpole is as good a speaker as he is a writer."—Darth Vader (a.k.a. Thomas H.)

"Mike Stackpole is one of my favorite writers; to be able to see him in person was great." —Tom, age 15.

"This is so cool! The library should do this every weekend!"—Levi, age 17.

"This is such a wonderful idea. It teaches kids that the library is more than just boring old books."—Anne O., Adult Reference Librarian.

"It rocks being able to enter a Yu-Gi-Oh! Tournament for free. More libraries should do this."—Greg, age 13.

Merideth Jenson-Benjamin is a Youth Services Librarian at Glendale Public Library in Glendale, Arizona. Her library's young adult area, Club Fishbowl, was featured in YA Spaces of Your Dreams in **VOYA***'s June 2003 issue.*

Recommended Graphic Novels

As the mantra states, "Graphic novels are a format, not a genre." We have created several genre-based recommendation lists that serve a dual purpose: First, we want to recommend books to add to your library collections that teens would enjoy. Second, we want to provide a starting place for a novice graphic novel or manga reader. Taking these lists as a starting point, you will be exposed to a wide variety of writers, artists, and publishers. Reading through these recommended books, a librarian will get a good idea of what is out there for teens, and what might work for your community. There is no better education into this format than by picking up graphic novels and reading them.

Recommending graphic novels and manga in a static medium like a book is tricky business. Graphic novels are a capricious arm of the publishing world; books fall in and out of print, new editions come out, properties change publishers. Some of the books we included on this list as the volume goes to press could be little more than memories a few short months from now. Also, as the publication schedule for graphic novels gets a little more crowded every month, by the time this book sees the eyes of a reader, there will be dozens of new titles that the authors wish they could add to the list. Finally, there are just so many good books to choose from, it makes it hard to winnow it down to just a handful of recommendations.

In the listings, we have sorted the graphic novels alphabetical by the title and have noted if it is a series. After the brief synopsis of the title, we have marked in parentheses the age range for this particular graphic novel. A title noted with an * denotes that this graphic novel would be a good introduction of graphic novels for non-graphic novel readers.

All ages

E=elementary school aged reading on their own

M=middle school (grades 6-8)

J=junior high (grades 7-9)

S=high school (grades 10-12)

A/YA=adult marketed books with teen appeal

Now on to the lists!

Action Graphic Novels

Just like in the movies, these graphic novels focus on physical feats rather than dialogue. They want to do it—not talk about it!

Angelic Layer (series) by CLAMP. Angelic Layer is a battle game in which humans use their thoughts to control a doll's movements. When Misaki sees it, she wants to play, since it's a game where even a small girl like her can win. With the help of her new school friends, Misaki slowly works her way up the ranks of Angelic Layer. (all ages)

Black Lagoon (series) by Rei Hiroe. If you need something delivered in Southeast Asia, you go to the crew of Black Lagoon. They'll deliver anything, anywhere. This series is the action manga most like a shoot 'em up movie. (A/YA)

Bleach (series) by Tite Kubo. Ichigo can see what others cannot—ghosts. One night he finds Rukia, a Soul Reaper in his bedroom. Soul Reapers destroy "hollows" —ghosts that attack and consume souls. When Rukia is injured protecting Ichigo, she infuses her soul into Ichigo, giving him the powers to be a Soul Reaper. Stuck on Earth, she trains Ichigo to be a Soul Reaper in her stead. (J, S)

Dragon Ball Z (series) by Akira Toriyama. Goku is the greatest fighter on earth until one day he discovers the truth—he's an alien that was sent to destroy Earth! Goku must defeat his alien family and other aliens to keep peace on earth. (M, J, S)

Flame of Recca (series) by Nobuyuki Anzai. Recca is a ninja geek. He's been training all of his life to be a ninja, but one day he discovers he has always possessed a secret power—the ability to control flame. (S)

Fullmetal Alchemist (series) by Hiromu Arakawa. After an attempt to use alchemy to bring their mother back to life ends disastrously, Edward and Alphonse Elric work for the military. They fight fellow alchemists in search of the Philosopher's Stone, which will hopefully restore their bodies to normal. (J, S)

*Gunsmith Cats (series) by Kenichi Sonoda. "Rally" Vincent and "Minnie" May are heavily armed bounty hunters living in Chicago. While running a gun store, they work on their cars and explosives. Their many adventures are filled with guns, cars, bombs, and more! (S, A/YA)

Naruto (series) by Masashi Kishimoto. Naruto is a junior ninja determined to be the best of them all. Teamed up with Kakashi, his instructor, and his two classmates—the best, Sasuke, and Sakura, a girl Naruto has a crush on—they face many difficult challenges, both in their jobs and exams as ninjas. (M, J, S)

One Piece (series) by Eiichiro Oda. Monkey D. Luffy dreams of being the King of Pirates, even though he can't swim because of the gum gum devil's fruit he ate as a kid. Now an adult, he's off to the Grand Line to find his crew and search for the ultimate pirate treasure "One Piece." (J, S)

Tsubasa: RESERVoir CHRoNICLE (series) by CLAMP. A mystical encounter causes Sakura's life force and all her memories to leave her body and scatter through multiple dimensions. Syaoran, Sakura, Fai and Kurogane travel through the dimensions to retrieve Sakura's memories one by one. Each dimension gives the group a new adventure and has characters from many of the CLAMP manga titles, including Yuko (the space-time witch from *xxxHolic*), who helps the adventuring group. (M, J, S)

Drama/Realistic Fiction Graphic Novels

It seems counterintuitive to ask an artificial medium (comics) to accurately portray reality. However, some of the most powerful and moving sequential art stories are tales of everyday people. Try these to start.

American Born Chinese by Gene Luen Yang. Danny, an all-American tween, Jin Wang, a first generation American of Taiwanese decent, and the Monkey King of Asian folklore each struggle with wanting to be something they are not. Simple, slightly cartoonish artwork beautifully melds with these parallel stories to tell an absorbing tale of assimilation and acceptance. (M, J, S)

Antique Bakery (series) by Fumi Yoshinaga. This slice of life drama focuses on the lives of four workers in a bakery: Tachibana, the owner; Ono, the gay head chef; Kanda, the boxer chef wanna-be; and Chikage, the waiter. The sparse, clean black and white artwork focuses on the characters and the yummy treats. (S, A/YA)

B.P.M.: Beats per Minute by Paul Sizer. Roxie is a mediocre club DJ, but under the tutelage of club legend Robbie, she becomes a star. However, Roxie's passion for music may lead her to difficult choices. Clean, candy colored artwork illustrate this coming of age story that will echo through the hearts of music loving teens. (S, A/YA)

Distant Neighborhood (series) by Jiro Taniguchi. Middle-aged Hiroshi is given the chance to right wrongs of his past when he is sent back to his life as an eighth grader. (S, A/YA)

Emiko Superstar by Mariko Tamiki. Teenage babysitter Emiko seeks to enliven her suburban existence by joining a local "freak show." Using her employer's diary as source material, she becomes a performance art sensation. Cleanly realistic artwork shows the changes Emiko undergoes, as questions about the morality of her actions and the complexity of new relationships make Emi find her own voice. (J, S A/YA)

Hopeless Savages (series) by Jen Van Meter, Bryan Lee O'Malley, Christine Norrie, and Chynna Clugston-Major. Punk legends Dirk Hopeless and Nikki Savage met, fell in love, and had a few kids. Now retired and living in the 'burbs, the focus shifts to the Hopeless-Savage children, Rat Bastard, Arsenal Fierce, Twitch Strummer, and Skank Zero. These three collections feature some comic and caper elements, as well as a who's who of indie artists, but are, at their heart, stories of family, and how it shapes us. (J, S, A/YA)

I Kill Giants by Joe Kelly and J. M. Ken Niimura. Jittery black and white art illustrates the story of proudly antisocial fifth grader Barbara. Tasked with finding and removing giants, she ignores anyone who won't believe her. However, when a classmate named Sophia earns a place of trust in Barbara's life, she must ask herself if the giants are real. (J, S, A/YA)

Kitchen Princess (series) by Miyuki Kobayashi and Natsumi Ando. Najika, a great cook, is determined to find her prince who saved her as a child. Following her only clue to his identity, she enrolls in the prestigious Seika Academy. Can she fit in with her special cooking talent and find her mystery prince? (J, S)

La Esperanca (series) by Chigusa Kawai. In an all boys' Catholic school, Georges, the quiet, devout, and popular student, is thrust against the selfish, rebellious newcomer, Robert. Georges's goal is to make people happy, as it is the only way he can be happy. When Robert comes to school, he immediately sets his sights on Georges. (J, S)

Maison Ikkoku (series) by Rumiko Takahashi. Ronin student, Yusaku, has fallen madly in love with Kyoko, the young widow landlady of his apartment complex. He has a terrible time showing his affections and has to vie for her with the stunningly handsome tennis coach. Adding to his troubles are the strange people living in his apartment building who can't help but meddle in his affairs! (J, S)

Nana (series) by Ai Yazawa. This story focuses on two women named Nana who meet on the train to Tokyo and become roommates as they each pursue their dreams. The hip, punk character designs are a trademark Yazawa style. (S, A/YA)

Othello (series) by Satomi Ikezawa. A split-personality drama. Yaya is a sweet high school girl who secretly loves to cosplay. Yaya's friends are cruel and abusive to her. When she reads a letter that she wrote as a six-year-old, something triggers inside her. Now when she gets mad at her friends and sees her reflection, she becomes Nana, a tough and confident personality. (J, S)

*The Plain Janes by Cecil Castelluci and Jim Rugg. Survivor of a terrorist attack, Jane does not look forward to "safety" in suburbia. However, at the loser table in the lunch room, she finds four other girls named Jane. Convincing them to join her, Jane sets out to save herself and community through art.

Refresh Refresh by Danica Novgorodoff, James Ponsoldt, and Benjamin Percy. Boys on the brink of manhood struggle with adult responsibilities and the burden of absent fathers. As the war in Iraq rages on, three small town teens refresh their e-mails, hoping for news of their absent parents. Removed from politics and rhetoric, this simply drawn graphic novel illustrates the weight of war on those left behind.

Re-Gifters by Mike Carey, Marc Hempel, and Sonny Liew. Dixie, a poor girl living on the edge of Koreatown in L.A., is a potential hapkido champion. However, when she spends her tournament fees on a gift for an unresponsive crush, she must fight her way back, not only into the tournament, but into her sense of self. (J, S, A/YA)

Skim by Mariko and Jillian Tamiki. Artwork reminiscent of Japanese watercolors illustrates the tale of a confused goth girl in a private school, who is only starting to discover who she is. Excellent use of grey tones and a very spare line will pull in readers, who will stay to experience Skim's painfully honest and authentic voice. (S, A/YA)

Special A (S. A) (series) by Maki Minami. Hikari has always wanted to beat her rival, Kei, in something—anything, but she always comes in second to him. Now part of the top seven students at their private school, she will stop at nothing to defeat him. The traditional *shojo* artwork allows for interesting panel work. (J, S)

Swallow Me Whole by Nate Powell. Ruth and Perry struggle with mental illness and adolescence in this absorbing graphic novel. Sweeping, flowing artwork illustrates this unique volume that is both a coming of age story and a tale of schizophrenia and obsessive compulsive disorder.

Tenshi Ja Nai (series) by Takako Shigematsu. Haunted by her memories of being bullied, Hikaru only wants to be left alone. When she moves into the dorm at her new school, her roommate is a TV idol, Izumi, who has a dark secret. Hikaru's life becomes chaotic as classmates try to get her to give them info about Izumi. (S)

What a Wonderful World by Inio Asano. Interconnected vignettes detail the small moments of life of disconnected young adults. This manga title is particularly good for traditionally non-manga readers. (S, A/YA)

Fantasy Graphic Novels

Beautiful ladies! Dashing rogues! Magic and mayhem! Fantasy is a well-represented genre in graphic novels and manga. Here are a few of our favorites.

After School Nightmare (series) by Setona Mizushiro. Mashiro, an intersexed teen, is assigned to a new class which sends him into a dream world. There he must find a key before his classmates do, in order to graduate and, within the dream world, come to terms with his gender identity issues. (S)

Amulet (series) by Kazu Kibuishi. Following the tragic death of their father, Emily and Navin are drawn into a dangerous fantasy world in this well-paced, tightly plotted adventure. The fantasy/steam-punk/ alternate world setting lets Kibuishi create fantastic monsters and mechanical marvels that are rendered in beautiful soft tones. (All Ages)

Basara (series) by Yumi Tamura. In the distant future, Sarasa must lead her people and become the Child of Destiny, after the Red King's army kills her twin brother, Tarata. Masquerading as Tatara, Sarasa must find the strength to protect her people and take revenge upon the Red King. (S)

Bayou (series) by Jeremy Love. 1933 Mississippi is not a safe place for African-American child Lee. Seeing her (white) best friend Lily abducted by a monster is bad, but the townspeople turning on her father is worse. As Lee ventures into the swamp to save both her friend and her father, she discovers a beautifully drawn, terrifying world of fantasy. (J, S, A/YA)

Bone (series) by Jeff Smith. In this sweeping epic, the three Bone cousins, Fone, Phoney, and Smiley, stumble upon a beautiful valley menaced by an ancient evil. Each finding their way to the heart of the action, the Bones discover a world of magic, dragons and "stupid, stupid rat creatures!" The high adventure is perfectly illustrated by deceivingly simple art. (All Ages)

Cardcaptor Sakura (series) by CLAMP. One day fourth grader, Sakura, opens a book with a set of tarot-like cards. As she reads aloud a word on the first card, it activates the magic and scatters the cards. Kero, the cards' guardian, awakens and gives Sakura the duty to capture the cards before they wreck havoc in the world. Costumes play a big role in this *shojo* artwork. (All Ages)

Fables (series) by Bill Willingham, Mark Buckingham, Lan Medina, et al. By turns a romance, a mystery, a thriller, and a fantasy, this ongoing series posits that the characters of fables and fairy tales are alive and well, and living on the Lower East Side of Manhattan. Forced from their homelands by a nameless Adversary, the "Fables" attempt to blend in with the "mundys," governing and policing themselves as they live out their immortal lives. (S, A/YA)

Foiled by Jane Yolen and Mike Cavallaro. Clean, uncomplicated art provides a perfect match for this story of fencing and fantasy. Aliera Carstairs is a dedicated fencer, whose passion for the sport sets her apart. However, when a handsome classmate begins to take an interest in her, she learns not everything is as it seems.

Fruits Basket (series) by Natsuki Takaya. When the Sohma family finds Tohru living in a tent, they offer her a place to stay in exchange for housework. The family has their own secrets to bear—they are the reincarnations of the original Chinese Zodiac signs. When hugged by a member of the opposite sex, they turn into their Chinese Zodiac identity. Tohru quickly discovers their secret and must deal with the consequences of her newfound knowledge. (J, S)

Fushigi Yugi (series) by Yu Watase. When Miaka finds and begins reading a book called *The Universe of the Four Gods*, she is transported into the world of Ancient China, becoming the main character of the book. As the Priestess of Suzaku, she is requested to find the seven Celestial Warriors and call upon the god Suzaku to save their country. If she does so, she can ask for anything and the god will give it to her. (J, S)

InuYasha (series) by Rumiko Takahashi. Modern teen girl Kagome falls into an old well transporting her to the warring period. There she meets InuYasha, a half demon-half human and discovers that she is the protector of the Shikon jewel. After the gem gets shattered into hundreds of pieces and scattered throughout the land, Kagome and InuYasha must work together to get the pieces back. (J, S)

Magic Knight Rayearth (series) by CLAMP. On school trips to the Tokyo Tower, Fuu, Umi, and Hikaru are transported to the Cephiro. There Lord Zagato has kidnapped Princess Emeraude, whose prayers keep the world safe. In order to save the Princess from Zagato and Cephiro from destruction, the three girls must become the Legendary Magic Knights. Fantasy and *mecha* (giant robots) meld together seamlessly in this artwork. (M, J, S)

Mushi-shi (series) by Yuki Urushibara. Mushi are invisible dangerous creatures that haunt people, but the mushishi Ginko can combat them with his own special abilities. (S, A/YA)

Negima! Magister Negi Magi (series) by Ken Akamatsu. Ten-year-old Negi, a recent graduate from wizardry school, is working in Tokyo. Teaching and living in the dorms at an all-girls school, he has been ordered not to show his magic. All the girls adore him but one, and she knows his secret. (S)

Rapunzel's Revenge and *Calamity Jack* by Shannon Hale, Dean Hale, and Nathan Hale. In this wild west/steampunk retelling of Rapunzel and Jack and the Beanstalk, Rapunzel is a whip wielding girl of action and Jack is a native confidence man. Fantasy author Shannon Hale knows how to write a compelling narrative, and Nathan Hale's expressive artwork brings her characters to life. (All Ages)

Sandman (series) by Neil Gaiman, Dave McKean, Sam Kieth, et al.. Morpheus, the king of Dream, must make a choice that will alter fate forever in this sweeping fantasy series. Trapped for a mortal lifetime, Dream begins to set his kingdom to rights and along the way visits the past and future, worlds real and imaginary. Featuring more artists than your average local con, this series is the gold standard for modern adult comics. (S, A/YA)

Stardust: Being a Romance Within the Realms of Faerie by Neil Gaiman and Charles Vess. Ethereal, transcendent artwork is the highlight of this charming story of love and magic. Tristan Thorn, an awkward young man of uncertain birth, travels to the realms of faerie to retrieve a fallen star for his lady love. The star is in no mood to be retrieved, and Tristan is not the only one seeking her. (J, S, A/YA)

Tegami Bachi (series) by Hiroyuki Asada. Under a pitch black sky, letter bees travel across a dangerous land filled with giant metal insects to deliver packages from one city to another. Lag was one of those packages being delivered by Gauche, a letter bee who inspires Lag to become one too. (J, S)

The Wonderful Wizard of Oz by Eric Shanower, L. Frank Baum, and Skottie Young. Bouncy, colorful art sets off a faithful adaptation of the beloved fantasy classic. (All Ages)

Historical Fiction and Biographic Graphic Novels

Is it true? Sometimes it is. Sometimes it could be. Here are our picks for the best historical fiction, biographical, and reality based graphic novels and manga.

The 9/11 Report: A Graphic Adaptation by Sid Jacobson and Ernie Colón. The dense and confusing 9/11 Commission Report is streamlined into an accessible and comprehensive graphic novel, featuring straightforward artwork. (J, S, A/YA)

Barefoot Gen (series) by Keiji Nakazawa. Based loosely on the author's experiences surviving the bombing of Hiroshima. Gen is six when Hiroshima is bombed and he is left to deal with the fallout, after losing everything but his mother. (S, A/YA)

Blade of the Immortal (series) by Hiroaki Samura. Manji, an immortal assassin swordsman, must slay a thousand evil men before he can be allowed to die. In search of redemption, he assists Rin to exact revenge on the Itto-Ryu, a school of swordsmen. Breathtaking pencil artwork adds another layer to this violent samurai period piece set in feudal Japan with a fantasy twist. (S, A/YA)

Buddha (series) by Osamu Tezuka. Tezuka creates fictionalized characters and intertwines them with the biography of Siddhartha, the prince who becomes Buddha. (S, A/YA)

Cantarella (series) by You Higuri. In this historical fantasy, Higuri brings to life the power struggles between religious and political players of the Italian Renaissance. Damned at birth for his father's ambitions, Cesare Borgia is followed by demons only he can see and he struggles against succumbing to the darkness within him. (S, A/YA)

Emma (series) by Kaoru Mori. Victorian London is the backdrop of this romance between a young maid and the man above her station in life. (J, S)

Fun Home: A Family Tragicomic by Alison Bechdel. The popular creator of *Dykes to Watch Out For!* tells the story of her closeted father and her own coming out in a circular, sprawling narrative featuring Bechdel's communicative, spare art. (S, A/YA)

Japan Ai by Aimee Major Steinberger. The subtitle, *A Tall Girl's Adventures in Japan,* sums this work up nicely. This graphic novel follows Japanese culture fan Steinberger throughout the Land of the Rising Sun.

Laika by Nick Abadzis. A moving, slightly sentimental biography of the first dog in space and the lives of those who cared for her. Slightly cartoony art and muted colors give the narrative a sense of place and time. (M, J, S)

Me and the Devil Blues (series) by Akira Hiramoto. Blues legend Robert Johnson gets his life re-imagined in this supernatural tale of RJ, the 1920's farmer who wanted to play guitar so badly that he sold his soul to the devil. (S, A/YA)

Mom's Cancer by Brian Fries. A family's struggle with cancer provides the plot for this touching and uplifting graphic memoir, given life by clean and accessible artwork. (S, A/YA)

Ooku: The Inner Chambers (series) by Fumi Yoshinaga. Edo period Japan is reworked with the roles of power being held by women. A disease has decimated the male population. A woman is the Shogun and her Inner Chamber is filled with the most handsome of men. (A/YA)

The Photographer: Into War-Torn Afghanistan with Doctors Without Borders by Emmanuel Guibert, Didier Lefévre, Frédéric Lemercier, translated by Alexis Siegel. A photojournalist traveling with the relief group is profoundly changed by his experiences in the war ravaged country. The unique format, which contrasts Lefevre's photos with Guibert's artwork, brings immediacy and understanding to an area of the world that is enigmatic for many. (S, A/YA)

Pitch Black by Youme Landowne and Anthony Horton. A deeply powerful graphic novel, the black and white images of this book stay with you long after you've read it. Anthony Horton was homeless and lived in the subway tunnels of NYC. This is the story of the people he met there, how he survived, and what he created. (J, S, A/YA)

Rurouni Kenshin (series) by Nobuhiro Watsuki. Kenshin, a wandering swordsman with a reverse blade sword that cannot cut people, was once known as *Hitokiri Battosai*, an assassin during the *Bakumatsu*, the warring period of Japan. Now eleven years later, Kenshin protects people with his sword. (J, S)

Satchel Paige: Striking Out Jim Crow by James Sturm and Rich Tommaso. Sparsely colored illustrations perfectly illustrate the tale of a black sharecropper, whose life was touched by baseball legend Satchel Paige. By avoiding a strict biographical treatment, Sturm manages to place Paige in the context of his time without seeming dry or preachy. (M, J, S, A/YA)

*Smile by Raina Telgemeier. Following a freak accident which knocked out her two front teeth, Raina underwent years of embarrassing and painful dental surgeries. Using bright and open art, Telgemier details not only her tooth pain, but the pains of adolescence in this gentle and fun memoir. (M, J)

Stagger Lee by Derek McCulloch and Shepherd Hendrix. The song "Stagger Lee" has been recorded by everyone from Duke Ellington to Beck. Using sepia toned artwork, this graphic novel interweaves the facts of the murder of Billy, analysis of versions of the song, and fictionalized narratives of those associated with the case to paint a picture of turn of the century America. (A/YA)

*Vagabond (series) by Takehiko Inoue. Adapted from a fictionalized biography, the life and times of Miyamoto Musashi come to life in this long-running, award-winning manga series. The story follows Tekezo as he changes his name to Musashi, searches out the greatest swordsmen to improve his own swordsmanship, and slowly becomes the master swordsman and founder of the famous Niten Ichi sword style. Inoue's departure from his normal artwork style adds to the maturity of this series. (A/YA)

Horror Graphic Novels

Things that go bump in the night bump around manga and graphic novels quite a bit. Maybe it's because the graphic format lends itself well to horror stories. Or maybe it's because the dramatic tension of horror appeals to creators. Or maybe horror stories are just cool. Whatever the reason, these graphic chillers will keep you up at night.

Black Hole by Charles Burns. In 1970s Seattle, teen sex can lead to horrific mutations, as a sexually transmitted virus sweeps through the senior class. Detailed artwork, featuring a horrifying exactness, illustrates a quietly terrifying tale. (Mature Readers)

Buffy the Vampire Slayer: Season Eight (series) by Joss Whedon, Georges Jeanty, Jo Chen et al. Geek icon Joss Whedon continues the tale of Buffy and the slayers in this extension of the defunct television series. Picking up where TV left off, Buffy must face a new threat, one that seeks to wipe magic from the world. Comic art that mirrors the look of the series will endear these volumes to *Buffy* fans. (S, A/YA)

Dark Entries by Ian Rankin and Werther Dell'Edera. John Constantine, the one man in the universe who doesn't watch reality TV, is suckered into **investigating supernatural shenanigans on the set of a scripted reality show. Jagged black-and-white art takes full advantage of the plot's ambiguities, with the shading slowly getting darker as the plot does the same.** (S, A/YA)

Dead @ 17 (series) by Josh Howard. Once thought to be murdered, Nara Kilday inexplicably returns from the dead to fight an ancient evil. Animated, manga-esque art illustrates this tale of axe-wielding schoolgirls. Parallels to *Buffy* are inevitable, but at its heart, this is a tale of friendship and sacrifice. (S, A/YA)

Demon Ororon (series) by Hakase Mizuki. One rainy day, Chiaki brings home and heals the injured Ororon, who turns out to be the King of Hell. In gratitude, he grants her a wish and she asks him to stay with her. With their cosmic differences—he, a demon who kills; she, a half-angel pacifist—is there any way they can be together happily? The hip, lanky character designs are the focus of the artwork. (S)

Future Diary (series) by Sakae Esuno. Yukiteru is a loner who keeps detailed accounts on her cell phone diary. His imaginary friend Deux Ex Machina invites Yukiteru to play a game of survival. Twelve cell phone diary users will receive future messages from themselves and use them to defeat the other diary users to become the next Deux. (S)

The Goon (series) by Eric Powell. A redneck mob enforcer faces ghosts, ghouls, pie crazed skunk-apes, extra-dimensional aliens, and mad scientists in this funny and outrageous series. Exaggerated, cartoony artwork that befits the zany premise adds to the appeal of this series. (A/YA)

Hellsing (series) by Kouta Hirano. Hellsing is an organization created to protect British soil and citizens from vampires and ghouls. Their greatest weapon is a vampire himself, Alucard, who is loyal to the Hellsing family. The dark, chaotic artwork portrays this vampire action manga perfectly. (S)

Kieli (series) by Yukako Kabei and Shiori Teshirogi. Eighty years have passed since the bloody war that created the Undying Soldiers. Now the Church obliterates any Undying they find by destroying their hearts. Kieli is a teen girl who spends most of her time with ghosts until she meets Harvey, an Undying. (S)

Le Chevalier D'Eon (series) by Tou Ubukata and Kiriko Yumeji. In 1750's Paris, virgin women are being brutally murdered for their blood, which a cult uses to write poetry called "Psalms." D'Eon de Beaumont, secret agent of the king, who uses the possession of his dead sister's soul to become Chevalier Sphinx, is the only one who can stop this cult. (S, A/YA)

Life Sucks by Jessica Abel, Gabe Soria and Warren Pleece. Dave is a vampire, working the graveyard shift at his master's convenience store, and pining for goth girl Rosa. However, when another vampire has Rosa in his sights, Dave must find his inner blood sucker. A sardonic worldview and Technicolor art make this the perfect antidote to teen vampire romances. (S, A/YA)

Locke and Key (series) by Joe Hill and Gabriel Rodriguez. What if traveling anywhere, leaving your body, or learning any skill was as easy as turning a key? The Locke children, reclaiming their lives after the brutal murder of their father, find that their new home, the Keyhouse, can make all of this happen and more. However, they also learn that nothing is simple in this smartly illustrated series. (S, A/YA)

Parasyte (series) by Hitoshi Iwaaki. Aliens have taken over human bodies with no one the wiser, until Shinichi discovers one attempting to take him over. As he fights to control his own hand where the alien lives, other humans controlled by aliens are out to get him. (S, A/YA)

Uzumaki (series) by Junji Ito. Kirie and her boyfriend, Shuichi, live in Kurozu-cho, a small coastal town. Shuichi's father became obsessed with spiraled items and killed himself trying to become one large spiral. Since his cremation, the town crematory's smoke spins into hypnotic spirals before the ashes fall into the town's lake. Other spiral-obsessed individuals have appeared and they all seem to fixate on Kirie. A traditional Japanese horror manga with realistic artwork adds to its *Twilight Zone* feel. (S)

Vampire Knight (series) by Matsuri Hino. Cross Academy has day and night classes. Yuki and Zero are the disciplinary committee that keeps the two classes separated, to prevent the day class from learning the night class' secret—they're vampires. Both Yuki and Zero are survivors of vampire attacks, but Zero has slowly been changing into the beast that he hates. Now it's up to Yuki to protect the students from the night class and Zero from himself. With *Shojo* artwork and vampire romance, this will appeal to supernatural romance fans. (J, S)

Walking Dead (series) by Robert Kirkman. Small-town cop Rick Grimes wakes from a coma to discover the world as he knew it overrun with zombies. He sets out to not only stay alive but find his wife and son. Realistic artwork illustrates this gory but poignant story of survival at any cost. (S, A/YA)

xxxHOLIC (series) by CLAMP. Kimihiro Watanuki has always seen spirits and ghosts, but when he approaches a particular building, the spirits back away from him. In the building, he meets Yuko, a witch who can make wishes come true—for a price. When he is tricked into having his wish—not to see the spirits—come true, Kimihiro's payment is doing work for Yuko. (J, S)

Zombie-Loan (series) by Peach-Pit. Michiru can see rings around people's necks. When the rings turn black, the people die. Two of her classmates have black rings, and after she decides to save them, she finds out that they already saved themselves—but gained a huge debt in the deal.

The Zombie Survival Guide: Recorded Attacks by Max Brooks and Ibraim Roberson. Queasily realistic artwork illustrates short stories detailing zombie attacks throughout history. Zombie fans unfamiliar with Brooks' other zombie tales, *World War Z* and *The Zombie Survival Guide*, will find this an irresistible introduction to the undead virtuoso. (S, A/YA)

Zombies Calling by Faith Erin Hicks. Joss knows the rules—the Rules of Zombie movies that is. When her college campus is invaded by the undead, she and her two friends must put her knowledge to use. Facial expressions and Hicks supple artwork make for a fun, tongue in cheek read. (J, S, A/YA)

Humor Graphic Novels

We all love to laugh. Whether it's the situational comedy, the over the top slapstick, or the truthful satire, graphic novels have something to tickle your funny bone.

*Azumanga Daioh (series) by Kiyohiko Azuma. Four-panel comic strips detail the everyday lives of five high school students and their teachers that are realistic, but laugh out loud funny. (J, S)

Black Butler (series) by Yana Toboso. Sebastian is the perfect butler. He can salvage any disaster, his suave public manners melt every heart, and he can easily protect his young master from any trouble—all thanks to his demon bloodline and his contract with his master. The humor plays out in the other staff's mistakes and how Sebastian cleans up said mistakes. (S, A/YA)

Gals! (series) by Mihona Fujii. Ran is a kogal in Shibuya with dreams of being the greatest gal. With her sense of justice ingrained from her police officer family, she and her friends stand up against those making a bad name of kogals in Shibuya. This goofy, over the top situational comedy is set in the city of Shibuya, the hippest part of Tokyo. (J, S)

Otomen (series) by Aya Kanno. Asuka loves girly things, but he hides his passion and acts the part of the jock. Ryo is terrible at all things girly and likes manly men. Can Asuka ever be true to himself and his feelings for her? The *shojo* artwork and the humor play on the gender issues in this romantic comedy. (J, S)

Ouran High School Host Club (series) by Bisco Hatori. Haruhi Fujioka, a scholarship student at the elite Ouran Academy, winds up passing as a boy and working as a host in this comical series that satirizes and celebrates the clichés of shojo manga. (J, S, A/YA)

Ranma ½ (series) by Rumiko Takahashi. This wacky martial arts romantic comedy revolves around Ranma Saotome and Akane Tendo, fiancés who fight constantly. Ranma and many other characters have been cursed during their training. When doused with cold water, they turn into something different— for Ranma, he turns into a girl; for his dad, a panda bear. Over the top situations with artwork that has perfect comedic timing will have many chuckling over this series. (S, A/YA)

Sayonara, Zetsubou-Sensei (series) by Koji Kumeta. *The Power of Negative Thinking* is the subtitle to this satirical manga series. Nozomu Itoshiki is a depressed teacher loved by his students, but can he be a good teacher for them when he's just searching for the proper place to die? (S, A/YA)

Sgt. Frog (series) by Mine Yoshizaki. Sgt. Keroro is on a secret mission to invade and take over Earth. Unfortunately for the frog-like alien, his cover has been blown and he is now living with the enemy! In exchange for room and board, he does the household chores while secretly planning his world domination plots! This series satirizes many science fiction manga and anime series with hilarious results. (J, S)

Wallflower (series) by Tomoko Hayakawa. In this twist on the harem story with lots of pop culture references, four *bishonen* (beautiful boys) teens get to live in a wonderful mansion for free if they can turn the owner's niece into a lady. Unfortunately, the niece loves horror movies, is afraid of the outdoors, and gets nosebleeds when she looks at a handsome person. (S, A/YA)

*Yotsuba&! (series) by Kiyohiko Azuma. Yotsuba and her daddy have moved to a new town. As she explores all the new things around her, the reader is reintroduced to childhood through the eyes of a wacky, inquisitive, high energy, and hilarious little girl with green hair. (All Ages)

Mystery/Crime Graphic Novels

Is it the puzzles? The intrigue? The suspense? We don't know, but we're suckers for a good mystery. This list features some of the best to be found in manga and graphic novels.

100 Bullets (series) by Brian Azzarello, Eduardo Risso, Grant Goleash et al. A mysterious figure with one hundred untraceable bullets and an intriguing proposition is the catalyst for a twisting mystery that winds throughout history and politics. Shadowy, stylized art brings a noir feel to this ambitious series. (A/YA)

20th Century Boys (series) by Naoki Urasawa. As kids, they wrote a story about the destruction of the world. As adults, one of them is trying to bring about that destruction. It's up to Kenji to gather his old childhood friends to stop the one who created the Friends cult. (S, A/YA)

Banana Fish (series) by Akimi Yoshida. New York, 1985: Youth gang leader, Ash Lynx, receives an address and drug samples from a dying man whose last words are "Banana Fish." Behind this mysterious mind control drug is a violent conspiracy that involves the mafia and the Chinese Triad, but begins with the US Government and the Vietnam War. Ash finds himself against the crime world in which he was raised and with only a handful of associates, he fights against those who want to use Banana Fish for ill purposes. The dated artwork may be hard for some readers to get into. (S, A/YA)

Black Cat (series) by Kentaro Yabuki. Train Heartnet traded his life as the assassin Black Cat for a simpler life as a small time bounty hunter—but will the Chronos organization give up their best assassin so easily? (J, S)

Case Closed (series) by Gosho Aoyama. Teen sleuth, Jimmy, met his match when men caught him snooping and forced him to take a strange drug. Instead of killing him, the drug shrunk Jimmy into the body of an elementary school kid! Taking a pseudonym, Conan, and moving in with a friend, Rachel, and her detective father, Conan works on various mysteries while searching for clues to his own. (J, S)

Death Note (series) by Tsugumi Ohba and Takeshi Obata. Light Yagami discovers a Death notebook of a *Shinigami*. Write any human's name in the notebook while thinking of their image and the person will die. Light decides to use the notebook to rid the world of evildoers. As criminals begin dying all over the world, Interpol authorities investigate. Heading the investigation is L, a mysterious teen detective. (S, A/YA)

Fake (series) by Sanami Matoh. A police procedural boys' love manga. Ryo and Dee are NYPD partners. Can they deal with being partners both on the job and at night? (A/YA)

From Hell by Alan Moore and Eddie Campbell. Comics god Alan Moore unspools his scrupulously researched take on the Jack the Ripper case in this creepy, gothic tale. Stark, realistic black and white artwork brings the Whitechapel murders to life in all their disturbing, visceral detail. (A/YA)

Godchild (series) by Kaori Yuki. In late 1800's London, the young Earl Cain Hargreaves solves mysteries and murders with his two close companions, as he searches for ways to destroy his presumed dead father's secret organization Delilah. Gothic artwork enhances this Victorian manga series. (S, A/YA)

Gotham Central (series) by Ed Brubaker, Greg Rucka, Michael Lark, et al. Gotham central is the stomping ground of Batman and his rogues gallery of colorful villains. Realistic superhero style artwork illustrates the stories of the ordinary men and women who make up the Gotham police department. (J, S, A/YA)

*Monster (series) by Naoki Urasawa. Dr. Tenma, an expert surgeon, chooses to save the life of a child instead of an influential politician. Years later, Tenma discovers that the child was the murderer of hospital personnel that opposed him and is still killing. It's up to him to clear his own name and stop the monster he saved in the operating room. (S, A/YA)

Switch (series) by Naked Ape (Saki Otoh and Nakamura Tomomi). Kai and Hal are rookie narcotic investigators. Their job is to track down the drugs from the user to the drug trafficker. Jurisdictional nightmares with the police, annoying partners, and undercover work is all part of their jobs. (S, A/YA)

Queen and Country by Greg Rucka, Steve Rolston, Brian Hurtt, et al. Tara Chace's life is far removed from the world of glamorous super spies. A "minder," her life is full of danger, but also has its share of politics and paperwork. A variety of art styles bring this realistic tale of espionage to life.

Will Eisner's The Spirit by Darwyn Cooke, Sergio Aragones, Mike Ploog, et al. Will Eisner's masked man, the Spirit, makes his modern debut in this charmingly old fashioned series. Dashingly square Denny Colt patrols Central City in artwork that pays homage to Eisner's original work.

Yellow (series) by Makoto Tateno. Taki and Goh work as "snatchers" who steal drugs from the "bad guys." Partners on the job and roommates at home, but when Goh wants more from Taki, can Taki reciprocate the feelings? A gritty crime romance boy's love manga. (A/YA)

Romance Graphic Novels

Love crosses all the barriers of genres and formats. Unrequited love, destined love, girl-next-door-meets-her-Prince-Charming love. Here are some romance stories that explore love in all its forms.

Absolute Boyfriend (series) by Yu Watase. After her latest rejection, Riiko goes online and signs up for a free trial run of Night, a lover figure. The next day, a large box containing a very handsome, very naked man—Night, the living doll—arrives. (S)

*Boys Be (series) by Itabashi Masahiro and Hiroyuki Tamakoshi. First crushes, high school romance, and blundered relationships through a guy's point of view are the subjects of this series of vignettes. (S)

Dramacon (series) by Svetlana Chmakova. Romance and comics fandom collide in this delightful OEL manga. Christie is a budding manga writer, traveling to her first con. There she meets Matt, a complicated and brooding cosplayer. The two connect but are kept apart by age and distance. Meeting only once a year, at a comics convention, can Matt and Christie ever find love? (S, A/YA)

Hana Kimi (series) by Hisaya Nakajo. Mizuki Ashiya admires the high jump champion Izumi Sano so much that she becomes an exchange student at his school—his all boys school. Masquerading as a boy, and rooming with her idol, Mizuki realizes that there's more to Sano than just his high jump. (J, S)

Kare First Love (series) by Kaho Miyasaka. An encounter on the subway with a boy named Kiriya leaves brainy Karin flustered and unsure of herself. When her friend, Yuka, meets Kiriya, she decides that *she* wants him and tries to get close to him. Her plans backfire, though, since Kiriya only has eyes for Karin. (S)

Kare Kano: His and Her Circumstances (series) by Masami Tsuda. Yukino is perfect, or so everyone thinks. In reality, she's vain and wants everyone's approval. Her rival in perfection is Arima, the boy who is first in her class. When Arima discovers Yukino's true colors, he still likes her, and she begins to realize that maybe being perfect isn't what she really wants—maybe what she really wants is Arima. (J, S)

Love As a Foreign Language Volume 1 & 2 by J. Torres and Eric Kim. Teaching English in Korea seemed like a great idea, but weird people, weird food, and homesickness have Joel ready to scrap the whole thing. Then he meets Hana. Is love enough to keep Joel in Korea? Realistic manga-style artwork illustrates what happens when romance meets culture shock. (J, S, A/YA)

Love the Way You Love (series) by Jaime S. Rich and Marc Ellerby. Simple but evocative artwork brings this rock and roll romance to life. Broken hearted Tristan meets his dream girl at a show. Life would be good, if only she wasn't engaged to the record exec who wants to sign his band! (J, S, A/YA)

Oh My Goddess (series) by Kosuke Fujishima. College student Keiichi dials the wrong number and ends up on a goddess hotline which brings him Belldandy, a beautiful goddess. When he jokingly wishes she would be with him forever, his wish is granted. Unfortunately, having a female goddess brings about lots of chaotic problems into his life. (S)

Only the Ring Finger Knows by Satoru Kannagi. At Wataru's school, wearing matching rings with your lover shows that you are dating. Wataru wears a ring, but it doesn't have a match, at least he thought so, until he accidentally switches rings with the most popular guy in school, Kazuki. (J, S)

Scott Pilgrim (series) by Bryan Lee O'Malley. Twenty-something slacker Scott has a band and a high school age girlfriend. However, his world is rocked by Ramona, the girl of his dreams. To win Ramona, Scott must defeat her seven evil exes. O'Malley's bold, loose artwork illustrates this oddly sweet gaming inspired series. (J, S, A/YA)

Socrates in Love by Kyoichi Katayama. Thrust together as class representatives in middle school, Aki and Sakutaro slowly grow from a close friendship into a loving one as they mature into high school students. When Aki is diagnosed with leukemia, Sakutaro stays by her side through it all. (S)

Train_Man: Densha Otoko (series) by Hidenori Hara. The story of an uber-geek's courting of a woman, Lady Hermes, who he saves from a drunken passenger on a train. With the help and support of his anonymous, online friends on 2channel, the largest Japanese Internet forum, he works his way through phone calls, e-mails, dinners, house visits, and confessing his love to her. (J, S, A/YA)

Science Fiction Graphic Novels

Imagining the future, its technology, space travel, and more, science fiction graphic novels are a staple in the publishing world.

Akira (series) by Katsuhiro Otomo. In post-WWIII Neo-Tokyo, Tetsuo is taken for military testing of his psychic abilities, which occurred after a bizarre motorcycle accident. His gang leader, Kaneda, is concerned for Tetsuo, but once Tetsuo's powers grow out of control, the gang must stop him from connecting with Akira, a paranormal boy who caused World War III—and becoming as powerful as Akira. (S, A/YA)

Astro Boy (series) by Osamu Tezuka. Originally created in 1951, the futuristic year of 2003 finds Japan filled with robots and technology. Dr. Tenma created a robot, Tobio, to replace his deceased son. The doctor soon realizes that Tobio is not his son and throws the robot away. Rescued by Professor Ochanomizu, he is given a new name, Astro Boy, and a new goal—protect humankind from any kind of threat. Classic manga artwork tends to be harder to get into for new manga readers. (All Ages)

Atomic Robo (series) by Brian Clevinger and Scott Wegener. Created by Nikola Tesla, and possessing "automatic intelligence," Atomic Robo fights Nazis, vampires, and other n'er-do-wells. Animated-style artwork is a perfect match for the humorous tone of this pulp-inspired sci-fi adventure series. (M, J, S, A/YA)

Battle Angel Alita (series) by Yukito Kishiro. Ido finds a damaged cyborg head in a trash heap, rebuilds the cyborg, and names her Alita. She has no memory of her past, but her body remembers one thing—an amazing fighting move called the Panzer Kunst. Soon her past begins to haunt her, so she must search for answers. (S, A/YA)

Bokurano: Ours (series) by Mohiro Kitoh. Fourteen seventh graders at a summer camp stumble into a cave and are offered the opportunity to play a game. The objective of the game is to pilot a giant *mecha* robot and defeat fifteen invading aliens. Placing their hands on an object seals the contract for the game. When the first alien appears, they quickly realize it's not a game, and there's a great cost to fighting the aliens. *Mecha* and realistic artwork blend well together. (S, A/YA)

Chobits (series) by CLAMP. Hideki finds a Persocom, a humanoid computer, in the trash. After turning her on, he discovers that she has no memory of her previous owner and has strong firewalls protecting her. Hideki names her Chi and discovers that beneath her childlike behavior lies something more powerful than other persocoms. (S, A/YA)

Clover by CLAMP. Sue, a person with terrifying super powers, is freed from her seclusion to visit the Fairy Park. Kazuhiko is assigned to escort her and protect her from organizations that would try to capture and exploit her abilities. The sparse artwork is different than CLAMP's usual ornate style. (S)

DMZ (series) by Brian Wood, Riccardo Burchielli, Kristian Donaldson, et al. Manhattan has become a demilitarized zone. As the Free States and the US fight out their Civil War, the poor and disenfranchised roam the abandoned streets, surviving by any means. Novice reporter Matty Roth is the only journalist in the DMZ, a career making assignment—if he can survive. Disturbing and topical, this series is brought to life by realistic art.

Echo (series) by Terry Moore. The metallic rain that covered Julie after the explosion was more than just a meteorological quirk. Having bonded to her skin, the metal can heal, protect, and seems to be imbued with the spirit of its last wearer. Realistic black and white artwork details Julie's flight from her enemies and discovery of her abilities. (A/YA)

Gankutsuou: The Count of Monte Cristo (series) by Mahiro Maeda. This science fiction re-imagining of the classic Dumas novel is set in space in 5053. The series features some gorgeous design work, but we wish it were in color in some instances. (S, A/YA)

Girl Genius (series) by Phil and Kata Foligo. This "gaslamp fantasy" combines elements of steampunk, history, sci-fi, and romance with dramatic, flowing art. Agatha Heterodyne, thought to be nothing more than a mediocre student at Transylvania Polygnostic University, is drawn into a full-fledged war among the "sparks" —scientists with extraordinary abilities. (M, J, S, A/YA)

*Maximum Ride (series) by James Patterson and NaRae Lee. This adaptation of Patterson's massively popular novel series follows Max and her mutant family as they try to stay away from "The School." (J, S)

Planetary (series) by Warren Ellis, John Cassaday, Alan Moore, et al. The Wildstorm universe is the setting for these "archeologists of the impossible." In this beautifully drawn series, a three-person super-powered team seeks out the unexplained and inexplicable

Pluto: Urasawa X Tezuka (series) by Naoki Urasawa and Osamu Tezuka. Based on a storyline in *Astro Boy*, robot detective Gesicht investigates the destruction of robot Mont Blanc and a human murder only to discover they are connected and more murders are to come. (S, A/YA)

Sentinel (series) by Sean McKeever and UDON. Brightly colored, manga-influenced artwork depicts Juston Seyfert, a much bullied teen, finding the remains of a mutant hunting robot in his father's junkyard. By rebuilding the machine, Juston hopes for a ticket to a better life, if he can evade the government agents who want their robot back. (M, J, S)

Star Wars: Clone Wars Adventures by Haden Blackman, Ben Caldwell, et al. Fast paced and humorous, these tales from the *Star Wars* universe expand on the story of the films and animated series. Artwork that mimics the style of the TV show will endear these trade paperbacks to young readers (E, M)

Trigun & Trigun Maximum (series) by Yasuhiro Nightow. Vash the Stampede, the "Humanoid Typhoon," is wanted for the destruction of a town. Insurance agents, Meryl and Millie, are sent to investigate and hopefully stop Vash from other destructive events. All that is known about him is his blonde hair and red coat. (J, S)

We3 by Grant Morrison and Frank Quitely. Scenes of sweetness and horrific violence are juxtaposed in this thoughtful, disturbing work. Bandit, Tinker, and Pirate—a dog, a cat and a rabbit—are trying to make their way home. Bioengineered as weapons, the three deal with their basic needs and the abnormal abilities they have been given. (S, A/YA)

Y the Last Man by Brian K. Vaughan. An unknown event has simultaneously killed everything with a Y chromosome—everything except for Yorrick Brown and his pet monkey Ampersand. As society struggles to move forward, and answers are sought, the Last Man is hunted by friends and foes. Plain artwork helps to raise serious issues of gender, responsibility, and ethics. (S, A/YA)

Sports Manga

Sports and competition is a big genre of manga. The emphasis is on the training, endurance, and end result of the competition.

Air Gear (series) by Oh!Great. Itsuki, the strongest kid on the Eastside, gets badly beaten in a fight against the Skull Skaders, an Air Treck Team. His housemates buy him a pair of Air Trecks, roller blades with motors inside that allow the wearer to fly. With their help, he is able to save his school from the Skull Skaders and get his dignity back. And now with Air Trecks, he can enter a completely foreign world to him. (S, A/YA)

Crimson Hero (series) by Mitsuba Takanashi. Nobara loves volleyball so much that she chose a high school that highlighted their volleyball team and court. But when she gets there, she discovers that the girls' team has been dismantled and the boys' team is the glory of the school. It will be up to her to restore the girls' team to its former glory. (J, S)

Eyeshield 21 (series) by Riichiro Inagaki and Yusuke Murata. Shrimpy Sena has always been an "errand boy" for bullies which has trained him to be super fast. Just starting high school, he joins the American football team as the manager, but quickly becomes a running back once the other members witness his speed. (J, S)

Hikaru no Go (series) by Yumi Hotta and Takeshi Obata. This game title is all about the board game Go. Hikaru, a sixth grader, is connected to the ghost of Sai, a skilled player from hundreds of years ago. Having killed himself after a terrible match, Sai's soul is stuck on earth until he can perfect the "Divine Move." Hikaru plays the moves Sai tells him so Sai is happy, but soon Hikaru desires to become a Go player as well. (All Ages)

One Pound Gospel (series) by Rumiko Takahashi. Kosaku is a promising young boxer with one really bad habit—he overeats all the time. With the sweet nun Sister Angela's assistance, will he be able to withstand the temptation of food? (S)

Prince of Tennis (series) by Takeshi Konomi. Seventh grade tennis player, Ryoma, has moved from America to compete with older teen tennis players at the Seishun Gakuen Middle School, which has one of the best tennis clubs. Ryoma's determined to be the best in the world, but he still has a ways to go. (M, J, S)

Real (series) by Takehiko Inoue. Wheelchair basketball is told through the eyes of the players, each dealing with their own issues of being paraplegic. (S, A/YA)

Slam Dunk (series) by Takehiko Inoue. Hanamichi has girl woes—they all see this tall scary looking guy and reject him. That changes with Haruko, his newest crush, and she wants him to play basketball. The introduction changes his life. (J, S)

Whistle! (series) by Daisuke Higuchi. When Sho is cast to the third string on an amazing high school soccer team, he switches schools for a chance to play his favorite sport. When his new teammates assume that he's a star player from his old school, he completely embarrasses himself and leaves school to train to become better. Once training is finished, he comes back with a great attitude and starts to be a team player to whom everyone looks up. (E, M, J)

Superhero Graphic Novels

The category that made comics possible is a tough one to recommend books in. Do we recommend specific writers? Our favorite characters? Series that we love? By taking a kind of a shotgun "all of the above" approach, we've managed to nail down our favorite superhero GNs.

1602 by Neil Gaiman and Andy Kubert. The familiar characters of the Marvel universe receive an Elizabethan makeover in this innovative and beautifully drawn collection. (J, S, A/YA)

52 Vol. 1-4 by Geoff Johns, Grant Morrison, Greg Rucka, et al. What would the DC universe be like without Superman, Batman, or Wonder Woman? This series focuses the spotlight on the "B List" of the superhero world, with writing and art from a who's who of comics luminaries. (J, S, A/YA)

All Star Superman (series) by Grant Morrison and Frank Quitely. Freed from continuity, Morrison creates his own version of the Man of Steel and his contemporaries, accompanied by subtle artwork from Quietly. Attempting to foil a plot to cause a global water shortage, Superman is exposed to a potentially lethal amount of solar energy. Could the Kryptonian be facing death? (J, S, A/YA)

Astonishing X-Men by Joss Whedon, John Cassaday, Warren Ellis, et al. A continuation of Grant Morrison's *New X-Men,* this ongoing series featuring the mutant superteam focuses on anti-mutant sentiment in the Marvel universe and the inter-team dynamics of the X-Men. (J, S, A/YA)

Astro City (series) by Kurt Busiek, Brett Anderson, and Alex Ross. Sure, there are superheroes, but the focus of these beautifully illustrated graphic novels is on the normal people—what is it like to live in a world of superpowers? Mature and nuanced, this graphic novel series focuses more on storytelling, and less on action. (J, S, A/YA)

Batman: RIP by Grant Morrison and Tony Daniel and *Batman: Whatever Happened to the Caped Crusader?* by Neil Gaiman and Andy Kubert. Batman must fight for his sanity and visit key scenes from his past in Morrison's sweeping tale that has major repercussions for the DC Universe. The story takes a quieter turn in Gaiman's depiction of Batman's wake, with artwork that pays homage to the many artists who worked on the iconic character. (S, A/YA)

Batman: The Long Halloween by Jeph Loeb and Tim Sale. A tightly plotted and intricate murder mystery, featuring unforgettable artwork. As Jim Gordon, Harvey Dent, and the Batman collaborate to convict mob boss Carmine Falcone, their efforts are confounded by a string of murders, all committed against employees of Falcone, by a mysterious assailant known as Holiday. (J, S, A/YA)

Batman: Year One by Frank Miller and David Mazzucchelli. The early years of Batman are revisited in this collection featuring spare but realistic artwork. As young Jim Gordon joins the Gotham Police, he is faced with corruption and greed and a strange masked vigilante. (J, S, A/YA)

DC: The New Frontier Vol. 1 & 2 by Darwyn Cooke. Dynamic, retro style art accompanies this tale of silver age superheroes. As the cold war begins, public sentiment begins to turn against superheroes. Batman, Superman, and Wonder Woman each deal with the changing world in their own way, and a new generation of heroes rises up.

Invincible (series) by Robert Kirkman, Cory Walker, and Ryan Ottley. Mark Grayson is a typical teen, except that his father is Omni-man, the world's greatest superhero. When Mark begins developing powers, he joins a team of teen heroes as Invincible. However, being a superhero brings a heavy cost, as Mark soon learns. Written by fan favorite Kirkman, this series features clean, brightly colored artwork.

Invincible Iron Man (series) by Matt Fraction and Salvador Larroca. Tony Stark, Iron Man, receives a reboot in this ongoing series with detailed, heroic artwork. Tony must face his enemies and his personal demons to protect his friends and himself. Great for fans of the 2008 movie and its sequel!

Nextwave: Agents of H.A.T.E. by Warren Ellis. Five lesser known heroes are recruited to be part of H.A.T.E—Highest Anti-Terrorist Effort—a government agency committed to the destruction of BWMD's—Bizzare Weapons of Mass Destruction. However, their employers are not what they seem. The frenetic and slightly angular art style conveys all of the absurdist action well. (S, A/YA)

*Rising Stars by J. Michael Straczynski. One-hundred thirteen children, all in-utero at the time of a mysterious comet, are born with extraordinary gifts. For some, this is a blessing, for others, a burden. The lives of these "Specials" are inexorably intertwined, particularly when someone starts killing them. This three volume series takes a gripping look at superheroes, and how power is defined by character and circumstances. (S, A/YA)

Runaways (series) by Brian K. Vaughan, Adrian Alphona, Joss Whedon and Terry Moore. All teens know their parents are up to something, but what if they actually were? Seven teens discover that their parents are actually supervillains and choose to run away rather than follow in their path. Written, in turn, by a geek who's who of creators, with manga influenced art, this ongoing series features teens making difficult decisions when everything they know has overturned. (M, J, S, A/YA)

Secret Six (series) by Gail Simone, Brad Walker, Jimmy Palmiotti, et al. Spinning out of the *Villains United* collection, this unusual superhero team takes on assignments of questionable morality and lethal consequences. What could be a typical anti-hero revenge fantasy becomes a nuanced tale of character and choice in the hands of writer Simone. (S, A/YA)

The Umbrella Academy by Gerard Way and Gabriel Bá. The members of the Umbrella Academy were gathered together as children by their adopted father. As they grew, the group split up due to differing interests and personalities. It is only at the death of their father that the group reunites, to face a threat that is much closer to home than they realize. (S, A/YA)

X-23: Innocence Lost by Craig Kyle, Christopher Yost, and Billy Tan. Brought up in a harsh environment and trained to be the ultimate assassin, X-23, a female clone of Wolverine escapes from her captors, with tragic results. The beautiful and fluid artwork, with manga influences, illustrates the cruel circumstances of X-23's life. (S, A/YA)

Young Avengers (series) by Allan Heinberg, Jim Cheung, Andrea Di Vito, et al. In the wake of *Avengers Disassembled* a new team of teen superheroes faces the greatest threat of all: adults. This series featuring teen versions of popular Marvel characters could have gone horribly, horribly wrong; however, sharp writing and clean superhero style art present a compelling look at the trials of young heroes.

Non-Fiction about Graphic Novels

As we've mentioned before, graphic novel and manga fans are not only consumers of their favorite format, many of them desire to become creators. Give aspiring manga-ka and future Eisner nominees a roadmap with these how-to guides and other nonfiction titles about graphic novels.

The DC Comics Guide to Digitally Drawing Comics by Freddie E Williams II.

The DC Comics Guide to Writing Comics by Dennis O'Neil.

Drawing Words & Writing Pictures: Making Comics: Manga, Graphic Novels, and Beyond by Jessica Abel and Matt Madden.

Graphic Storytelling and Visual Narrative by Will Eisner.

How to Draw Comics the Marvel Way by Stan Lee and John Buscema.

How to Draw Manga (series) by The Society for the Study of Manga Techniques.

How to Make Webcomics by Scott Kurtz, Kris Straub, Dave Kellett and Brad Guigar.

Making Comics: Storytelling Secrets of Comics, Manga and Graphic Novels by Scott McCloud.

The Manga Cookbook by The Manga University Culinary Institute; Illustrated by Chihiro Hattori.

Manga Mania: Chibi and Furry Characters by Christopher Hart.

Manga: The Complete Guide by Jason Thompson.

The Rough Guide to Anime by Simon Richmond.

The Rough Guide to Manga by Jason S. Yadao.

Shojo Beat's Manga Artist Academy by Hiroyuki Ilzuka; Art by Amu Sumoto, Shoko Akira, Yuu Watase, and Mayu Shinjo.

Writing for Comics and Graphic Novels with Peter David by Peter David.

Glossary

Alternative Comics: Comics published by non-mainstream publishers. More often than not, they are black and white and deal with non-traditional subjects.

Animated Art: Artwork that resembles the animation style used in television shows like *Batman: The Animated Series* or *Justice League.* Characters drawn in this style look both cartoony and realistic, facial details are minimized, and people often have an unnatural angularity.

Anime: Animation from Japan. Many anime titles were adapted from manga. Anime is both singular and plural, like "goose." The term is taken from French, meaning "animated."

Bat-family: Any member of the extended group of crime fighters springing from the Batman comic. Batman, Robin, Red Robin, Nightwing, Batgirl, Oracle, Catwoman, and to a lesser extent Black Canary, Huntress, Batwoman, and the Question are all part of this group.

Bishojo: From the Japanese, meaning "beautiful young girl."

Bishonen: From the Japanese, meaning "beautiful young boy."

Boys' Love: A sub-genre of manga and anime that focuses on relationships of two males. The sub-genre is traditionally marketed to women and teen girls, not necessarily gay males. Also called BL, *Shonen-ai* and *Yaoi*, but Boys' Love or the abbreviated BL is the preferred terminology.

Comics Code, The: The guidelines for so-called "clean" comics, self-imposed by the comics industry since the 1950s. Although the Code has become much less restrictive over the years, titles that bear the Code's symbol today avoid harsh language, gore (though not violence), most sex, and truly mature themes. Since submitting comics to the Code Authority is voluntary, many publishers ignore it completely.

Comics: Generically used to refer to any story that combines sequential art and text. Comics usually refer to staple bound monthly publications.

Con: A comics convention. A large gathering of comic book creators, artists, publishers, and fans. The largest con in the U.S. is Comic-Con International in San Diego, held every summer. Other notable cons are AnimeExpo, DragonCon (Atlanta) and WonderCon (San Francisco).

Cosplay: A combination of the words "costume" and "play." Fans dress up as anime, manga, or video game characters and often re-enact scenes during the anime conventions' masquerade competitions.

Creative Team: The combination of artist and writers who work together to create a graphic novel. This can include writers, pencilers, inkers, letterers, colorists, a cover artist, designers, and editors.

Crossover: When a character or group of characters from one ongoing series makes an appearance in another character's ongoing series. Crossovers are often featured in mini- or maxi-series or in one-shots. The most celebrated crossovers are probably those that happen between characters from the DC and Marvel universe.

Doujinshi: The Japanese phrase for the very popular field of self-published or fan comic books. It can be based on characters not "owned" by the writer/artist. Like CLAMP, many *manga-ka* start out in the *doujinshi* field first. There are major comic conventions in Japan just to promote this type of comic. The manga and anime, *Comic Party*, focuses on this convention world.

Dub: Anime whose original dialogue is replaced with dialogue in another language. For a show to be seriously considered for broadcast in America, it has to be dubbed. For a good dub, try Hayao Miyazaki's *Spirited Away*.

Ecchi: This Japanese term means perverted and is a milder term than *hentai*. *Ecchi* (basically how you pronounce the letter "H" in Japanese) applies to works that are erotic in nature, but not pornography.

Eisner Awards, The: The Will Eisner Comic Industry Awards. The best known of the comics awards and arguably the most prestigious, the

Eisners award publications and creators of the previous year in more than two-dozen categories. A panel of comics industry professionals chooses the nominees, and voting is open to members of the comics industry community. The awards are given out at Comic-Con International San Diego, in July or August of each year. For a FAQ and brief history of the award try *http://www.comic-con.org/cci/cci_eisnersfaq.shtml*; *http://users.rcn.com/aardy/comics/awards/eisner.shtml* has a list of previous winners.

Fanboy/Fangirl: A person, who is completely focused on comics as a hobby and can be obsessive about small details of comics. Considered a derogatory remark, the term fanboy/fangirl indicates a person who has an immature taste in comics. *The Simpsons'* character, Comic Book Guy, is a fanboy.

Fan Service: This refers to extraneous scenes in anime or panels in manga that have mild erotic content (i.e. panty shots or shower scenes) and have nothing to do with the plot.

Fansub: An anime that has been translated and subtitled in English by fans for fans' use. This occurs before the rights of an anime have been bought by an American company. Typically, the fansubbing group requests that the fansub is destroyed once the American product is available, but there is no way of enforcing this request. Fansubs are available for downloading on the Internet using Bit Torrent and other sources. Technically, fansubs are in the gray area of copyright.

Funny animal comic: A comic that uses anthropomorphic animals, such as *Maus*, *Mouse Guard* or *Pride of Baghdad*, but not necessarily in a humorous manner.

Golden Age, The: The first wave of true comic books, arising in the late 1930s and 1940s when such legendary characters as Superman and Batman first appeared.

Gutter: The white space in-between the panels on a comics page, or the white space in the margins of a comic.

Graphic Novel: A book length narrative, of any genre, for any audience, which uses sequential art, either by itself or in combination with text elements in order to tell a story. Graphic novels can be collected editions of previously published serials, or original work. Graphic novel refers to a format, not a genre.

Harvey Awards, The: An award for comics excellence, the Harvey Awards are presented in more than twenty categories at the Museum of Comics and Cartoon Art Festival Weekend. Unlike the Eisner awards, the Harveys are both nominated by and selected by the full body of comic book professionals. For information on the award and past winners, visit the official Web site at *http://www.harveyawards.org.*

Hentai: A Japanese term meaning "pervert." This refers to pornographic manga or anime.

Independent: A comic book not published by a mainstream press like Marvel, DC, TOKYOPOP, VIZ, etc. "Indie" can also refer to a creator who does not work for a mainstream company.

Inker: Person who inks over penciled work.

J-Pop: Short for "Japanese Pop," used to refer to the genre of popular Japanese music. While not always directly related to anime, J-Pop songs may be sung by Japanese voice actors or used as the theme songs/background music of anime

series. This term is also sometimes used as a general category of Japanese popular culture.

Josei: A sub-category of manga geared towards older teen females and women.

Kodomo: A Japanese term literally meaning "child" or "children." This usually refers to anime or manga that aims at little children like *Hamtaro* or *Hello Kitty.*

Letterer: Person who physically writes the text of the comic. Many comics are being lettered digitally.

Limited Series: A mini-series or a maxi-series.

Mainstream: This usually refers to comics publishers Marvel and DC and their subsidiaries; however it can also refer to any comic that is produced for a general audience.

Magical Girl: This term refers to a subgenre of the *shojo* genre. The main characters use magical powers, usually to protect Japan (or the world).

Manga: The Japanese term for comics. In America, it is used to distinguish English-translated Japanese comics from other countries' comics.

Manga-style: A comic that utilizes artwork or storytelling conventions from manga, but is produced in America or another Western country, sometimes called Ameri-manga, Original English Manga (O.E.L.), or faux-manga.

Manga-ka: A Japanese term for comic book artist.

Manhua: Chinese and Tawainese comics. Some examples are *Shaolin Soccer, Storm Riders,* and *Real/Fake Princess.*

Manwha: Korean comics. Some examples are *Priest* and *Demon Diary.*

Mature Readers Line: A subsidiary of a publishing company that produces comics intended for adults.

Maxi-Series: A comic book series that is scheduled to run only a certain number of issues (usually more than six) and then end.

Mecha: A term abbreviated from the word "mechanical," it refers to giant robots or piloted armor suits found in anime and manga.

Mini-Series: A comic book series that is scheduled to run only a certain number of issues (usually less than six) and then end.

OAV: Original Animation Video—sometimes called OVA as well. This is the direct to home video or DVD.

OEL: Original English Language.

One-Shot: A comic book that is produced as a single issue. Often this is used for "special events," such as crossovers, or to introduce a character in advance of that character being used in a regular series. Some one-shots are later republished as brief graphic novels.

Ongoing Series: A comic book series that has no ending planned and will continue until sales dictate its cancellation. Ongoing series can have a frequency from weekly to semi-annually. Most are monthly or bi-monthly. Superman is the star of the longest running ongoing series in the United States, *Action Comics.*

Otaku: A fanatic usually referring to anime fans. In Japan, it has a negative connotation, meaning more of an obsessed fan. In America, fans have taken this phrase and made it their own. It means anyone who likes anime. Otaku is both the singular and plural form, like "goose."

Panel: A box that contains comics art. It is not necessarily square, and sometimes the entire page is a single panel. Panels are used sequentially to forward the story.

Penciler: The person who provides the basic art of a panel.

Relaunch: The reintroduction of an ongoing series, usually featuring a revised character.

Reuben Awards, The: National Cartoonists Society Awards. These are the oldest awards associated with American cartoons, commonly known as the "The Reubens." Excellence in the fields of newspaper strips, newspaper panels, TV animation, feature animation, newspaper illustration, gag cartoons, book illustration, greeting cards, comic books, magazine feature/magazine illustration, and editorial cartoons are chosen by the members of the National Cartoonists Society. The Web site of the National Cartoonists Society is http://www.reubens.com.

Revisionism: Taking an old character (usually a less popular superhero or a hero who never developed a following) and completely revamping him/her to make him/her more modern, relevant and/or realistic. Revisionist stories tend to be darker and grittier.

Scanlation: A term that combines the words "scan" and "translation," referring to any manga, which has been translated from the original Japanese, scanned, and posted online. Scanlations are considered illegal by both American and Japanese companies, because they are reproductions of the original, distributed for free rather than bought in the store.

Screentones: Plastic adhesive film that has designs printed on it, primarily used in manga for quick shading and backgrounds. More information about screentones can be found in the many "how to draw Manga" books.

Seinen: A sub-category of manga geared towards older teen males and men.

Seiyuu: A Japanese term for voice actors in anime and video game voice-overs.

Sequential Art: Static images placed in a progression to impart meaning, such as the passage of time, a specific action, or an event.

Shojo: A Japanese term for "young girl." The genre called *shojo* is a style of anime or manga created for teenage girls. The plots tend to focus on relationships, and the artwork tends to be more fluid and expressive than *shonen* tales.

Shonen: A Japanese term for "young boy." The genre called *shonen* is a style of anime or manga aimed at young teenage boys, usually stories involving action and adventure.

Silver Age: Comics from the mid 1950s until approximately 1970, beginning with the appearance of *The Flash* in Showcase #4 (1956) and other reimagined heroes from the DC universe. These were followed by more realistic characters produced by Marvel (such as Spider-Man and the Hulk) who had as many problems as powers, and changed the rules for superheroes.

Story arc: A specific story told in an ongoing series over the course of many issues of an ongoing series.

Sub: Short for "subtitled." This refers to anime left in the Japanese dialogue and subtitled in English instead. Most anime DVDs have both dubbed and subbed versions available on them.

Super-Deformed: This is when an anime or manga character is drawn in squashed, miniaturized versions of themselves, typically for comedy. This is sometimes referred to as "chibi" or "SD."

Tankobon: The Japanese term for a trade paperback compilation of a manga series.

Trade Paperback: Bound editions of previously published issues of an ongoing comics series, mini-series or maxi-series. Sometimes abbreviated as TPB.

Universe: The fictional setting of a comics line. Each comics publisher has its own universe. Some comic publishers, such as Marvel, set their comics in real locales (i.e. New York City). Others, such as DC, create fictional locations modeled on real locales (i.e. Gotham). Usually, characters can move about in a publisher's universe; for example, although Superman lives in Metropolis, he can visit Gotham. Rarely do characters from different universes appear in comics together, unless it is in a crossover event.

Web-comic: A comic published on the Internet, either on a Web page or through an e-mail subscription service. It is more and more common for web-comics to have print anthologies.

Writer: Person who provides the basic storyline for a comic, as well as all of the dialog and narration. Sometimes different writers provide the plot and the script.

Women in Refrigerators: Disproportionate violence against female characters depicted in comics. The term originated with Gail Simone and refers to Kyle Rayner (Green Lantern) finding his girlfriend dismembered in his refrigerator.

Yaoi: This Japanese term is an acronym for "*yama nashi, ochi nashi, imi nashi,*" meaning "no climax, no resolution, no meaning." Originally this referred to *doujinshi* that focused on homosexual relationships between two male characters. In America, publishers have used this phrase for male-male sexual relationships/ romance with disregard to the more readily acceptable term Boys' Love. Some publishers refer to Yaoi as containing more hardcore sexual content than Boys' Love.

Yuri: A Japanese term that means "lily." Rarer than Boys' Love, these stories involve female-female sexual relationships.

Subject Index

Age ratings, 62-66
    in American graphic novels,
        63-64
    and collection development,
        62-66
    in manga, 42, 65
    and popularity, 66
Amazon.com, 3, 103
American Library Association
    (ALA), 19, 92
Anime, 27
    Festivals/Screenings, 120-121
Arizona Library Association, 29
Artwork, 3
    Evaluating, 94-95
Awards, 90-93
Bindings, 113-114
Book Jobbers, 103-104
Bookstores, 33, 103
Borders Books, 33, 103
Boys'love, 41-42
Brenner, Robin, 42
Burns, Robert A., 50
Cary, Stephen, 52
Challenges, 66-72
Chofu City Library, 30-31
CMX, 65
Closure, 56-57
Collection development, 59-68
    Age ratings, 62-66
    Challenges, 66-67
    Current collection, 89
    Deselection, 67-68
    Media tie-ins, 60
    Non-comics material,
        60-61
    Policy, 46-47, 59-68
    Selection criteria, 60-66
    Series, 61-62
    User group, 57
Colorist or Letterers' Work, 95

Comic Books
    Event comics, 62
    Perception of, 2
Comics, Comix, & Graphic Novels:
    A History of Comic Art, 5
Comics Code, 8-9, 10
Comics specialty store, 12, 17,
    101-103, 111,
Comix - *see Underground comics*
Contests, 126-128,
Conventions
    in the library, 125-126
Cosplay, 120-122
Dark Horse Comics, 17, 32, 109
DC Comics, 7, 9, 15, 29, 61, 63,
    89, 109,
Diamond Comic Distributors,
    104
    Diamond Bookshelf, 107
    Diamond Previews, 105-106
Digital Manga Publishing, 41, 109
Direct Market - *see Comics*
    specialty store
Displays, 127
EC Comics, 8
English language learners (ELL),
    51-52
Expansion effect, 52-56
Expansion effect—manga, 54-55
Evaluating for purchase, 89-100
    Artwork, 94-95
    Awards, 90-92
    Creators, 89-90
    Current collection,93-94
    Physical characteristics,
        93-94
    Popularity, 87-88
Fantagraphics, 18, 109, 124
Faster than a Speeding Bullet: The
    Rise of the Graphic Novel, 5
Flow, 95

Fredric Wertham and *Seduction of*
    the Innocent, 8
Gekiga, 27
Getting Graphic @ Your Library
    Preconference, 33
Glendale Public Library, 52, 59, 60,
    64, 65, 66, 67, 69, 73, 88, 94,
    112-113, 114,116, 120,
    122-123, 124, 125, 136, 138,
    148-150
GNLIB-L, 19, 68-69, 71
Golden Age, 7
Graphic novels
    Action, 152-13
    Awards, 90-93
    Benefits, 49-57
    Biographic, 160-163
    Cheat sheet, 73-83
    Crime, 169-171
    Definition, 2-4, 60
    Difference between
        manga and American
        comics, 43
    Fantasy, 157-160
    Historical fiction, 160-163
    Historically important, 16
    Horror, 163-167
    Humor, 167-169
    Mystery, 169-171
    Parts, 2
    Realistic fiction, 154-157
    Romance, 172-174
    Science fiction, 174-177
    Sports, 177-179
    Superhero, 179-182
The Great Comic Book Heroes, 11
Great Graphic Novels for Teens,
    19, 87, 92-93
Hayes, Donald P., 51
Hiroshima City Library, 31
Horner Fellow, 29

Image Comics, 17, 109
Independent publishers, 18
Josei, 42-43
Kodomo, 36-37
Krashen, Stephen, 51
Kyoto Seika University Library and Information Center, 30
Libraries, 18-19
    Japan, 29-31, 46-47
Literacies
    Graphic, 56
    Visual, 50-51
MAD magazine, 8
Magnificent 24s, 40
Manga
    Age ratings 42, 63-65
    Authentic/Japanese style, 32, 34
    Characteristics, 34-36
    Conventions, 33
    Definition, 4
    Expansion effect, 54-55
    Flipped, 32-33
    History, 23-27
Marvel Comics, 9, 13, 62-63, 91, 104, 109
Mature readers, 62, 66,
McCloud, Scott, 19, 56
Mending, 92, 113-117
Mile High Comics, 103
National Diet Library, 29-30
New Comics Release List, 107
Newspaper, 5-6
Non-comics material, 60-61, 182-183
Oni Press, 64, 109, 113, 123,
Online retailers, 103
Panel, 2, 32, 34,40
Prebinding, 117
Programming, 119-
    Active, 119-126
    Anime festivals/
        Screenings, 119-121
    Author visits, 123-124
    Contests, 121, 126-128
    Cosplay, 120-121
    Create your own comic
        book, 124

Discussion Groups, 124-125
    Mini-convention, 125-126
    Passive, 126-128
    Trivia, 121, 122, 123, 128-134
Publishers' web sites, 108-111
Ratings — *see Age ratings* and *Manga*
Readers
    Active, 56
    Advisory to, 38,41
    Benefits to, 49-57
    Reluctant, 50-51
Reading level, 49
Reviews, 96-100
    Fans, 96-97
    Library journals, 99-100
Revisionism, 13
Right Stuf International, 103
Sabin, Roger, 5
Scholastic, 16
Sequential Art, 2-3, 5
Shojo, 39-41
    Cross-dressing, 41
Shojo Beat, 41, 70, 89
Shonen, 37-38
Shonen-Ai - see Boys' love
Shonen Jump, 38 54,
Sienen, 39
Silver Age, 9
Slave Labor Graphics, 89, 109
Staff
    Challenges, 69, 71
    Education, 69-71
    Resistance, 68-72
Story Arc, 61-62
Synecdoche – *see Closure*
Tokyo Metropolitan Library, 24
TOKYOPOP, 23, 32-33, 37, 63, 63-64, 94, 109, 113, 147
Trivia, 121, 122, 123, 128-134
Udon Kids, 37
Ukiyo-e, 23, 24
Underground comics, 10
Vendor Catalogs, 110
Vertigo, 89,108
VIZ, 23, 31, 36, 39, 41, 54, 64, 89, 109,113

Visual Literacy - *see Literacies*
Weekly Shonen Jump, 28, 35
Weiner, Stephen, 5
Yaoi, 41
Young Adult Library Services Association (YALSA) - *see American Library Association*

Manga and Graphic Novel Title and Creator Index

The 9/11 Report: A Graphic Adaptation, 161
52, 179
100 Bullets, 73, 169
300, 78
1602, 179
1985, 87
20th Century Boys, 39, 169
Abadzis, Nick, 162
Abel, Jessica, 165, 183
Absolute Boyfriend, 172
After School Nightmare, 157
Air Gear, 178
Akahori, Satoru, 63
Akamatsu, Ken, 64, 159
Akira, 73, 174
Alice 19th, 73
All Star Batman and Robin, 95
All Star Superman, 180
Alphona, Adrian, 181
American Born Chinese, 3, 19, 154
Amulet, 74, 157
Anderson, Brett, 180
Ando, Natsumi, 155
Angel, 42
Angelic Layer, 37, 74, 152
Anno, Moyocco, 43
Antique Bakery, 154
Anzai, Nobuyuki, 153
Aoyama, Gosho, 170
Apocalypse Meow, 74
Aragones, Sergio, 171
Arakawa, Hiromu, 153
Aro, Hiroshi, 66
Asada, Hiroyuki, 160
Asano, Inio, 157
Astonishing X-Men, 68, 85, 180
Astro Boy, 74, 174
Astro City, 18, 74, 180

Atomic Robo, , 174
Azuma, Kiyohiko, 37, 167, 169
Azumanga Daioh, 74, 167
Azzarello, Brian, 73, 169
Bá, Gabriel, 182
Bakegyamon, 37
Banana Fish, 40, 74, 169
Barefoot Gen, 23, 32, 161
Basara, 74, 158
Bastard!, 39
Batgirl, 74, 81
Batman: RIP, 180
Batman: Whatever Happened to the Caped Crusader?, 180
Batman: The Long Halloween, 180
Batman: Year One, 180
Battle Angel Alita, 74, 175
Battle Royale, 55, 63, 74
Bayou, 142
Bechdel, Alison, 161
Bendis, Brian Michael, 75
Big O, 75
Birds of Prey, 75
Black Butler, 167
Black Cat, 170
Black Hole, 164
Black Lagoon, 39, 152
Blackman, Haden, 177
Blade of the Immortal, 32, 75
Bleach, 38, 75, 152
Bokurano: Ours, 175
Bone, 16, 17, 75, 158
The Book of Genesis, 4
Books of Fairie, 75
Books of Magic, 75
Boy Princess, 41
Boys Be, 75, 172
Boys over Flowers, 75

B.P.M.: Beats per Minute, 154
Brain Powered, 76
Brooks, Max, 167
Brubaker, Ed, 171
Buckingham, Mark, 158
Buddha, 76, 161
Buffy the Vampire Slayer, 4, 76, 164
Burchielli, Riccardo, 175
Burns, Charles, 164
Buronson, 76
Busiek, Kurt, 16, 170
Calamity Jack, 160
Caldwell, Ben, 177
Cantarella, 41, 161
Captain America, 76
Captain Tsubasa, 38
Cardcaptor Sakura, 76, 158
Carey, Mike, 156
Case Closed, 170
Cassaday, John, 176, 180
Castelluci, Cecil, 156
Castle in the Sky, 74
Catwoman, 76
Cavallaro, Mike, 158
Ceres, Celestial Legend, 76
Chen, Jo, 164
Cheung, Jim, 182
Chi's Sweet Home, 37
Chmakova, Svetlana, 172
Chobits, 76, 175
CLAMP, 37, 40, 76, 77, 84, 152, 153, 158, 159, 166, 175
CLAMP School Detectives, 84
Claremont, Chris, 78
Clevinger, Brian, 174
Clover, 175
Clugston-Major, Chynna, 155
Colon, Ernie, 161

Confidential Confessions, 77
A Contract with God, 11-12
Cooke, Darwyn, 172, 181
Cowa, 37
Crimson Hero, 40, 89, 178
Crumb, R., 4, 10
Daniel, Tony, 180
Daredevil, 13, 16, 77
Dark Entries, 164
The Dark Knight Returns, 14, 16
DC: The New Frontier Vol. 1 & 2, 181
Dead @ 17, 164
Deadpool, 77
Dear Myself, 41
Death: The High Cost of Living, 52, 83
Death: The Time of Your Life, 83
Death Note, 170
Dell'Edera, Werther, 164
Demon Ororon, 63, 77, 164
Diary of a Wimpy Kid (series), 3-4
Dinosaur Hour, 37
Distant Neighborhood, 154
A Distant Soil, 73
Ditko, Steve, 9
Di Vito, Andrea, 182
DMZ, 175
D.N. Angel, 40, 77
Donaldson, Kristian, 175
Doran, Colleen, 73
Dragon Ball, 65, 77
Dragon Ball Z, 38, 75, 153
Dramacon, 172
Earthian, 41
Echo, 176
Edwards, Tommy Lee, 87
Eerie Queerie, 41, 63
Eiki Eiki, 41
Eisner, Will, 11-12, 16, 155, 183
Elektra, 77
Elfquest, 16, 77, 93
Ellerby, Marc, 173
Ellis, Warren, 176, 180, 181,
Emiko Superstar, 154
Emma, 161
Emura, 41

Ennis, Garth, 78
Essential Spider-man, 77
Essential X-Men, 78
Esuno, Sakae, 165
Excel Saga, 78
Eyeshield 21, 178
Fables, 53, 78, 158
Fake, 41, 170
Flame of Recca, 78, 153
Foligo, Kata, 176
Foligo, Phil, 176
Foiled, 158
Fraction, Matt, 181
Fries, Brian, 162
From Hell, 16, 18, 73, 170
Fruits Basket, 40, 55, 70, 159
Fujii, Mihona, 168
Fujishima, Kosuke, 173
Full Metal Panic, 78
Fullmetal Alchemist, 120
Fun Home: A Family Tragicomic, 161
Fushigi Yûgi, 39, 78, 159
Futaba-kun Changes, 66
Future Diary, 165
Gadget, 78
Gaiman, Neil, 15, 16, 18, 19, 52, 75, 81, 95, 160, 179, 180
Gals!, 168
Gankutsuou: The Count of Monte Cristo, 176
Gibbons, Dave, 14, 16,
Girl Genius, 176
Gloom Cookie, 78
Godchild, 170
Goleash, Grant, 169
Golgo 13, 27
The Goon, 165
Gorgeous Carat, 41
Gotham Central, 171
Gotoh, Shinobu, 41
Gravitation, 42, 63
Green Arrow, 75, 79
Green Lantern, 79
GTO: Great Teacher Onizuka, 79
Guibert, Emmanuel, 162
Gundam, 79

Gunsmith Cats, 79, 153
Hagiwara, Kazushi, 39
Hale, Dean, 160
Hale, Nathan, 160
Hale, Shannon, 160
Hana-Kimi, 41, 75 79, 172
Hands Off!, 41
Happy Happy Clover, 37
Happy Mania, 42
Hara, Hidenori, 174
Hatori, Bisco, 40, 168
Hayakawa, Tomoko, 169
Heinberg, Allan, 182
Hellsing, 79, 109
Hempel, Marc, 156
Hendrix, Shepherd, 163
Hicks, Faith Erin, 167
Higuchi, Daisuke, 89, 179
Higuri, You, 41, 161
Hikaru no Go, 178
Hill, Joe, 109
Hino, Matsuri, 40, 166
Hiramoto, Akira, 162
Hirano, Kouta, 165
Hiroe, Rei, 39, 152
Hopeless Savages, 79, 155
Horton, Anthony, 163
Hotta, Yumi, 178
House of M, 62
Howard, Josh, 164
Hurtt, Brian, 171
I Kill Giants, 155
Ihara, Shigekatsu, 37
Ikegami, Ryoichi, 39
Ikezawa, Satomi, 125, 156
Il Gato Sul G, 41
Imadoki, 79
Inagaki, Riichiro, 178
Incredible Hulk, 79
Initial D, 80
Inoue, Takehito, 38, 39, 55, 163
InuYasha, 37, 80, 130
Invincible, 181
Invincible Iron Man, 181
Invisible Boy, 41
Iron Man, 61, 80
Ishihara, Satoru, 41

Ito, Junji, 166
Iwaaki, Hitoshi, 166
Jacobson, Sid, 161
Japan Ai, 162
Jeanty,Georges, 164
Johnny the Homicidal Maniac, 66
Johns, Geoff, 179
Justice League, 54, 80
Juvenile Orion, 80
Kabei, Yukako, 165
Kanari, Yozaburo, 95
Kannagi, Satoru, 41, 173
Kanno, Aya, 168
Kare First Love, 172
Kare Kano, 63, 80, 173
Kasane, Katsumoto, 41
Katayama, Kyoichi, 174
Kawai, Chigusa, 41, 155
Kaze Hikaru, 40
Keith, Sam, 160
Kelly, Joe, 155
Kibuishi, Kaza, 74, 157
Kieli, 165
Kilala Princess, 37
Kim, Eric, 157
Kim, Seyoung, 41, 173
Kimi-Shiruya: Dost Thou Know?, 41
Kindaichi Case Files, 80, 95
Kingdom Come, 18
Kirby, Jack, 9
Kirkman, Robert, 82, 166, 181
Kishimoto, Masashi, 37, 153
Kishiro, Yukito. 175
Kitchen Princess, 155
Kitoh, Mohiro, 175
Kobayashi, Miyuki, 1155
Kodaka, Nao, 37
Kodocha, 80
Konami, Kanata, 37
Konomi, Takeshi, 37, 89, 178-179
Kouga, Yun, 41
Kubert, Andy, 179, 180
Kubo, Tite, 37, 152
Kumeta, Koji, 168
Kurtzman, Harvey, 8
Kyle, Craig, 182
La Esperança, 41, 155

Laika, 162
Landowne, Youme, 162
Lark, Michael, 171
Larroca, Salvador, 181
Le Chevalier D'Eon, 165
Lee, Jim, 17, 18, 94-95
Lee, NaRae, 176
Lee, Stan, 9, 16, 183
Lefevre, Didier, 162
Lemercier, Frederic, 162
Liew, Sonny, 156
Life Sucks, 165
Locke and Key, 166
Loeb, Jeph, 180
Logicomix, 4
Lone Wolf and Cub, 31, 59, 80
Los Bros. Hernandez, 16, 18
Love and Rockets, 16, 18
Love As a Foreign Language Volume 1 & 2, 173
Love Hina, 64, 80
Love, Jeremy, 158
Love the Way You Love, 173
Loveless, 41
MAD Magazine, 8
Maeda, Mahiro, 176
Maeda, Shunshin, 37
Magic Knight Rayearth, 77, 81, 159
Maison Ikkoku, 81, 155
Marmalade Boy, 81
MARS, 63, 81,
Marvels, 16, 18
Masahiro, Itabashi, 172
Matoh, Sanami, 41, 170
Maus, 14-15, 16, 74
Maximum Ride, 176
Mazzucchelli, David, 180
McCulloch, Derek, 163
McFarlane, Todd, 16, 17
McKean, Dave, 94, 160
McKeever, Sean, 176
Me and the Devil Blues, 162
Medina, Lan, 153
Millar, Mark, 87, 90
Miller, Frank, 13-14, 16, 17, 77, 78, 94, 180
Minami, Maki, 40, 156

Miyagi, Tohko, 41
Miyasaka, Kaho, 172
Mizuki, Hakase, 164
Mizushiro, Setona, 157
Mom's Cancer, 162
The Moon and the Sandals, 41
Moore, Alan, 13-14, 16, 18, 73, 170, 176
Moore, Terry, 16, 18, 176, 181
Monster, 171
Mori, Kaoru, 161
Morrison, Grant, 78, 177, 179, 180
Murakami, Maki, 41
Murata, Yusuke, 178
Mushi-shi, 159
Nakajo, Hisaya, 41, 172
Nakazawa, Keiji, 161
Naked Ape, 171
Nana, 42, 64, 73, 166
Naruto, 37, 55, 81, 153
Nausicaa of the Valley of the Wind, 81
Negima! Magister Negi Magi, 159
Neon Genesis Evangelion, 81
Nextwave: Agents of H.A.T.E., 181
New Teen Titans, 83
Nightow, Ysuhiro, 177
Nightwing, 75, 81
Niimura, J.M. Ken, 155
Ninja Baseball Kyuma, 37
Norrie, Christine, 155
Novgorodoff, Danica, 156
Obata, Takeshi, 170, 178
Oda, Eiichiro, 28, 153
Odagiri, Hotaru, 41
Oh! Great, 65, 178
Oh My Goddess, 81, 173
Ohba, Tsugumi, 170
O'Malley, Bryan Lee, 155, 173
One Pound Gospel, 178
Ooku: The Inner Chambers, 162
One Piece, 28, 81, 153
Only the Ring Finger Knows, 41, 173
Othello, 124, 156
Ottley, Ryan, 181
Otoh, Saki, 171
Otomen, 168
Otomo, Katsuhiro, 174

Ouran High School Host Club, 40, 168

Outcault, R.F., 6

Outsiders, 81, 82

Palmiotti, Jimmy, 182

Palestine, 18

Parasyte, 166

Patterson, James, 176

Peach Girl, 63, 82

Peach-Pit, 167

Percy, Benjamin, 156

Petshop of Horrors, 82

The Photographer: Into War-Torn Afghanistan with Doctors without Borders, 162

Pitch Black, 162

The Plain Janes, 156

Planetary, 176

Planetes, 82

Pleece, Warren, 165

Ploog, Mike, 171

Pluto: Urasawa X Tezuka, 176

Pokémon, 35

Ponsoldt, James, 156

Powell, Eric, 165

Powell, Nate, 157

Powers, 75, 82

Preacher, 78, 82

The Prince of Tennis, 37, 89, 178

Punisher, 82

Queen and Country, 171

Quitely, Frank, 177, 180

Rankin, Ian, 164

Ranma ½, 37, 66, 70, 82, 168

Rapunzel's Revenge, 160

Raw, 15

Real, 179

Refresh, Refresh, 156

Re-Gifters, 156

Reiber, John, 75

Rich, Jaime S., 173

Rin!, 41

Rising Stars, 181

Risso, Eduardo, 169

Roberson, Ibraim, 167

Robin, 82

Rodriguez, Gabriel, 166

Rolston, Steve, 171

Ross, Alex, 16, 18, 73, 180

Rucka, Greg, 78, 171, 179

Rugg, Jim, 156

Rurouni Kenshin 34-35, 37, 54, 83, 163

Runaways 83, 181-182

S. A (Special A), 40, 156

Sacco, Joe, 16, 18

Sailor Moon, 28, 113

Saito, Takao, 27

Sakurazawa, Erica, 42

Sale, Tim, 180

Same Cell Organism, 41

Samura, Hiroaki, 32, 161

Sandman, 15, 16, 17, 52-54 81, 83, 95, 160

The Sandman Presents, 83

Satchel Paige: Striking Out Jim Crow, 163

Sato, Fumiya, 95

Sayonara, Zetsubou-Sensei, 168

Scott Pilgrim, 173

Secret Six, 182

Sentinel, 176

Sgt. Frog, 168

Shigematsu, Takako, 157

Shioya, Hitoshi, 37

Shiozu, Shuri, 41

Simone, Gail, 85, 182

Sin City, 16, 17, 78, 83

Sizer, Paul, 154

Skim, 156

Slam Dunk, 38, 179

Smile, 163

Smith, Jeff, 16, 17, 19, 75, 158

Sonoda, Kenichi, 153

Sorcerer Hunters, 63

Socrates in Love, 174

Soria, Gabe, 165

Spawn, 16, 17, 83, 95

Spider-man, 9, 16, 83

Spiegelman, Art, 14-15, 16, 18, 74

Stagger Lee, 163

Stardust: Being a Romance within the Realms of Faerie, 160

Star Wars: Clone Wars, 83

Star Wars: Clone Wars Adventures, 83, 177

Steinberger, Aimee Major, 162

Stitches, 3

Straczynski, J. Michael, 181

Strangers in Paradise, 16, 18

Sturm, James, 163

Sugisaki, Yukiru, 40

Swallow Me Whole, 157

Swamp Thing, 13, 16

Switch, 171

Takahashi, Rumiko, 37, 50, 66, 80, 81, 90, 155, 159, 168, 178,

Takami, Koushun, 66

Takanashi, Mitsuba, 40, 89, 178

Takaya, Natsuki, 40, 159

Tamakoshi, Hiroyuki, 172

Tamiki, Gillian 156

Tamiki, Mariko, 154, 156

Tamura, Mitsuhisa, 37

Tamura, Yumi, 158

Tan, Billy, 182

Tanaka, Rika, 37

Taniguchi, Jiro, 154

Tateno, Makoto, 41. 171

Tatsuyama, Sayuri, 37

Teen Titans, 82

Tegami Bachi, 160

Telgemeier, Raina, 163

Tenshi Ja Nai, 157

Tenchi Muyo, 84

Tenjho Tenge, 65

Teshirogi, Shiori, 165

Tezuka, Osamu, 26, 39, 76, 161, 174, 176,

Time Lag, 41

Toboso, Yana, 167

Tokyo Mew Mew, 84

Tommaso, Rich, 163

Tomomi, Nakamura, 171

Toriyama, Akira, 37, 73, 153

Torres, J., 173

Train_Man: Densha Otoko, 174

*Train*Train*, 41

Transmetropolitan, 84

A Treasury of Victorian Murder, 84

Trigun, 84, 177

Tsubasa RESERVoir CHRoNiCLE, 40, 153
Tsuda, Masami, 173
Ubukata, Tou, 199
UDON, 176
Ultimate Spider-Man, 75, 84
Ultimate X-Men, 84
Ultimates, 84
The Umbrella Academy, 3, 182
Until the Full Moon, 41
Urasawa, Naoki, 39, 169, 171, 176
Urushibara, Yuki, 159
Uzumaki, 166
V for Vendetta, 73
Vagabond, 39, 55, 84, 163
Vampire Knight, 40, 166
Van Meter, Jen, 155
Vasquez, Jhonen, 66
Vaughn, Brian K., 177, 181
Vess, Charles, 160
W Juliet, 40-41, 84
Waid, Mark, 18
Walker, Brad, 182

Walker, Cory, 181
The Walking Dead, 4, 82, 85, 150, 166
Wallflower, 169
Watanabe, Taeko, 40
Watase, Yu, 39, 73, 76, 79, 159, 172, 183
Watsuki, Nobuhiro, 37, 163
Watchmen, 14, 16, 73
Way, Gerard, 182
We3, 177
Weekly Shonen Jump, 28
Wegener, Scott, 174
What a Wonderful World, 157
Whedon, Joss, 164, 180, 181
Whistle, 89, 179
Will Eisner's The Spirit, 171
Willingham, Bill, 53, 158
Wolverine, 62, 85
Wonder Woman, 85
Wood, Brian, 175
X-Men, 85
X-Men Noir, 64
X-23: Innocence Lost, 182

xxxHOLIC, 166
Y The Last Man, 85, 177
Yabuki, Kentaro, 170
Yang, Gene Leun, 19, 94 154
Yazawa, Ai, 42, 73, 155
Yellow, 41, 171
The Yellow Kid, 6
Yolen, Jane, 158
Yoshida, Akimi, 40, 169
Yoshinaga, Fumi, 41, 154, 162
Yoshizaki, Mine, 168
Yost, Christopher, 182
Yotsuba&!, 37, 85, 169
Young Avengers, 182
Yu Yu Hakusho, 85
Yu-Gi-Oh!, 85
Yuki, Kaori, 159
Yumeji, Kiriko, 165
Zap, 10
Zombie-Loan, 167
Zombie Survival Guide: Recorded Attacks, 167
Zombies Calling, 167

VIZ Media – Manga Image Copyrights

About the Authors

Kristin Fletcher-Spear is a teen librarian at the Foothills Branch Library in Glendale, Arizona. She has a Bachelor degree in English and a Master in library science, both from Indiana University. She always read comic strips, but began reading graphic novels in college, starting with *Maus* by Art Spiegelman. She became interested in manga and anime when her boyfriend, now husband, made her watch the first episode of *Ranma ½* on their first date. After that show, she was hooked on anime, which lead her to reading manga. Kristin reviews graphic novels for *Voice of Youth Advocates, Library Media Connection*, and ICv2. com. She also reviews anime for ICv2.com. Kristin has written several articles on anime and graphic novels, and has been making presentations on these topics since 1999. An active member of Young Adult Library Services Association, the Arizona Library Association, and the Assembly on Literature for Adolescents, Kristin can be found at most American Library Association conferences attending meetings and sneaking over to the graphic novels section of the exhibits! She can be reached at kfletcherspear@gmail.com.

Merideth Jenson-Benjamin is a teen librarian at the Glendale Public Library in Glendale, Arizona. She received a Master of Arts in Information Resources and Library Sciences and a Bachelor of Arts in Women's Studies from the University of Arizona. One day she woke up a rampaging comics geek, which came as a surprise, as it was never really a goal. She blames youthful exposure to *Ameythst: Princess of Gemworld*, a younger brother who collected the Marvel trading cards, and the accidental discovery of Neil Gaiman as an adult for her current comics obsession. Merideth reviews graphic novels and other materials for *Voice of Youth Advocates* and *GraphicNovelReporter.com*. She is also a frequent panel member at Comic-Con International: San Diego. Merideth lives with her equally geeky husband and warrior-princess daughter in a very messy house stuffed to capacity with comics, Star Trek memorabilia, and toys. You can reach her at meridethlibrarian@gmail.com and hear more of her opinions on her blog, *http://meridethsays. blogspot.com*.

LaVergne, TN USA
10 April 2011
223362LV00002B/1/P